# Therapeutic Communities for the Treatment of Drug Users

leaving behind most of the lifestylers in the original Santa Monica facility, that things began to go wrong:

> I think that when Synanon residents left Santa Monica to escape the influ- ences of the city, they lost more than they gained, because they left the rest of us behind: those Squares and Lifestylers who could always be counted on to comment that the King had neglected to button his fly.

In those early years too, Synanon offered a warm welcome to an almost endless procession of professionals (in its later years the welcome became in- creasingly less warm), some of whom, like the sociologist and psychodramatist Lew Yablonski, stayed for protracted periods as residents. Many returned to their areas of operation, both throughout the USA and elsewhere in the world, and established modified versions of the community (see Kooyman in this volume).

One of the major reasons for the excitement felt by these early visitors was the fact that Synanon appeared to be not only working, but actually thriving as an organization, with little or no state funding.

Bassin (1978) has described the despair that many professionals were feeling during that period at the failure of existing treatment programs to do more than 'contain the whirlwind' of destruction which howled around the drug addict. While some research (Robins and Murphy 1967; Winick 1962) pointed to a natural 'maturing out' of addicts in their thirties, there was little hope that existing treatment practice could achieve more than a minimal impact on the dramatic increases in levels of addiction.

America's major treatment facilities were recording depressingly high levels of relapse. Figures show that the relapse rate for the Riverside Hospital in New York was almost 100 per cent (Vaillant 1966), while in the much vaunted methadone experiment at the Rockefeller University Hospital, New York (Dole and Nyswander 1965), almost 20 per cent of those in the program for six months or more had been arrested – and this despite a screening process which rejected approximately 50 per cent of volunteers to the program as being 'unmotivated'. Indeed, in a similar experiment in Canada, with less rigid selection criteria, of 321 addicts recruited, a stagger- ing 264 dropped out of the program (Louria 1968).

After the passing of the Harrison Act in 1914, much of the American treatment response (in contrast to that in Europe, where addiction was largely seen as a health matter) had developed within the penal system. Lexington, Kentucky, a US prison given over almost entirely to addiction treatment was recording relapse rates of 95 per cent (Louria 1968). In Cali- fornia, Corona, with capacity for 1,900 men and 400 women, was recording similarly depressing reconviction rates of almost two thirds, despite a rigid treatment regime which lasted up to ten years (Louria, *ibid.*). Puzzlingly, the harsh regime which appeared to work so well within Synanon led only to re-sentment and relapse in correctional facilities. Some, like the psychotherapist Carl Rogers, speculated that this was possibly due to the fact that in Synanon addicts were themselves responsible for the harshness of the regime and that participants instinctively knew that what happened to them was motivated by love (Bassin 1978).

American treatment and service planners were desperate for a rehabilita-tion intervention which worked. Synanon, with its heady mix of spiritual community, boot-camp rigour and self-made citizenship aspiration, was en-thusiastically embraced by an impressive array of senior authorities on drug treatment. Detractors might point to the fact that 50 per cent of Synanon residents left the community without graduating (Louria 1968), but this radical, self-help regime appeared to work and the negative aspects were largely ignored. Moreover, the harshness of the approach ensured that the new therapeutic communities were an attractive option for politicians, who instinctively felt that since drug addiction was wrong, the treatment response ought to contain an element of retribution.

## The cultural background in Europe

In Europe too, the therapeutic community methodology pioneered by Synanon was warmly welcomed, despite its very American ethos and the apparent brutality of some of its practices (verbal assaults, haircuts and placard-wearing humiliations). The ease with which American therapeutic community methodology established itself in the very different culture of the European drugs field has been the subject of some debate.

A number of authorities have speculated upon the links between this in-novation and the legacy of the 'democratic therapy' pioneered by Maxwell Jones, Tom Main and others at Northfield Hospital after World War II. However, Jones' version of the 'therapeutic community' differs in significant respects from that pioneered at Synanon; a development of which Jones himself was completely unaware until the late 1970s (Jones 1979). Moreover, Kooyman (1993) and others have pointed out that the model initiated at Northfield and subsequently developed at the Henderson Hospital was ineffective with an addict population.

However, the work begun at Northfield with traumatized ex-servicemen, did fit into an established tradition of radical psychiatry which ensured that there was, in the late 1960s, a significant group of free-thinking psychiatrists prepared to experiment with new approaches (Bloor, McKeganey and Fonkert 1988). Among these, both Lacan in France and Laing in the UK were already bringing together existential philosophy and psychiatry (Laing 1994).

In the UK, R. D. Laing had already implemented his theories, first in the establishment of the so-called 'rumpus room' in Gartnavel Hospital, Glasgow, and later, in conjunction with David Cooper and other members of the left-wing Philadelphia Association, by taking his patients out of the hospital environment altogether and launching the influential and anarchic therapeutic community, Kingsley Hall, in London's East End (Cooper 1967; Laing, Esterton and Cooper 1965). Much of this work was influenced by – and, in its turn, influenced – movements such as People Not Psychiatry, in the UK and Democratica Psychiatrica in Italy (Basaglia 1988; Wilkinson and Cox 1986), significant movements for the reform of mental health services, which brought together mental health patients, radical health workers and social and political activists.

Outside the confines of psychiatric medicine, there was a long tradition within Western Europe of the use of small, self-governing communities, particularly in the treatment of maladjusted children. Indeed, it is this work, focusing as it did upon therapeutic interventions with a resistant and antisocial group of young people, which offers the most compelling antecedent for the American therapeutic community model imported into Europe in the early 1970s.

Among the earliest innovators was August Aichhorn, a Viennese schoolteacher in charge of a complex of reformatories for violent young men. His innovative approach in allowing a limited system of self-governance was noted by Freud and was promoted in the UK by Freud's daughter Anna, who influenced the early work of Maxwell Jones (Mohr 1996).

Of equal if not greater importance was the work of the American innovator Homer Lane, in London in 1913. A former woodwork teacher, Lane was a charismatic freethinker who had led the self-governing Boys' Republic. Impressed by Lane's approach to working with the most aggressive and delinquent children, George Montagu (later Lord Sandwich) invited him to the UK, where he established the Little Commonwealth. The Little Commonwealth, on Montagu's 200-acre estate, accepted 'unmanageable' children both from the courts and from their parents. Lane's approach, much influenced by Steiner, Montessori, Pestalozzi and others, was a mixture of tough love (including some corporal punishment), extensive self-government and hard manual labour. Residents were divided into self-regulating 'families' and paid a wage for their work. This wage was pooled and used to clothe and feed the family. Those who idled and thus reduced the family's income were forcefully reprimanded by their peers in family meetings (Bridgeland 1971).

Lane's work was both radical and exciting and influenced the later work of A. S. Neill at Summerhill School. The parallels with Dederich's work are striking. Not only did the two communities they founded employ a remarkably similar methodology, but, like Dederich, Lane was a charismatic figure who, in practice, exercized total control over the establishment he had set up. Like Dederich, Lane eventually spiralled out of control. In 1917 the Home Office withdrew support following unsubstantiated allegations against him of sexual impropriety by two female residents (Lane had become fascinated by the work of Freud and Jung and had embarked on a program of rather amateurish psychoanalytic sessions with some of the children), and Lane, accused on a technical charge of failing to register as an alien, agreed to go into voluntary exile. Without Lane, the Little Commonwealth collapsed within a year.

The legacy of Lane's Little Commonwealth is an impressive one. A. S. Neill claims that such was Lane's influence on him, that he felt himself incapable of independent thought until Lane's death broke the spell (Bridgeland 1971). Lane was also a major influence on the work of radical educationalist J. H. Simpson, who later remarked: 'The measure of my personal debt to Mr. Lane is incalculable' (Simpson 1917).

Of all who inherited the Little Commonwealth innovations, the most important was perhaps David Wills. Wills, a former Borstal housemaster, was employed by the Q Camps Committee (later to evolve into the Planned Environment Therapy Trust) to manage a new experiment with delinquent youths, called the Hawkspur Experiment. Wills, who freely acknowledged his debt, drew heavily upon the work of Lane. The Hawkspur Camp was founded in 1936, with staff and residents living in tents and building their own accommodation. Much of the ethos of the camp was drawn from the open-air school movement, but the tough love regime and the self-governing economy were pure Lane (Wills 1967).

Prominent on the Q Camps Committee was Norman Glaister, one of the originators of the pacifist camping organization established, in part, to counter the militarism of Baden Powell's Boy Scouts: the Order of Woodcraft Chivalry. Glaister was passionately committed to the notion of the 'multi-mental group' and to the Lane mix of self-governance and tough love, to which the Hawkspur Camp added a formal groupwork component (Pines 1999). Glaister went on to work (at the Tavistock) with Harold Bridger, another of the Northfield collaborators and a central figure in the establishment of concept-based therapeutic communities in Italy (see Kooyman in this volume) and with Mandlebrote, who not only worked under Maxwell Jones, but was the originator of the Oxford-based concept house, Ley Community.

The work of these early pioneers was replicated in work with malad-justed children across Europe, although its influence upon the emergent democratic therapeutic community movement is rarely acknowledged. What does seem likely is that this tradition of confrontative groupwork and self-governance with young delinquents facilitated the establishment of the early concept houses as they began to be imported into Europe in the early 1970s, and ensured that these apparently new ideas were accepted more readily than might otherwise have been the case.

## Concept houses as a major influence on European drugs work

These new therapeutic communities soon began to exert an influence upon the field of drug treatment in Europe which greatly outstripped their actual practical involvement in the field. By the mid-1970s, concept-based thera-peutic communities accounted for almost half of the residential rehabilita-tion beds in the UK (Yates 1981). While this is an impressive 'territorial' claim, in terms of numbers of drug users presenting for treatment, therapeu-tic communities were inevitably a very small player. However, their influence was felt throughout the treatment field.

The links between these new communities and medically based treatment services were strong throughout Europe, and it is significant that many were initiated by psychiatrists (Broekaert *et al.* 1996). By the mid-1970s, medical staff working in specialist centres were beginning to incorporate some of the techniques of the therapeutic communities into the clinical setting. The aim was to provide a more therapeutic regime than the sterile interaction which had developed, largely dominated by staff–patient manipulation around the dosage and type of substitute prescription (Mitcheson 1994).

Non-residential treatment services, too, were influenced by the therapeu-tic communities, with some developing pre-entry 'induction programs' (Strang and Yates 1982; Yates 1979), while others began to undertake groupwork modelled upon that found in therapeutic communities. In the Netherlands a non-residential therapeutic community was established, and in a number of European countries existing non-residential services re-styled themselves as providers of 'non-residential rehabilitation'.

Similarly, residential services were keen to adopt some of the therapeutic community practices, and a number of Christian-based houses began to develop a more hard-edged, confrontative approach to the interactions between residents and staff (Wilson 1978).

In part, this imbalance between scale and influence appears to have resulted, as in the USA, from a perception that therapeutic communities were the only organizations actually successfully achieving abstinence for the residents they were working with. There was widespread dissatisfaction in medical circles at a role that appeared to offer little more than the provision of a steady drip-feed of substitute drugs to prevent the escalation of a black market (Mitcheson 1994).

In the non-medical ambulatory services, the majority of the clients were at what would later be described as the 'pre-contemplative stage' (Prochaska and DiClemente 1998), which created similar tensions with the staff in those agencies. Often, staff would feel cheated and abused by a client group which showed little motivation for change and used every opportunity to take advantage of the system for their own objectives. Moreover, staff tended to feel resentful that on many occasions, when clients had moved on to become residents of therapeutic community programs (often after many years of attendance at non-residential services), success would inevitably be credited to the therapeutic community, where change was generally more visible and often quite dramatic (Yates 1992).

The therapeutic community was also in the vanguard of integrating new and alternative therapies – e.g. psychodrama, bioenergetics and transactional analysis – into the treatment regime. Kooyman (1993) has written of how these new developments began to influence the original programs in America, but they also had a great impact upon other drug services (Yates 1992). Throughout the European drug treatment field, services began to experiment with these alternative approaches and, while much of this work was often ill-informed and amateurish (Toon and Lynch 1994), it did enrich the field and encourage an ethos of exploration and experimentation which has characterized this work in Europe ever since.

## The waning of the influence of the therapeutic community in Europe

By the beginning of the 1980s in Europe, the drug treatment field was beginning to experience significant and dramatic changes which would, eventually, see therapeutic communities pushed out to the periphery.

At this time, drug consumption and supply began to increase dramatically both across Europe (Arlaachi 1998; Henman, Lewis and Malyon 1985) and throughout the world (UNDCP 1997). These changes led to a much increased political profile, with drug prevention policies dominating many of the debates surrounding the development of the European Community (Dorn, Jepsen and Savona 1996) and widespread revision of drug policy throughout Europe (Berridge 1999).

With an increased political and public profile came pressure to further finance drug prevention and enforcement activities, rationalize national drug treatment networks and establish evaluative criteria for treatment efficacy. Coming at a time of increasing unemployment and a European-wide tightening of the public purse, therapeutic communities came under increasing pressure to shorten programs and modify program content to ensure increased throughput and enhanced retention rates.

At the same time, many countries were rationalizing the ways in which public money was spent on healthcare. In a number of legislatures, this process brought those seeking funding for residential drug rehabilitation into direct competition with funding demands for other groups – children, the elderly, etc. – generally regarded as more 'deserving', and this trend put considerable pressure upon therapeutic communities (Kooyman in this volume; Toon and Lynch 1994).

What is more, the increase in the numbers of young people using drugs naturally affected the ratio of 'normal' to 'damaged' individuals within that population (Gilman 1988; Yates 1992), with a number of treatment services reporting an influx of drug users apparently less physically and psychologically distressed than earlier populations. Again, this development had the effect of further marginalizing the therapeutic communities. More and more, the traditional therapeutic communities and the hospital based treatment services came to be seen as yesterday's solution, and community-based ambulatory services – accessible, dynamic and, crucially, relatively inexpensive – were viewed as the way forward.

When, in the UK, the British Government embarked upon a major central government-funded pump-priming initiative to establish a national network of drug treatment services, residential rehabilitation services were unable to secure more than 10 per cent of the new money, with the lion's share (56.2 per cent) going to community services (MacGregor 1994).

Perhaps most importantly during this period, intensifying public concern regarding the spread of HIV/AIDS and the potential for the drug-injecting population to create an 'infection route' between the drug-using community and wider society, led to a shift in priority away from abstinence and towards harm reduction. Harm reduction, of course, was not a new phenomenon (Berridge 1996; Velleman and Rigby 1990). Substitute prescribing had been a part of drug treatment in many countries for much of the twentieth century, needle exchanges had been established in the Netherlands in the early 1970s in response to the spread of the hepatitis virus, and Turner (1994) has recorded how early British day centres regularly issued clients with clean injecting equipment and, in some cases, provided 'fixing rooms'.

What was new, however, about this shift in emphasis in the 1980s was the scale of the change and the fact that, for the most part, it received tacit, and occasionally overt, political support (Berridge 1996). Substitute prescribing (in almost all cases, of methadone hydrochloride for the treatment of heroin dependence), which had fallen somewhat into disrepute in the late 1970s (Mitcheson 1994), staged a remarkable comeback in many countries. This emphasis on a program of long-term stabilization further limited the sphere of influence of those treatment services which, like therapeutic communities, had traditionally been wedded to a philosophy of abstinence.

## The future for therapeutic communities

This volume comes at a time when the therapeutic community is experiencing a period of extremely mixed fortunes. On the one hand, the public health imperative which has driven the drug treatment field for the past decade has proved increasingly intolerant of those treatment modalities which do not easily fit into its infection control matrix. On the other hand, a number of context-specific therapeutic communities have been established, with increasing interest in the use of the therapeutic community approach for populations such as drug users in prison (Martin 1999).

Indeed, a new emphasis in the western world on the connections between drug use and crime (Stimson 2000), coupled with concern over the growing incidence of drug use within custodial establishments, appears to have sparked a new interest in abstinence-based modalities such as concept-based therapeutic communities, within the criminal justice system.

Therapeutic communities will need to show that they are able to be flexible in offering services in these contexts; although it should be noted that the therapeutic community movement has had a long history of working alongside the criminal justice system. Even Synanon, with its strong emphasis on voluntary commitment to the group, recognized the need for a pragmatic approach to coerced treatment, accepting referrals through the courts from its earliest days (Kooyman 1993).

In addition, an impressive number of studies (see Wilson and Yates in this volume) have indicated that there are high levels of psychiatric co-morbidity among those entering residential treatment services. The European research study *Improving Psychiatric Treatment in Residential Programs for Emerging Dependent Groups (IPTRP)* (Kaplan, Broekaert and Frank 1999) examined residents presenting for treatment at over thirty therapeutic communities across Europe and concluded that a significant number were experiencing multiple problems. Indeed, Toon and Lynch (1994) noted that during a period when many ambulatory services were seeing a more normalized influx of clients (Gilman 1988) and some were adapting their practices to meet the needs of a new generation of 'recreational' users of so-called 'dance' drugs (Yates 1992), therapeutic communities continued to see a client group whose problems were both deep-rooted and complex, extending far beyond their dependence upon drugs.

It seems entirely appropriate that intensive and unavoidably expensive treatments such as therapeutic communities – although, in fact one recent study (Unell and Vincent 1994) has suggested that the costs of community-based treatment, when calculated as a whole, are actually higher than those for residential rehabilitation – should be reserved for the treatment of clients with more difficult and deeply-entrenched problems. Wilson and Yates (in this volume) have speculated that it is chiefly in this area that the future for the therapeutic community will be realized.

Finally, the IPTRP study previously cited, noted that the mean age of clients presenting to the therapeutic communities in the study was significantly higher than among other samples (Kaplan, Broekaert, Frank and Reichmann 1999). While, at this stage, we can do little more than speculate, it may be that just as substitute prescribing can reduce the incidence of drug-related acquisitive crime but not entirely eliminate it, it may delay but not totally undermine the 'maturing out' phenomenon noted by Robins and Murphy (1967) and by Winick (1962).

In many countries in the western world, substitute prescribing has in the last decade become the dominant treatment response to spiralling drug use. Some have argued (Yates 1992) that this development is more to do with concern over rising crime and the fear of AIDS than any genuine compassion for drug users themselves. Whatever the rights and wrongs of this argument, it seems probable that within the next ten years, many of those currently receiving such long-term prescriptions will grow tired of an existence which offers little more than an artificial stabilization of their drug use and will wish to 'mature out'.

If, as we have speculated, the next decade is marked by an increase of those on long-term prescriptions seeking detoxification and associated rehabilitative inputs, then it is vital that those sectors of the treatment field best able to provide such inputs be protected, nurtured and learned from. Whatever their faults, concept-based therapeutic communities have shown over the past four decades that they are able to work effectively and compassionately with those who wish to change. They have proved their worth in a world which has often been hostile to their ideals and aspirations, and they have shown that they can survive and change while maintaining the core values which underpinned those early days in a Santa Monica waterfront hotel.

## Overview of the book

In bringing together these chapters, we have tried to achieve a number of aims. Importantly, we wanted to give an impression of the growth and change in concept-based therapeutic communities for drug users throughout the world, rather than focusing on just Europe, or, as is more common in this field, just North America. Over the years, the therapeutic community model has lodged itself in many different countries and regions, with different languages, different cultural traditions and different funding mechanisms, and we have tried to reflect some of the diversity that stems from this, beginning with a general overview of therapeutic community organization and practices by Eric Broekaert. Three of the chapters report specifically on developments in different parts of the world: George De Leon describes the situation in the USA, Clive Lloyd and Frances O'Callaghan focus on Australia and New Zealand, and Martien Kooyman outlines what has been happening in Europe. In addition, we have deliberately looked for authors from the USA, Britain and Europe, so that the diversity which comes from geographical location will be evident throughout the book.

We also wanted to describe the variety of arrangements and modifications which can now be found around the therapeutic community model. The traditional, community-based, strongly hierarchical self-help model is no longer the only therapeutic community treatment offered for drug users, and even that traditional model has changed to accommodate some of the very needy and fragile clients who now present themselves to drug treatment services.

Rowdy Yates and Jane Wilson describe the discovery of high rates of personality disorder and post-traumatic stress disorder among therapeutic community residents, and the kinds of changes in treatment and regime that have been made to accommodate and retain such residents. Peter Mason, Diane Mason and Nadia Brookes describe the recent introduction of therapeutic communities into the British prison system, and the monitoring and evaluation work which they carried out during the early days of their operation. Paul Goodman and Karen Nolan focus on the issue of resettlement after treatment, and describe the Ley Community resettlement program and the work of the resettlement workers, who need to work outside in the community while maintaining close links with the Ley.

We also wanted to say something about what it is actually like to live and work in a therapeutic community. Two papers capture the thoughts and feelings of practitioners going about their work. Alan Woodhams, who joined a staff team as a professional counsellor, writes about what the work of a staff member entails, and about the problems and rewards which he has experienced while working in a therapeutic community. A group of ex-residents from the Ley Community, who in the self-help tradition of therapeutic communities have gone on to join the staff team, document their motivations for doing this, and the particular hurdles they have confronted in returning as staff members. To complete this 'experiential' theme, we also wanted to give the residents a say. In a chapter which reports on a study he carried out at Phoenix House in Durham, Keith Burnett presents a description of residents' views of treatment and of the various rules, procedures and sanctions which shape and create their experience.

In any treatment modality today, research into the effectiveness of the provision is becoming more and more important to survival and growth, and to the improvement of services. Barbara Rawlings outlines the variety of evaluation studies which has been conducted for therapeutic communities, and provides a backdrop for two studies, one by Edle Ravndal of residents in a community-based therapeutic community in Norway, and one by James Inciardi, Steven Martin and Hilary Surratt of the CREST post-prison work-release program in the USA. In the USA in particular, outcome research has been a major feature of therapeutic community development, and has helped to establish and maintain the profile of therapeutic communities as an effective treatment for drug users.

When we began this book, we were unsure what to call the therapeutic communities we wanted to describe. Should they be called 'concept-based' or 'hierarchical' or 'concept houses'? We found that the people who actually work in them just call them 'therapeutic communities'. But this caused problems of authorship, because this is not the only type of therapeutic community in existence. There is a whole other world of therapeutic communities, based on the democratic psychiatric model of Maxwell Jones (1968) and Tom Main (1946), which exists not to treat drug addiction (except as a symptom of other pathology) but to treat personality disorder and sometimes mental illness. People who work in this world generally refer to their organizations simply as 'therapeutic communities' as well. As Martien Kooyman points out in his chapter, once you start to look for the differences between the two, they are not so easy to spot: democratic therapeutic communities are 'democratized' rather than democratic (Rapoport 1960), and modifications to concept-based therapeutic communities have softened the rigid lines of the original model. The distinction between the two types of community may sometimes have less to do with organization and more to do with the practice of people sticking with the kind of therapeutic community they have become used to. There is a gap between the two, and while no particular purpose may be achieved by bridging it, this book may go some way towards informing people from each type of community about the existence and present-day methods of the other. We decided in the end to use the term 'concept-based', and if this sounds a little old-fashioned in some circles, we apologize.

Finally, our aim was to put together a book which a number of different audiences will find readable, interesting and informative. We hope it will come to the attention of therapeutic community members, drug treatment professionals who want to know more about therapeutic communities in general, care professionals who are looking for somewhere to place their clients, and service managers who want a broad understanding of a range of provision. We hope this book will provide enough good glimpses of what is going on in therapeutic communities today, for anyone who is interested to want to browse and find out more.

## References

Amish Acres (2000) *A Chronology of Anabaptist and Amish History.* http://amishacres.com/aa_history/Chronology.htm: Amish Acres.

Arlaachi, P. (1998) 'The role of UNDCP in the international effort against drug abuse.' In U. Nizzoli (ed) *Drug Use and the Crisis of European Societies: Reviewing the Quality of Interventions.* Bologna: ERIT.

Basaglia, F. (1988) 'Italian psychiatric reform as a reflection of society.' In S. Ramon and M. Giannichedda (eds) *Psychiatry in Transition: The British and Italian Experiences.* London: Pluto Press.

Bassin, A. (1978) *The Miracle of the T.C: From Birth to Post-partum Insanity to Full Recovery: 2nd World Conference of Therapeutic Communities.* Montreal: McGill University.

Berridge, V. (1996) *AIDS in the UK: The Making of Policy 1981–1994.* Oxford: Oxford University Press.

Berridge, V. (1999) 'European drug policies: the need for historical policy perspectives.' In J. Derks, A. van Kalmthout and H.-J. Albrecht (eds) *Current and Future Drug Policy Studies in Europe.* Freiburg: Max-Planck Institut.

Bloor, M., Mckeganey, N. and Fonkert, D. (1988) *One Foot in Eden: A Sociological Study of the Range of Therapeutic Community Practice.* London: Routledge.

Bridgeland, M. (1971) *Pioneer Work with Maladjusted Children: A Study of the Development of Therapeutic Education.* London: Staples Press.

Broekaert, E., Bracke, R., Calle, D., Cogo, A., van der Straten, G. and Bradt, H. (eds) (1996) *De Nieuwe Therapeutische Gemeenschap.* Leuven, Belgium: Garant.

Cooper, D. (1967) *Psychiatry and Anti-Psychiatry.* London: Tavistock.

Dole, V. and Nyswander, M. (1965) 'Medical treatment for diacetylmorphin (heroin) addiction: a clinical trial with methadone hydrochloride.' *Journal of the American Medical Association 193*, pp.646–650.

Dorn, N., Jepsen, J. and Savona, E. (eds) (1996) *European Drug Policies and Enforcement.* London: Macmillan Press.

Gilman, M. (1988) 'Joining the professionals.' *Druglink 3*, 2, pp.10–11.

Henman, A., Lewis, R. and Malyon, T. (1985) *Big Deal: The Politics of the Illicit Drugs Business.* London: Pluto Press.

Inglis, B. (1975) *The Forbidden Game: A Social History of Drugs.* London: Hodder and Stoughton.

Jackson, P. (1997) 'The rise and fall of Synanon.' *The Daily News Current.* http://morrock.com/synanon.htm: Morrock News Service

Jones, M. (1968) *Social Psychiatry in Practice.* Harmondsworth: Penguin.

Jones, M. (1979) 'Therapeutic communities: old and new.' *American Journal of Drug and Alcohol Abuse 6*, 2, pp.137–149.

Kaplan, C., Broekaert, E. and Frank, O. (1999) *Biomed 2 IPTRP Project on Improving Psychiatric Treatment in Residential Programs for Emerging Dependency Groups: Final Report 1996–1999.* Maastricht: University of Maastricht.

Kaplan, C., Broekaert, E., Frank, O. and Reichmann, S. (1999) 'Improving psychiatric treatment in residential programs for emerging dependency groups: approach and epidemiological findings.' In *NIH-NIDA Community Epidemiology Work Group, Los Angeles, December 17 1999.* NIH-NIDA, forthcoming.

Kooyman, M. (1993) *The Therapeutic Community for Addicts: Intimacy, Parent Involvement and Treatment Outcome.* Lisse: Swets and Zeitlinger.

Kurtz, E. (1979) *Not God: A History of Alcoholics Anonymous.* Center City: Hazelden Educational Services.

Laing, A. (1994) *R. D. Laing: A Life.* London: HarperCollins.

Laing, R., Esterton, A. and Cooper, D. (1965) 'Results of family oriented therapy with hospitalized schizophrenics.' *British Medical Journal II*, pp.1462–1465.

Louria, D. (1968) *The Drug Scene.* New York: McGraw-Hill.

MacGregor, S. (1994) 'Promoting new services: the central funding inititiative and other mechanisms.' In J. Strang and M. Gossop (eds) *Heroin Addiction and Drug Policy: The British System.* Oxford: Oxford University Press.

Main, T. (1946) 'The hospital as a therapeutic institution.' *Bulletin of the Menninger Clinic 10*, pp.66–70.

Martin, P. (1999) 'Flexibility in treatment provisions.' *IV European Conference on Rehabilitation and Drug Policy, Marbella, February, 22–26*, 1999. PlanMarbella/EFTC, 2000.

Miles, B. (1989) *Ginsberg: A Biography.* New York: Simon and Schuster.

Mitchell, D., Mitchell, C. and Ofshe, R. (1980) *The Light on Synanon: How a Country Weekly Exposed a Corporate Cult and Won the Pulitzer Prize.* New York: Seaview Books.

Mitcheson, M. (1994) 'Drug clinics in the 1970s.' In J. Strang and M. Gossop (eds) *Heroin Addiction and Drug Policy: The British System.* Oxford: Oxford University Press.

Mohr, G. (1966) 'August Aichhorn.' In F. Alexander, S. Einstein and M. Grotjahn (eds) *Psychoanalytic Pioneers.* New York: Basic Books.

Pines, M. (1999) *Forgotten Pioneers: The Unwritten History of the Therapeutic Community Movement.* http://www.pettarchiv.org.uk/atc-journal-pines.htm: Association of Therapeutic Communities.

Prochaska, J. and Diclemente, C. (1998) *Changing for Good.* New York: Avon.

Rapoport, R. (1960) *Community as Doctor.* London: Tavistock.

Robins, L. and Murphy, G. (1967) 'Drug use in a normal population of young negro men.' *American Journal of Public Health* 57, pp.1580–1586.

Simpson, J. H. (1917) *An Adventure in Education.* London: Sidgwick and Jackson.

Stevens, J. (1993) *Storming Heaven: LSD and the American Dream.* London: Flamingo.

Stimson, G. 'Blair declares war on the unhealthy state of British drugs policy.' In *Methadone and Beyond: Expanding and Exploring Drug Treatment Options: Methadone Alliance Conference London, March, 22, 2000.* Methadone Alliance, forthcoming.

Strang, J. and Yates, R. (1982) *Involuntary Treatment and Addiction.* Strasbourg: Council of Europe (Pompidou Group).

Toon, P. and Lynch, R. (1994) 'Changes in therapeutic communities in the UK.' In J. Strang and M. Gossop (eds) *Heroin Addiction and Drug Policy: The British System.* Oxford: Oxford University Press.

Turner, D. (1994) 'The development of the voluntary sector: no further need for pioneers.' In J. Strang and M. Gossop (eds) *Heroin Addiction and Drug Policy: The British System*. Oxford: Oxford University Press.

Unell, I. and Vincent, J. (1994) *The Costs of Residential Care and Services in the Community for Problem Users of Drugs and Alcohol*. Loughborough: Loughborough University of Technology.

United Nations Drug Control Program (UNDCP) (1997) *World Drug Report*. Oxford: Oxford University Publications.

Vaillant, G. (1966) 'A twelve-year follow-up study of New York narcotic addicts.' *American Journal of Psychiatry 122*, pp.727–735.

Velleman, R. and Rigby, J. (1990) 'Harm minimization: new wine in old bottles?' *International Journal on Drug Policy 1*, 6, pp.24–27.

Wills, D. (1967) *The Hawkspur Experiment*. London: Allen and Unwin.

Wilkinson, K. and Cox, A. (1986) *Principles into Practice: A Developmental Study of a Community Mental Health Service*. Manchester: Youth Development Trust.

Wilson, F. W. (1978) 'Spiritual therapy in the therapeutic community.' In P. Vamos and D. Brown (eds) *Proceedings of the 2nd World Conference of Therapeutic Communities: The Addiction Therapist, Special Edition 2*, 3 and 4, pp.204–205.

Winick, C. (1962) 'Maturing out of narcotic addiction.' *United Nations Bulletin on Narcotics, 14*.

Yates, R. (1979) 'An experiment in multi-facility addiction.' *Addiction Therapist (Special Edition)*, Winter, 3, pp.25–30.

Yates, R. (1981) *Out From the Shadows*. London: NACRO.

Yates, R. (1992) *If it Weren't for the Alligators – A History of Drugs, Music and Popular Culture in Manchester*. Manchester: Lifeline Project.

Part 1

# Background

# CHAPTER 1

# Therapeutic communities for drug users: description and overview

## Eric Broekaert

## Basic description

### Definition

In 1991 in 'De Haan' (Belgium) a general meeting of the European Federation of Therapeutic Communities took place. The concept of a drug-free therapeutic community was defined as follows:

> A therapeutic community is a drug-free environment in which people with addictive (and other) problems live together in an organized and structured way in order to promote change and make possible a drug-free life in the outside society. The therapeutic community forms a miniature society in which residents, and staff in the role of facilitators, fulfil distinctive roles and adhere to clear rules, all designed to promote the transitional process of the residents. Self-help and mutual help are pillars of the therapeutic process in which the resident is the protagonist principally responsible for achieving personal growth, realizing a more meaningful and responsible life, and of upholding the welfare of the community. The program is voluntary in that the resident will not be held in the program by force or against his/her will. (Ottenberg *et al.* 1993, p.51–62)

It was also stated that even if every therapeutic community differs in significant aspects, there are nevertheless fundamental principles which must be respected. Every therapeutic community has to strive towards integration into the larger society; it has to offer its residents a sufficiently long stay in treatment; both staff and residents should be open to challenge and to questions; ex-addicts can be of significant importance as role models; staff must respect ethical standards, and therapeutic communities should regularly review their 'raison d'être'.

The last few years have brought about some changes. The 'new therapeutic communities' have largely developed in terms of complex networks dealing with special needs and specific target groups. Under certain conditions a more flexible treatment approach may be introduced, as in the case of residents with dual diagnosis or those with chronic addiction requiring appropriate psychotropic medication. Nevertheless these aforementioned characteristics remain of central importance (Broekaert *et al.* 1998).

## The philosophy

The therapeutic community philosophy is a statement of belief about the possibility of change and personal growth, and is explicitly stated by the therapeutic community, and referred to in daily activities. While the particular written philosophy of each therapeutic community may vary, each is based to some extent on a combination of different strands of thinking (Broekaert 1999). These include early Christian values (Broekaert and van der Straten 1997; Glaser 1977; Mowrer 1976; the 'first century Christian fellowship' and the Oxford group of F. Buchman (Lean and Buchman 1985), Alcoholics Anonymous (Bassin 1977), the Synanon movement (Garfield 1978) and the humanist psychologists such as Maslow (Maslow 1967) and Rogers (in Bassin 1977, p. 24).

The 'philosophy' was originally stated by Richard Bauvais, a resident of Daytop Village, New York. He wrote:

> I am here because there is no refuge, finally, from myself. Until I confront myself in the eyes and hearts of others, I am running. Until I suffer them to share my secrets, I have no safety from them. Afraid to be known, I can know neither myself nor any other; I will be alone. Where else but in our common ground, can I find such a mirror? Here, together, I can at least appear clearly to myself, not as the giant of my dreams, nor the dwarf of my fears. But as a person, part of the whole, with my share in its purpose. In this ground, I can take root and grow. Not alone anymore, as in death, but alive to myself and to others. (In O'Brien 1993, p.99)

In most therapeutic communities all over the world we can identify similar applications. Further, throughout the day and during morning meetings, seminars, and encounter groups, 'the philosophy' is discussed until it becomes an integrated part of one's personality. Residents strive for a positive lifestyle based on dedication, honesty, a sense of responsibility, showing concern, and acting 'as if' (i.e. as if they were already well-balanced, drug-free members of society). They strive to keep the therapeutic community environment free of drugs and violence (Kooyman 1992, pp.26–31).

## Residents

The therapeutic communities refer to drug users seeking treatment in their centres as 'residents'. They consider them as emotionally immature human beings needing to be educated through the therapeutic program. They define them as born manipulators who suffer from anxieties and fears, and who use aggression to disguise their weakness:

> I learned to manipulate people and I will continue doing so when it suits me. I have both a good and bad character. I'm suspicious. I manipulate people and provoke them with word games. I like people who can retaliate. I will continue to manipulate people in order to see how far I can trust them. I know that this has a lot to do with this basic distrust of mine. I have lots of friends now and they know that I become aggressive when I feel pessimistic. When I'm angry I blame this one scapegoat for everything. Sometimes I then start crying. The day after I feel so childish and regret having shown myself as so little a man. (Ex-resident; author's records)

On the other hand they attribute to them a great potential for positive change. Therapeutic communities make a clear distinction between 'residents' who can be educated and 'patients' who need to be cured. Residents in the therapeutic community often criticize previous treatments, where they were expected to act passively, as patients:

> In those days I lived alone. One day I wrote to my girlfriend telling her that I intended to commit suicide. However it was impossible for her to meet me as she was ill herself. I then made a suicide attempt with 'city gas' but this is not deadly. They found me twenty-four hours later and I was taken into hospital. There they treated me like a child. They gave me an injection every hour and didn't answer when I asked them what it was for. My father and my sister came to visit and threatened to have me locked up in a psychiatric hospital. I knew this hospital because of my situation with X, and certainly didn't want to go there. At midnight I was given a last injection, struggled to stay awake and then split. (Ex-resident; author's records)

Casriel was the first to consider them, in the first place, as people with personality disorders. Addicts suffer from anxieties and pain which they can neither 'fight' nor 'flee'. Instead they 'freeze' their emotions.

> Instead of disguising or distorting his basic emergency emotions, the character-disordered personality represses these emotions all together. He

detaches his feelings from his conscious awareness, encapsulating them in a shell of unawareness, unconsciously creating an emotional isolation. (Casriel 1976, p.158)

The classic therapeutic tools cannot reach these 'frozen' personalities and that is where the therapeutic community can come in.

### Treatment phases

#### Crisis intervention

Substance abusers in an acute stage of disturbance and crisis can contact a therapeutic community for crisis intervention and detoxification. Most of these people go into treatment and leave after a few days. Some of them can be motivated to go for treatment. Most of them go back to the streets, and immediately revert to using drugs. They deny their problem.

#### Ambulatory level

At this level, potential residents come in to the program several times a week, while still living outside. They have to come in drug-free, and are given simple tasks so that they can show their willingness to enter the therapeutic community. The ambulatory level brings some regularity into their lives, and it is expected that some initial modification of their behaviour occurs at this early stage.

#### Reception

Many substance abusers encounter much difficulty in their first step towards treatment. Most therapeutic communities have a low threshold program at their disposal. This is less challenging than the main program, and is designed to get a resident used to therapy. Over a period of several weeks, this more individualized approach prepares for induction to the community. It also functions as aid and support for early dropouts and leads to a better differentiation of available treatments, both at community level and at the level of specialized services aimed at specific target groups. At 'reception' the first social and psychological assessment takes place.

#### Induction

At induction the motivation for treatment is tested. Sometimes shortly after 'reception' or during a week at ambulatory level, the candidate is required to show his external motivation (stopping drug use, demonstrating acceptable behaviour and clothing). He also has to be willing to change.

### Treatment

At the treatment centre, 'community' is used as 'method' (De Leon 1997). During a period of one year the resident will live together with his peers. In a hierarchically structured environment, and in a sphere of safety and acceptance, he will learn to express his emotions and change his behaviour by means of 'encounter' groups and other therapeutic means. It is believed that through these means the resident will reach a new stage of personal identity and gain better self-insight.

### Social (re)integration

During a further half year, the resident will gradually move from a 'halfway house' (where he lives together with friends who have also been through the program) to his 'own housing'. The approach is much more individualized now and the resident slowly but surely resumes contact with the 'normal' outside world. After 'graduation' from the program the resident will reach a new stage of social identity, accompanied by a better insight into his place in the world.

### Treatment characteristics

#### Safety and acceptance

In the therapeutic community the drug abuser is no longer threatened by outside dangers such as drugs, pimps, dealers and criminals. Within the community the resident lives with caring staff members and, crucially, a group of people who share similar experiences. There are people there who understand what the residents have been through, and what they are going through now, because they have been through it all themselves. It is this recognition of common experiences which facilitates the development of trust.

> What they most need in order to open up in the group is trust. If you are really going to expose yourself to people then that sense of reciprocity and empathy, the feeling that you're not so different from everybody else, is of crucial importance. (Ottenberg 1999, p.25)

Explicit rules pertaining to no drugs in the community, no physical violence and (to a certain degree) no sex, add to an atmosphere of safety and acceptance.

If the rule is broken and there is any drug abuse in the house it is an inevitable rule that the resident has to leave the community. Various alternatives are available – he can live on his own and come back after a while if he remains drug-free, or he can go to the reception department, or start an ambulatory induction. Depending on the needs of the individual involved, an alternative form of treatment to the therapeutic community may be proposed, such as methadone maintenance, counselling or psychiatric hospital care.

Physical violence is also absolutely forbidden. It can erupt quickly and forcibly as there are many residents with a criminal record of violence in their past. Sex (in the community itself) is not permitted as it can lead to negative contracts between some residents and provokes anxieties in those residents with a past history of prostitution and sexual abuse.

*Hierarchical structure*

A therapeutic community consists of several work departments, such as the service crew, the kitchen, the administration, public relations, etc. Each department has its own specific responsibilities and internal hierarchy, and the different departments themselves are organized around an implicit hierarchical order. New residents gradually climb up from the lowest ranks of the service departments to the higher ranks of the public relations department. New residents begin as helpers; they follow orders and don't take responsibilities without permission. They are free to join the discussions relating to the philosophy and concept of the therapeutic community. Older residents become department heads; they check the work and helpers are permitted to speak with them about their feelings. The most senior member of this residents' hierarchy is the co-ordinator, who is responsible for planning the daily activities of all the different departments. The co-ordinator also keeps the staff informed and serves as a bridge between them and the residents. Together with the staff he prepares the 'encounter' group and proposes adequate approaches to individual residents. He is helped by assistants or 'expediters', who have to be aware of everything that happens in the community. The staff are the real decision-makers and the ones who take responsibility for the therapeutic and educational functioning of the community.

As the substance abuser is not used to an orderly life, the community offers a daily routine. Residents get up at six, take care of personal hygiene, and breakfast at seven. At eight, everyone reports at morning meeting. The 'philosophy' is stated and discussed, announcements are made, 'things forgotten to do' are brought to mind, and 'things to do' are summed up. At the end, usually in a spirit of fun and humour, commitments are reaffirmed and a good attitude for the day is established. After morning activities in the various departments, lunch is taken at noon, followed by some free time. The afternoon follows the same scheme of activities till dinner. After dinner the residents enjoy some leisure time, then go to bed. Within this daily routine, educational seminars are held and encounter groups and other specific therapeutic activities take place.

The responsibilities of the residents are hierarchically structured in order to create a situation of adapted therapeutic evolution. Tasks and orders must be direct and clear. Moving up the chain of command and assuming more responsibility stimulates the feeling of making progress in therapy. However, as nothing is constant but change, it is equally possible to go down in the hierarchy. This can warn against insufficient enthusiasm and dedication.

Bridger (1984, p.57) warns us not to confuse the concept of hierarchy with that of autocracy. The former seeks to guide through rank, while autocracy refers to absolute power. According to Kooyman (1992, p.50) the structure does not stand by itself but is in permanent balance with the emotion and individual expression which comes out in therapy groups. In this way therapeutic communities are different from hierarchically organized institutions such as prisons or armies, where the structures are characteristically static.

*Verbal reprimands and learning experiences*

In a therapeutic community it is not uncommon that residents act out during the day. In a sense they call for attention through a show of disinterest, by making mistakes, or by reacting against the process of recovery. The main reason for this is that they are charged with emotion, anxiety, pain and craving. Through the chain of command – department heads, expediters and co-ordinators – the staff are informed. After discussion a verbal reprimand is sometimes called for, or a learning experience. The former means that the staff or co-ordinators try to correct this behaviour through verbal explanation.

A learning experience requires that the staff look for certain specific projects or individual activities that could help the resident. It is important that the resident feels respected and understands why this correction is made. It may never be regarded as a sanction in the strict meaning of the term. Outsiders often misinterpreted these interventions. In the early American therapeutic community, and to some degree in Europe, residents were seen as offenders and were called into a separate room where they had to stand and listen to the reprimand without being given opportunity to reply. They might have had to wear a sign or perform an extra duty. This was part of the 'brutal honesty' (Maslow 1967) of the early therapeutic approach, which itself was considered a humanistic reaction against the punitive trend of the treatments which had existed before that (Bratter *et al*.1985).

Outside of encounter groups, residents are asked to act 'as if' they can stand it. Acting 'as if' requires that people behave as the person they should be, rather than as the person they have been. This gives responsibility to the resident for his behaviour, and inevitably it produces its own pressures:

> The first six months in the therapeutic community were a hell for me. I suffered physically very much; often I could not eat because of the tensions that built up in my throat. I cried almost every day as if experiencing a lot of grief that I had never previously expressed. Crying was a release; afterwards I could eat better. I felt tense because they always made remarks but I knew that in fact I needed this – it was something my father had never done. Even now I still need it, but am better equipped to find solutions. (Ex-resident; author's records)

These pressures are often saved up and expressed in the encounter group.

### Encounter

The encounter is the primary therapeutic tool of the therapeutic community. Three times a week, for approximately two hours, the therapeutic community is split up into separate groups of about eight to ten persons, consisting of new residents, older residents and staff. Those attending sit in a circle, on chairs or mattresses. There is no hierarchy at that moment. Everybody has full freedom of expression. However, staff members have specific tasks: they monitor the process and guarantee safety and support at difficult moments.

Confronting negative behaviour or attitude is an essential aspect of the encounter group in the therapeutic community. Confrontation has to be direct and open and clear. Negative behaviour by those confronted cannot be supported by other group members. Negative contracts between members have to be broken. Confrontation can be person to person, but often several group members will join and support the one confronting. When it is clear to the rest of the group that the person being confronted understands *why* he is being confronted, and agrees to look at his behaviour and try to change it, the roles can quickly be reversed. The confronters may themselves become the confronted. In a group that is functioning well, as much attention is paid to the person confronting as to the one confronted.

Experienced group members have at their disposal a lot of encounter tools which can be used to reach a person: tools such as humour, exaggeration, contradiction, acceptance and support. Confrontation is usually related to irresponsible behaviour during the daily activities. It takes place in 'the here and now'. The person can explain his behaviour in emotional terms, sometimes invoking the past or the background of his behaviour. But this 'past' has to be lived through in the 'here and now' and the 'past' can never be an excuse for current behaviour. Other group members can identify and give examples of how they experienced and resolved the same problems. The encounter can end warmly with a lot of shared emotion, and reference to the concept.

Over the years, confrontation has changed from a direct attempt to penetrate the encapsulation of the person to an advanced form of dialogue. Attempts to achieve clarity and understanding are combined with a lot of respect for the individuality of the person. If we adopt a more abstract approach we can identify the different phases of the encounter as follows: a building up of tension, followed by release and openness, concluding in the implementation of (new) values through identification with more experienced peers.

It is very important in this context that staff members act as group members and contribute their own experiences and beliefs. Acting from a position of power or using the 'concept' or 'philosophy' as an abstract tool could lead to a certain type of indoctrination. The group is essentially an instrument of social learning, as defined by Maxwell Jones (Jones 1984), and constitutes a 'transitional space of experience' as learned by Winnicott and Harold Bridger (Bridger 1984). In this sense the therapeutic community itself can be considered as the quintessence of the treatment, consisting as it does of positive peer pressure and social learning through interaction, the balance of hierarchy and the expression of emotion, an increasing ability to take responsibility for one's own behaviour, the growth of self-esteem, internalization of a new value system, and a new appreciation of the family – all culminating in (re)integration into society. Therapeutic community treatment can be considered as an intensified form of rebuilding a value system, one that uses the old principles of therapeutic education and social learning[1], and adapts them to the needs of a drug-abusing population.

*Family work*

The family is considered of essential importance to the good functioning of the resident in the therapeutic community. At the moment of enrolment, the first contact with the family is made. As much information as possible, pertaining to the family history and situation of the resident, is gathered. Residents are invited to phone and write to their relatives, who can visit the department at the resident's request. After admission to 'reception' and during their stay in the therapeutic community, supportive talks with the family are set up. The residents are carefully prepared for the meetings with their family, who often have a large impact on the therapeutic work. Families can meet other residents' families in order to discuss their common problems. At certain moments families are invited to parties and special events in the house. In Europe, Picchi (Picchi 1994) and his 'Progetto per l'Uomo' focus attention particularly on the family approach.

It has to be added that many communities are devoted to the contextual approach of Boszormenyi-Nagy (Boszormenyi-Nagy and Krasner 1986). This is based on the work of the Hungarian psychiatrist, who created a systematic approach to understanding family influences on individual behaviour, using a combination of psychodynamic theory and existentialist philosophy. Within this framework, the actual problems of the clients are placed into an intergenerational context, and understanding is reached through investigations of the loyalties and conflicts engendered by these complex family networks.

## Discussion
### The new therapeutic community

The last few years have brought about some changes. The 'new therapeutic communities' have largely developed in terms of complex networks dealing with special needs and specific target groups. (Broekaert et al. 1998). Whereas in the early therapeutic communities the simple indication 'character disorder' seemed sufficient, the 'new therapeutic community' expanded to other groups, such as people with dual diagnosis, children of abusers, homeless people, post traumatic disorders, prisoners, immigrants, prostitutes and HIV victims. This has involved a more adapted approach, known as 'the modified therapeutic community' (De Leon 1997). For example, in the case of residents with dual diagnosis or those with chronic addiction, appropriate psychotropic medication is accepted and the burden on the client is lowered. There has also been a move towards the creation of an integrative recovery strategy (De Leon 1996). This means that programs that aim at drug treatment, such as drug-free therapeutic communities, psychiatric treatment and methadone maintenance treatment, are no longer considered as aggressive competitors, but as collaborating partners.

### Staff challenges

In the early days of the therapeutic community, staff members adhered to the self-help principle whereby ex-addicts were very involved. Residents could identify with the staff and use them as role models.

In the European therapeutic communities, where professionals had played an important role from the beginning, a further professional integration took place. Those professionals followed special training and learned how to manage a therapeutic community. In the Belgian therapeutic community 'De Kiem' most of the staff were trained as interns in established

American or European therapeutic communities. In the phase that followed many ex-addicts suffered burnout, but those who remained became the protagonists of a new profession. However, regardless of the type of schooling followed, the job of therapeutic community staff member requires a lot of skill. Constant flexibility is required, together with focus and thoroughness. There is a complex interaction between one's own personality and daily exposure to extreme forms of psychological problems. Besides being emotionally resilient enough for the job, one also has to believe in the approach and yet maintain sufficient distance. Above all one must understand that one is simply a facilitator of the therapeutic process. The more 'superfluous' the staff members become, the better they are doing their job. In that sense their behaviour has to be transparent and open to challenge.

## Encounter and dialogue

The encounter was often described as a behaviourist reaction against psychoanalysis. 'Insight' can lead to a series of excuses not to change current 'behaviour' and can be seen as a way of using the past as an excuse for the present. 'Insight gives the client an out not to deal with his behaviour' (Bratter et al. 1985, p.478). In Synanon, the encounter was considered as 'an uninhibited conversation, an arena for discussing all human feelings'. In Synanon it was called 'the Game', and observers defined it as an unusual form of 'attack' or 'reality attack therapy'. Confrontation with one's behaviour was an essential aspect of the encounter group in the therapeutic community.

Confrontation had to be direct, without fear or inhibition. Many 'ex-addicts' still swear by the encounter groups of the past, and some (mostly American therapeutic communities in the prison system) continue to favour that approach. However, an evolution has undoubtedly taken place over the years. The groups have become less intensive and more sensitive. Bracke, an addiction therapist in the therapeutic community 'De Kiem' since 1977, makes a remarkable observation:

> The encounter and its hard confrontations strove to 'break' the image of the addict. However it often happened that this radical method did not destroy the 'image' but that the person himself felt broken, devalued, humiliated and without support. Many stopped their treatment prematurely because they did not get time to experience the support and comprehension that made the therapy tolerable. (Bracke 1996, p.73)

Recently the encounter has evolved into an intense form of dialogue where as much attention is given to the one confronting as to the one being confronted. The process has essentially become more rather than less sophisticated and this can make it difficult for young staff members, as it becomes less easy to understand and 'direct' an encounter. However the basic assumptions and mechanisms remain the same. All other forms of individual and family treatment in a therapeutic community are geared through the encounter.

### External researchers

In recent years the therapeutic community has been surrounded by 'science' and 'psychiatric diagnosis'. This is especially so in Europe, where the therapeutic community was and is largely subsidized by government money, and where an official request exists for medical diagnosis and assessment. Together with university researchers, more sophisticated assessment instruments have entered the therapeutic community. For example, the multi-centre trial study, Biomed II/ITPRP, introduced a number of standard assessment instruments into 29 therapeutic communities spread over eleven European countries.[2] About 3000 individual tests were carried out, and the results indicated that depression is a major problem for residents, that many of them have been sexually abused, that they have a lack of attachment, that they suffer from morbidity, and that many suffer from a psychiatric disorder as well as an addiction problem (Kaplan et al. 1999).

While such findings are helpful both from the point of view of directing treatment, and for continuing to attract funding, therapeutic community staff members often find that such an emphasis on assessment directly interferes with the planning of treatment and with their own vision of the residents. While a more psychiatric terminology has become relevant as therapeutic communities have become more professional, there is still a general feeling that the characteristics of the residents are of less importance than the questions which residents' day-to-day behaviour provokes within the team. It is this tradition of working closely with the issues and problems thrown up by the particular individuals who are in residence at the moment, and doing so within the familiar structured therapeutic community environment, which continues to form the basis of treatment.

### Notes

1. *Author's note.* The term 'social learning' is used here to refer to development in all activities of life, such as personal care, eating, working, playing and learning. Although the term 'social learning' is often used in therapeutic community material, it is used here as the nearest translation we can find for the Dutch phrase '*sociale pedagogiek*'.

2. ADAD (Adolescents Drug Abuse Diagnosis); youth MAPS (youth Monitoring Area and Phase System); DSM (the statistical manual); SCID (Structured Clinical Interview for DSM [Diagnostic and Statistical Manual of Mental Disorders]); MSMA (Maastricht Social Network Analysis); CTQ (Childhood Trauma Questionnaire); ASI (Addiction Severity Index); MAPS (Monitoring Area and Phase System); CMRS (Circumstances, Motivation, Readiness, and Suitability Scales); TUF (Treatment Unit Form); SEEQ (therapeutic community Scale of Essential Elements Questionnaire); VACT (Video Addiction Challenge Test).

## References

Bassin, A. (1977) *The Miracle of the Therapeutic Community: from Birth to Post-partum Insanity to Full Recovery.* In P. Vamos and D. Brown (eds) Second world conference of therapeutic communities. *The Addiction Therapist, Special Edition 2,* 3 and 4, pp.3–15.

Boszormenyi-Nagy, I. and Krasner, B. (1986) *Between Give and Take: A Clinical Guide to Contextual Therapy.* New York: Brunner/Mazzel.

Bracke, R. (1996) 'De encounter, het hart van de therapeutische gemeenschap.' In E. Broekaert, R. Bracke, D. Calle, A. Cogo, G. van der Straten and H. Bradt. (eds) *De Nieuwe Therapeutische Gemeenschap.* Leuven, Belgium: Garant.

Bratter, T., Collabolleta, E., Fossbender, A., Pennachia, M. and Rubel, J. (1985) 'The American self-help residential therapeutic community: a pragmatic treatment approach for addicted character-disordered individuals.' In T. Bratter, T. and G. Forrest (eds) *Alcoholism and Substance Abuse.* London: The Free Press, pp. 461–507.

Bridger, H. (1984) *The Therapeutic Community Today. Proceedings of the First World Institute of Therapeutic Communities.* Rome, Italy: Centro Italiano di Solidarietà.

Broekaert, E. (1999) 'History and basics of the therapeutic community (Die Entstehung der Therapeutischen Gemeinschaft).' In M. Colla, T. Gabriel, S. Milham, Müller-Teusler and M. Winkler (eds) *Handbook of Residential and Foster Care in Europe* (Handbuch Heimerziehung und Pflegekinderwesen in Europa). Neuwied, Kriftel: Luchterhand, pp.173–179.

Broekaert, E., Bracke, R., Calle, D., Cogo, A., van der Straten, G. and Bradt, H. (eds) (1996) *De Nieuwe Therapeutische Gemeenschap.* Leuven, Belgium: Garant.

Broekaert, E., Kooyman, M. and Ottenberg, D. (1998) 'The "new" drug-free therapeutic community: challenging encounter of classic and open therapeutic communities.' *Journal of Substance Abuse Treatment 15,* 6, pp. 595–597.

Broekaert, E. and van der Straten, G. (1997) 'Histoire, philosophie et dévélopement de la communauté thérapeutique en Europe.' *Psychotropes: Revue Internationale des Toxicomanies 3,* 1, pp.7–23.

Casriel, D. (1976) *A Scream Away from Happiness.* New York: Grosset and Dunlap.

De Leon, G. (1994) 'The therapeutic community approach to rehabilitation.' In *Therapeutic Communities of America. Paradigms: Past, Present and Future.* Proceedings of the Therapeutic Community Association 1992 Planning Conference. Washington D.C.

De Leon, G. (1996) 'Integrative recovery: a stage paradigm.' *Substance Abuse 17,* 1, pp.51–63.

De Leon, G. (1997) *Community as a Method: Therapeutic Communities for Special Populations and Special Settings.* Westport, Connecticut: Praeger Publishers.

Emerson, R. W. (1955) *Select Writings.* London: Walter Scott Publishing.

Garfield, M. (1978) *The Synanon Religion: The Survival Morality for the 21st Century.* Marshall, California: Synanon Foundations.

Glaser, F. (1977) *The International History and Evolution of the Therapeutic Community Movement. Proceedings of the Second World Conference of Therapeutic Communities.* Montreal, Canada: The Portage Press.

Jones, M. (1984) *The Two Therapeutic Communities. A Review. Proceedings of the Eighth World Conference of Therapeutic Communities.* Rome, Italy: Centro Italiano di Solidarietà.

Kaplan, C., Broekaert, E., Yates, R., Frank, O. *et al.* (1999) *Final Report of Biomed 2 on Improving Psychiatric Treatment in Residential Programs for Newly Dependent Groups Through Relapse Prevention.* Maastricht: University of Maastricht.

Kooyman, M. (1992) *The Therapeutic Community for Addicts: Intimacy, Parent Involvement and Treatment Outcome.* Rotterdam, the Netherlands: Universiteitsdrukkerij Erasmusuniversiteit.

Lean, G. and Buchman, F. (1985) *A Life.* London: Constable and Company Limited.

Maslow, A. H. (1967) 'Synanon and Eupsychia.' *Journal of Humanistic Psychology* 7, pp. 28–35.

Mowrer, O. H. (1976) *Therapeutic Groups and Communities in Retrospect and Prospect. Proceedings of the First World Conference on Therapeutic Communities.* Katrineholm, Sweden: Vallmotorp Foundation.

O'Brien, W. B. (1993) *You Can't Do it Alone.* New York: Simon and Schuster.

Ottenberg, D. (1999) 'The TC – Essentials.' In E. Broekaert, W. Vanderplasschen and V. Soyez (eds) *Proceedings of the International Symposium on Substance Abuse Treatment and Special Target Groups.* Ghent: University of Ghent, Department of Special Education.

Ottenberg, D., Broekaert and E. Kooyman, M. (1993) 'What cannot be changed in a therapeutic community?' In E. Broekaert and G. Van Hove, (eds) *Special Education Ghent 2: Therapeutic Communities.* Ghent: vzw OOBC.

Picchi, M. (1994) *Un Progetto per L'Uomo.* Roma: Centro Italiano di Solidarietà.

# CHAPTER 2

# Democratic and concept-based therapeutic communities and the development of community therapy

## Salvatore Raimo

## Introduction

Writing today about democratic and concept-based communities is not easy because this issue has always been imbued with ideological viewpoints and passion. Moreover, although it is helpful to clarify the two approaches, for the benefit of those who are not familiar with one or the other, it no longer seems such an important distinction. Concept-based therapeutic communities have changed, and in describing such therapeutic communities, it is important to explain how and why these changes have come about. This chapter will do just that. I will begin with a description of the two models (for a fuller description of both, see Kennard 1998). I will then go on to show how, in Italy at least, the therapeutic community is now part of a much wider concept: community treatment.

## The democratic model

When we talk about the democratic therapeutic community we usually refer to a model developed by psychiatrists. Maxwell Jones (Jones 1952) worked at the Belmont Industrial Neurosis Unit in England in the 1940s, which later became the Henderson Hospital, and is still a therapeutic community today. Bion and Foulkes, both psychiatrists, were working at an English army hospital in Northfield at about the same time (Bion 1960; Foulkes 1948). Though Belmont and Northfield were not connected, these two institutions separately began to change in similar ways. They provided their patients with information on their various complaints and gave them responsibility for each other's progress and treatment. Staff and residents were encouraged to become much closer, and more equal, and residents were given decision-making powers, through voting. Community issues were discussed daily in large groups, in which anyone could have a say. The group, rather than the individual psychiatrist, became the therapist (Main 1946; Rapoport 1960).

The big change represented by this so-called democratic approach was based on recognition of the patient as a person and not just as a subspecies that has to be locked into a clinic for protecting him/her and society. As the patients started to take part in decision-making processes, the former hierarchical structure of the psychiatric hospital became more horizontal. This created an atmosphere which had a therapeutic effect. Doors were unlocked, the exchange with the outside community increased, and so too did opportunities for the patients to have contact with their families and relations outside the clinic. The outside community became aware of the fact that the people inside the clinic were not a danger, but human beings with whom it was possible to establish a relationship.

This process changed not only the treatment but also the organization of the hospital, because the principles of sharing responsibility implied also the sharing of power. This changed the understanding of staff roles and changed their job descriptions. They became actors in the therapeutic process, not just guardians of sick people.

Nevertheless, I call this the 'so-called' democratic approach because the model has never been truly democratic: the roles were given and a patient could be cured and maybe healed, but he could not become part of the staff. The sharing of power and responsibility was never meant to be equal, so the adjective 'democratic' sounds a bit déplacé; it was not democratic but it was *more* democratic. It allowed for a very high level of participation by all members in the decision-making process, a high degree of information sharing, and a 'big ear' for listening to the others.

### The concept-based model

It was in 1958, in Santa Monica, California, USA that Charles Dederich started Synanon. He was an alcoholic, and a person with a strong charisma, with experience of Alcoholics Anonymous and their self-help concept. The Synanon community was very different from the therapeutic community of Maxwell Jones. Synanon was a self-help system. It was a community in the sense that all the people who lived and worked at Synanon during the day, also lived there in their free time. There were no trained, professional staff members, it was much like a big patriarchal family with a rigid hierarchy. Synanon had no patients. All people were residents and for a long time no professionals were admitted. This early period was described in detail by Lewis Yablonsky, a sociologist, and one of the first professionals to be allowed in (Yablonsky 1965).

'The Game' was the moment of catharsis for the community. This was a group meeting which emphasized confrontation and expression of feelings. Fear, anger and joy were expected to happen directly, without inhibitions or the mediation of self-control. Every member of the community, no matter how senior or junior, could be confronted during the Game. This moment could be seen either as an attempt to create a basic democracy or as a valve for aggression and a means of maintaining social control.

Although Synanon started well, and grew and became known as a viable treatment method for addiction, members felt it was shifting more and more towards a sect-like community, and was becoming too inward-looking and demanding of residents. In 1963 a group of people from Synanon, together with professionals and a Catholic priest, opened Daytop Village in New York (Sugarman 1974) which became the model for many more therapeutic communities.

Like Synanon, Daytop was very rigidly structured, based on the belief that a more democratic setting could not be handled by drug-addicted people. Like Synanon also, Daytop called themselves 'family'. Today it is still possible to attend an international meeting and hear the speaker start with a sonorous 'Good morning, family!'.

### The differences between the two models today

The attempt to make it clear where the differences really were and still are, is a delicate issue because it is coloured inevitably by factors of ideology, prejudgement and personal experiences.

What is clear is that the concept-based model has changed greatly over the past thirty years, and has become increasingly flexible and outward-looking. The clear distinction between the democratic and concept model no longer seems so easy to draw, although concept houses still retain their distinctive hierarchical resident structure and continue to use many of the rules which originated at Daytop. What has happened over the years is that different countries have adopted both models of therapeutic community, and altered them to suit their particular culture and needs. Thus for example, in Italy the democratic therapeutic community is particularly concerned with the treatment of mental illness, while in Britain it is mostly concerned with the treatment of personality disorder. In Italy, there seems to be more communication and overlap between democratic therapeutic communities and concept-based therapeutic communities, particularly at senior staff level, where directors and psychiatrists may attend the same conferences and belong to the same professional organizations. This is much less likely, even now, to happen in Britain. In Italy, both democratic and concept-based therapeutic communities are much more closely tied up with their local social communities, both as sources of referrals and as sources of ongoing support for residents and ex-residents. Two major enduring differences can, however, be distinguished. First there is the continuing fact that the concept house is almost always designed for people whose primary presenting problem is drug addiction, whatever 'secondary' or antecedent problems emerge during the course of their treatment. Democratic therapeutic communities, by contrast, are almost always designed for people who are classed as personality disordered or mentally disordered. Such people may also have an addiction to drugs, but not necessarily. The second major difference is that the staff of democratic therapeutic communities are all professionals, while many of the staff of a concept house will be ex-residents.

While it cannot be said that today the concept house has become democratic, any more than it could be said the democratic therapeutic community itself is truly democratic, it has certainly changed from the early model and become much more approachable and person-centred. To show in detail what this means, I will go on to describe the changes which have taken place in an Italian treatment centre for addicted people, the CEIS of Modena.[1] Originally a purely concept-based program, this community has opened up to include other ideas and skills, and now works with other agencies and resources, in order to provide individually-tailored treatment programs for a variety of addiction-related problems.

### The original concept-based program at Modena

The program in Modena started in 1982 as a therapeutic community, based very much on the American Daytop model, and adapted to the Italian context. That meant that residents' families were regarded as an important support in the therapy. It was structured in three main parts: *accoglienza* (reception, intake unit – non-residential); *comunità terapeutica* (therapeutic community residential treatment); re-entry (after care – residential or not).

The residential part was considered the most important treatment stage, and it was the facility in which most of the hierarchical and directive attitudes of this approach could be perceived. The hierarchy among the residents was very rigid and to take the step from one role to a higher one was something that had to be earned, mainly through acceptance of the rules and demonstration of faith in the therapeutic community system. The benefit for the resident was not just an improvement in social status; the real gain was the sense of belonging.

The whole system was very tight and exchange with the outside society was reduced to a minimum. The distance between the worlds inside and outside the therapeutic community was increased by the esoteric language used for describing events and actions: 'haircut', 'shot down', 'pull up board', 'take board', 'play game'... All these terms had a particular meaning inside the therapeutic community, and this made it difficult to describe to others what really happened there. Communication with other institutions was full of such barriers of language and meaning.

Respect for the rules and norms was a required attitude; infringement was followed inevitably by a sanction. The types of sanctions sometimes were very hard and could last for days. These sanctions could be individual or applied to the whole 'family', because everybody was considered responsible for the health and the safety of the therapeutic community and 'responsible concern' was one of the main therapeutic 'pillars'. The therapeutic community was managed by residents and many of the sanctions or interventions were decided by senior residents who had a certain hierarchical position but no specific knowledge, nor sufficient emotional distance. Understandably, they could react strongly to situations which they felt could threaten the health of the therapeutic community.

The staff group was mixed, and included former residents and professionals with different backgrounds. Staff training was provided by CEIS Rome with the help of teachers coming from Daytop Village, New York. The content of the training consisted of teaching the appliance of the therapeutic tools (haircut, pull up board, take board, encounter groups...) and the history of the therapeutic community movement (in which little time was lost on the work of Maxwell Jones or the work of other institutions except for Daytop, Alcoholics Anonymous and Synanon).

## The resident's experience in the early days

A new resident was admitted into this therapeutic community with the rite of the 'Interview'. This was a group session. The new member had to sit in front of five representatives of the 'family', tell them about his/her life and convince them that he/she wanted to be part of the family. This all had to be done in a very intense and emotional way, and the acting out of anger, fear and loneliness had to be perceived as genuine by everyone present in the room. The resident was required to shout and scream the need for help. Shouting and screaming was seen as a necessary part of the treatment.

At the end of the interview, which could last easily about four hours, the new resident would be given a warm and relieving hug in the entrance to the livingroom, where all the residents of the therapeutic community would be waiting. The 'older brother' or 'older sister' (one of the interviewers who would then be, for some weeks, the referral person for the new member) would then say to everybody: 'This is..., and from now on he/she is part of our family!'

Every new resident started out as labour in the cleaning brigade. The cleaning jobs were considered the most humble. Contact with the outside community was minimal: just the parole office, dentist, or church on Sunday. The resident was required to commit to the inside and to concentrate on just that. New residents were not allowed to be left on their own, nor were junior residents allowed to gather together without a staff member or a senior resident present to guide and control their talk. Control of the group was very strong and exclusive relationships were seen as dangerous. The demand was for the resident to conform to the rules and way of living of the therapeutic community, and not just to adapt to them, but to gradually internalize the values of honesty, respect and solidarity.

Every day started with the morning meeting of the family and the telling of the 'philosophy', which was the translation of the Daytop prayer into Italian. This morning meeting was designed to emphasize that everyone starts the day together, and to organize work and agree the 'open jobs'. An open job could be a job in a work sector but also a relational job, like talking to some other resident about something. For example, a resident might say to another: 'I want to share my feelings with you, because when you talked about your boyfriend I felt very close to you...' This would be spoken in front of everybody and a check would be made during the day or in the next morning meeting to see that it had been carried out.

Another important goal of the morning meeting was to establish the 'issue of the day', so that each member of the family could work towards achieving a common goal. It was held that this goal should not be abstract but concrete, so that it could be checked against a definite standard to see whether it had been achieved. (Unfortunately, sometimes the goal would be too vague: 'Let's be honest', or 'Let's think about our motivations for being here'.)

Several times a week residents would work in groups to express their feelings about each other and the pressures of the program. The main dynamic group (called dynamic because the people in it changed from group to group) was very similar to the original Game of Synanon, aggressive and confrontational. Other groups, with a more static membership, focused on issues more related to each resident's individual concerns: sexuality, family issues, biography and drug-taking career.

With time, and by fulfilling duties, and involving him/herself in the groups, a resident would climb the ladder of the therapeutic community hierarchy. He or she would gain privileges like not having to ask permission to smoke, being allowed to wear a watch, or make-up, or small jewels. With a higher hierarchical position a resident's contacts with the outside were also increased, first by shopping for the 'family' together with another resident, then independently.

## The need for change

When in 1984 the first AIDS cases were discovered among the residents, it was a terrible shock for the program. Increasingly, too, there were found to be residents with problems besides the addiction: eating disorders, dual diagnoses and families who were deeply dysfunctional in their relational patterns. The limits of treatment became evident and so did the need to connect with other agencies.

The first step was to define the task of the therapeutic community in this new situation. This can now be considered the starting point in the shift from a 'treatment in the therapeutic community' to a 'community treatment', which is what the change became. For the therapeutic community the problem became: what is a community treatment and how does the therapeutic community fit into it? The problem for the therapeutic community was to no longer have a treatment program which corresponded to a certain dogma, as it had done up till this point, but to have a program which permitted interaction with other services, especially medical services. At the same time it was important not to lose the identity and the strength which gave the therapeutic community its distinctive character, and its effectiveness as a treatment for addiction. This last issue has always been one of the most difficult tasks.

It was also realized that to be capable of working with this new situation, competencies were needed which had not been part of the usual therapeutic community staff training. New training was devised to enable staff to deal with more challenging residents, and to enable them to liaise with outside agencies. This training was attended by all staff members. Meetings with medical doctors and psychiatrists became part of the work. These meetings allowed staff to learn that there are other ways of describing situations and actions, and other ways of handling them than sanctions and shouting. Now, too, families were included in the program differently – and treated as a resource rather than a pathogenic factor.

What happened in Modena then was a growth in connection and co-operation with other helping systems in the field of public health. Whereas in the early days new residents had to fit in with the standard requirements of the therapeutic community, today there is no predetermined treatment plan which fits each client. A treatment plan has to be worked out for each individual, taking into consideration the resources of the person and his/her social system, the resources of the program and the resources of the larger community. The challenge for the therapeutic community has been to listen to people when they talk about their needs, without trying to tell them what their needs should be.

Now that change has happened, and we can look back, the differences between therapeutic community and community treatment can be outlined as shown in Table 2.1.

| Table 2.1: Differences between therapeutic community treatment and community treatment | |
|---|---|
| TREATMENT IN THERAPEUTIC COMMUNITY | COMMUNITY TREATMENT |
| ○ Program as a treatment process<br>○ Little exchange and interaction with the social community<br>○ Own language and terminology for describing situations and actions<br>○ Defined and fixed boundaries<br>○ Therapeutic community-centred staff training<br>○ Little use of the resources of the social community | ○ Program as part of a treatment process<br>○ Program as a part of the social community<br>○ Common language and terminology with other treatment professions<br>○ Permeable and flexible boundaries<br>○ Client-centred staff training<br>○ Strong connection with the existing resources of the social community |

During this process of change, the perception of inside–outside changed, the walls of the therapeutic community were lowered and became less visible. Professionals from the public health agencies started not just to visit the program, but to provide together treatment in different areas of the client's life. To set this up and co-ordinate contributions it was necessary to use a common language, and the effort to achieve this had to be made mainly by the staff members of the therapeutic community.

## The immediate effect of the change

This process of change created a crisis among the staff. The necessity for change was clear, but not the direction to take. This meant that a deep review of the work was required, and there was uncertainty about where everything was going. Many times the perception of the need for change was accompanied by a feeling of helplessness and confusion. Various members chose to leave and work in other programs. I think that this confusion among the staff was caused by a deep questioning of the role of the staff, and of the competencies that staff members need, in order to work in a therapeutic community. Skills and approaches which up till now had been considered 'good practice' were suddenly open to criticism and reform.

However, the effort was worthwhile because it opened the door to better treatment in the therapeutic community: better in the sense of being less exclusive. Clients who would never have been capable of staying in a rigid, hierarchical program were now able to do so.

One critical event was the opening of a house for terminal AIDS patients, since this brought about a confrontation with methadone. Up to that moment, methadone maintenance treatment had been considered by the therapeutic community in the same way as heroin addiction, while methadone treatment had always argued against the therapeutic community dogma of 'drug-free'. Now, with these new clients, the centre came to see that methadone could be useful in the treatment of certain people after all.

In the early 1990s the program started to have contacts with therapeutic communities from northern Europe. This resulted in further changes: the opening of a facility for addicted women with children, a higher tolerance in accepting differences, and membership of the European Federation of Therapeutic Communities.

The difference between treatment in the old style and the new-style therapeutic community will be illustrated in the following stories of two clients. One, F., is a hypothetical case, based on the author's experience of old-style methods and memories of many different residents. The second, G., is the true case study of a more recent client. There are similarities between the two. Both were young, drug-addicted women when they arrived at the therapeutic community, and both came from families which had migrated from other areas.

*The story of F*

F. was a young woman whose family had migrated from a suburb of Naples to a small town in the northern part of the country. There were seven children: three brothers and four sisters. F. was the youngest. The father, an unqualified workman, died in an accident at work three years after they left Naples, when F. was about seven years old.

The financial situation of the family collapsed and the mother had to do more than one job to make enough for them to live on. F. was placed in a boarding-school run by nuns. For her, this was a period of abandonment and loneliness. She started to rebel against school, until her mother was obliged to take her home.

The women of the family were educated to be submissive, but in a manipulative way. One of her older sisters became Miss Something in a local beauty contest. The brothers became bricklayers and truck drivers. F. left her new school and started to have experiences with older men. Some of them gave her money, and then drugs entered her life. She arrived at the treatment centre when she was 19 years old.

F. was admitted to this therapeutic community with the ritual of the interview. Like all new residents, she had to sit in front of five representatives of the 'family' and tell them about her life. Then she had to ask for their help to sort herself out. The representatives, however, were not initially convinced by her request for help, and felt she was playing games with them. They accused her of being manipulative and of being seductive towards them – tactics she had learnt in her childhood and which had been reinforced in her street life. The interview erupted into a crescendo of shouting, as the representatives tried to make F. 'cross the bridge' and ask for help in a 'real' way. Eventually the representatives thought they had made some progress and that F. was being more honest with them. They decided to end the interview and welcome her into the family.

In this way, F. came into treatment during a wave of 'the residents have to make a real choice about whether they are motivated to stay in the therapeutic community or not!' She continued to act out the survival strategy she had learned throughout her life: seduction. Seductive behaviour was seen in the therapeutic community as typical, negative, female behaviour, which had to be avoided, and so F. got sanctions for acting this way. She was smart enough to understand the expectations, and for a while she behaved 'well'. Meanwhile, the staff, who were busy with work inside the therapeutic community, saw F.'s family only once. This was not in the presence of F., because there was a 'tight house' at the time (a period of no contact for residents with the outside). This meeting with the family was difficult, because the cultural differences between Modena and Naples made it nearly impossible to create a real contact with the family, that would allow them (or at least one of them) to develop enough trust to participate as a resource in F.'s recovery. Although they asked for information about life in the therapeutic community, they did not participate at the parents' meetings, so they only understood a small part of what they were told. The family could not understand why they should not see their relative. They were not seen as a resource, nor did they feel like one. If anything, they were considered to be a danger.

After some months, F. was allowed to spend a weekend at home with her family. When she came back, she talked about it, saying that it had been great to be back home again, and that things with her family were much better than in the past. In a phone call (not in person) the family confirmed what F. said. This was repeated a few times.

However, it is clear now that the dramas of prostitution and abuse were never faced in an adequate way, because none of the staff members of the therapeutic community had enough experience to do this and there were no connections to women's associations or other agencies who could have provided help in these kinds of areas. The last time F. came back from her weekend at home, another resident asked her about 'guilt' and she answered that she was 'all right'. This did not convince the other resident and he went on asking about her guilt, while she denied having any. The next day this questioning went on until she admitted that she had taken drugs at various times during her weekends at home. Her family knew about it, but together they had decided not to say anything, because if the people from the therapeutic community knew about it, F. would be thrown out. (This is what F. had told them.)

F. got a hard sanction. She felt she could not take it, and she left the therapeutic community and went back to her family, relapsing continuously with heroin. With no support from the therapeutic community, it took the family a long time to develop enough trust in therapeutic communities to go to another program and ask for help. Meanwhile, F. had a very hard time, using drugs with all the humiliation and pain which are connected with that.

### The story of G

In contrast, this is the more recent experience of G., a drug-addicted woman in her twenties. The following description shows how differently the therapeutic community treats its clients today.

G. was a 26-year-old female client. She was born in Switzerland of Italian parents and was the first of three children. Both parents worked hard and had a very low level of integration with their environment. The isolation was created by language problems, cultural misunderstandings, feelings of inadequacy, and by the fact that the stay in Switzerland should have been temporary, and as short as possible, which was an obstacle to emotional involvement with colleagues or neighbours.

G.'s mother was overweight and depressed. Her father showed symptoms of alcohol abuse, but this was always denied by the family members. The younger sister (24 years) and brother (20 years) still lived with the parents. During meetings with the therapeutic community, every time one of the children started to talk about the day they would leave home, the mother started to weep and the father looked disappointed. In later sessions, the mother talked about her childhood and about the loss of her mother and how she had had to take over the nursing of her younger siblings. During these later sessions, much of the parents' behaviour became understandable, in the sense that it became clear what they were trying to gain, or better, to avoid...the crumbling of the family.

G. was a problematic child. At school she showed aggressive behaviour and she did not finish her vocational training because she was expelled and could not complete the Swiss compulsory education. Only a long time after the appearance of these symptoms did the family ask for help in a public consulting centre. However, when they did, the difficulties in understanding each other's language (in the widest meaning of the word) impeded the increase of confidence.

Various attempts by G. to leave her family failed, because the whole family was unable to cope with the 'loss' of a member. They finally asked for help from an Italian facility based in Switzerland. From there, G. entered the therapeutic community in Modena, while her family started to participate at self-help groups for Italian parents in Switzerland. From the very beginning it became evident that G. had great difficulties with the treatment. Her way of talking was different from that of the other residents, her way of interpreting situations was different. She left the centre several times and went back to her family. However, the family, with the help of a counsellor in Switzerland who was in contact with the treatment centre, had the strength to bring her back into treatment each time.

As time went on, some staff members began to think there was something else wrong with G. besides the problem of addiction. Then G. attempted suicide and was admitted to a psychiatric ward of the Modena hospital. The family was involved in this decision. While in the hospital, she was visited daily by members of the therapeutic community. She was discharged from hospital with a diagnosis of borderline personality disorder, and went back into the therapeutic community. After a month she relapsed again, and took drugs during a week spent with her family. It was decided that it was no longer possible to keep her in the program, because the group (and maybe the staff) were not willing to accept this behaviour, and she was asked to leave.

The family came over from Switzerland and they were told that the program was no longer able to help. They were advised to go to a specific psychiatrist when back in Switzerland. This psychiatrist (who was married to an Italian woman) was known to the centre before, and he was contacted and informed. Today, G. lives with her family and has reached a certain level of stability. She is in pharmacological treatment with the psychiatrist, and with her family she attends an Italian-speaking family counsellor who works in a Swiss treatment centre. From time to time she visits the program in Italy.

## Conclusion

Under the original concept-based regime, G. would have found it very difficult to stay in treatment, because of the relationship with her family. She would have had to choose between her real family and the therapeutic community family, and she would almost certainly have chosen the former. Once she had left the therapeutic community, she would have had no further contact with it, unless she herself had initiated it. As far as F. is concerned, we do not know what might have happened with her if the therapeutic community had been different. What we do know is that the more the therapeutic community is able to connect itself with other agencies and resources, the better equipped it is to deal with the varied challenges of drug addiction treatment.

In the treatment of G. it was necessary to orchestrate the action of the therapeutic community, the psychiatric hospital of the local health department, the psychiatrist in Switzerland, a self-help group in Switzerland and an Italian-speaking family counsellor in Switzerland. The therapeutic community had to interact with all these different parts, connect them up, and enable the family to use them. It also had to be satisfied with an outcome which the old therapeutic community would not have regarded as optimal, since G. was still being treated by drugs.

The connection with these outside agencies and resources has meant a shift from 'inside' to 'outside' thinking. The therapeutic community has had to develop a common language, so that the therapeutic community process can be described to professionals outside the organization and understood. Thus there has been a need to avoid the esoteric terminology of the past.

A comparison between concept-based treatment centres and democratic treatment is helpful in clarifying the terms and the differences and similarities between the two approaches. However, in terms of practice the distinction may not be so useful. The question is more: who is the person who comes to us and what are his or her needs? What are we capable of providing? How can we connect up with the people who can provide the missing parts of a treatment plan, the parts we have not got the resources for? Thus it is no longer the therapeutic community alone which is seen as the most effective treatment method for addiction, but the therapeutic community in conjunction with a whole range of other services. This is community treatment.

## Notes

1. The Centro Italiano di Solidarietà (CEIS) was founded in 1979 by Morio Picchi in Rome. Today there are about 50 programs in Italy, most of them strongly linked with the Catholic Church. The staff is a mixture of professionals and ex-addicts. CEIS works with addiction, alcoholism, minors, immigrants, juvenile delinquency, AIDS, psychiatric disturbances and drug abuse prevention.

## References

Bion, W. R. (1960) *Experiences in Groups.* London: Tavistock Publications.

Foulkes, S. R. (1948) *Introduction to Group Analytic Psychotherapy.* London: Heinemann.

Kennard, D. (1998) *An Introduction to Therapeutic Communities.* London: Jessica Kingsley Publishers (second edition).

Jones, M. (1952) *Social Psychiatry.* London: Tavistock.

Main, T. (1946) 'The hospital as a therapeutic institution.' *Bulletin of the Menninger Clinic 10,* pp.66–70. (Reprinted in *Therapeutic Communities,* (1996)*17,* 2, pp. 77–80).

Rapoport, R. N. (1960) *Community as Doctor.* London: Tavistock.

Sugarman, B. (1974) *Daytop Village: A Therapeutic Community.* New York: Holt, Rinehart and Winston.

Yablonsky, L. (1965) *Synanon: The Tunnel Back.* New York: Macmillan.

Part 2

# The Situation Worldwide

# CHAPTER 3

# The history of therapeutic communities: a view from Europe

## *Martien Kooyman*

## Introduction

During the 1960s Europe was faced with a new problem when a significant number of young people became involved with the use of illegal drugs. Up until this time drug abuse, particularly the use of opiates, was almost entirely confined to a small group of people working in the health field, such as physicians, nurses and pharmacologists. In most European countries, legislation prohibiting opiates had been operative since the 1920s, long before European society had to deal with the effects of widespread drug addiction.

Drug addiction was seen as a health problem. Drug addicts were referred to physicians, psychiatrists, mental hospitals and clinics for alcoholics. In the mid-1960s the drugs most commonly used by youngsters were cannabis, LSD, amphetamines and opium. In most European countries heroin was not introduced before the 1970s. In Great Britain heroin was prescribed to adolescent drug addicts by physicians and, from 1968, by special clinics linked to psychiatric hospitals or psychiatric wards of general hospitals. Actually, this so-called 'British system' never was a system; it was a result of the British tradition to allow doctors to prescribe drugs for their addicted patients. The restriction to specialist (psychiatric) clinics from 1968 was the direct result of increasing public and political concern at the large amount of surplus prescribed heroin finding its way on to the black market. (Glatt *et al.* 1967; Spear 1994).

In the Netherlands, where in 1968 methadone was introduced in maintenance programs for youngsters addicted to opium, heroin appeared on the black market in 1972 and soon replaced amphetamines and opium to become the most popular hard drug (Kooyman 1984). As heroin and methadone programs did not cure patients of their addiction, and the traditional general and psychiatric hospitals proved to be even less successful in this respect, new methods to treat the growing addict population had to be developed.

Among the new treatment methods being developed, one of the most successful had been created in the 1960s in North America: the drug-free therapeutic communities, with Synanon as their predecessor. In his book on Daytop Village in New York, the first therapeutic community modelled on Synanon, Sugarman termed the birth, growth and subsequent proliferation of therapeutic communities in the United States and in other parts of the world as one of the most fascinating social developments of our time (Sugarman 1974).

## The origin of the American therapeutic communities

The roots of the American therapeutic communities are in Synanon (Casriel 1963; Yablonsky 1967; Endore 1968). This self-help community was influenced greatly by the Alcoholics Anonymous (AA) movement. The founders of AA initially had links with the Oxford Group Movement, a spiritual organization founded by Frank Buchman, which after 1938 became known as the Moral Rearmament Movement (Buchman 1961; Marcel 1960). This movement had a religious character, proclaiming honesty to oneself and others and self-examination in group meetings (Glaser 1974; Glaser 1977).

The founder of Synanon was Charles (Chuck) Dederich, a former businessman and member of AA. A charismatic and forceful leader, Dederich found that the regular AA meetings were not nearly enough for him. In January 1958 he began to hold a Wednesday night discussion group in his apartment. Over the years, AA meetings had changed from telling everything that happened in one's life to simply recounting personal behaviour related to drinking. In addition, AA did not admit drug addicts as members. Dederich's Wednesday night meetings abandoned these restrictions. During one of the Wednesday night meetings, the participants started to scream loudly at each other in a heated confrontation. After this emotional outburst group members experienced feelings of great relief. It was decided to repeat this experiment at further meetings and to call these groups 'games'. Dederich believed that the fact that no professional had been present to calm them down might have made it possible for feelings to reach a point where such relief was possible (Dederich 1974). The regular participants were by now managing to abstain from alcohol and heroin and a decision was taken to start a community where they could live together. In 1958 the group founded their new community in Santa Monica, California, and gave it the name Synanon.

'The Game' became the heart of the community. The acceptance of the expression of verbal aggression between group members in the Game helped to resolve interpersonal conflicts and to express emotions. The cardinal rules in the community were: no violence or threat of violence, no use of alcohol or other mind-altering chemicals. The concept of self-reliance described by the American philosopher R. W. Emerson greatly influenced Dederich's ideas at this time. His vision was to create a better society. Traditional values such as honesty and responsibility were an important part of the Synanon Philosophy (Patton 1973). Residents of the Synanon community were not supposed to return to the society which they had renounced, although many did leave (Broekaert 1996). Within Synanon they created an ideal society (Maslow 1967). The residents had no private property, worked for seven days followed by seven days free time, and adopted several other community living patterns. At any time, work could be stopped to have a game to resolve conflicts. There was no money in the community, although the community owned and ran several businesses and farms. Synanon became a fascinating social experiment.

When the author visited Synanon in 1975 it had several large facilities, the main one being at Tomales Bay, north of San Francisco, where 16,000 people, including both former addicts and so-called 'lifestylers' attracted to the Utopian community ideals, were living and working together. They had their own schools, fire brigade, ambulances, farms, factories and other businesses. The centre of the community was 'the temple', a building with a library where members could study literature and tapes to become a 'Synanon fanatic'. In this building there was for many years an ongoing group discussion held in the form of a game. The weekly Monday night games of the elders also took place in this building. These were broadcast in Tomales Bay by closed circuit television and by radio to the other facilities.

It was Dederich's opinion at that time, that he, as the leader, had become a sort of demigod: in the games he was only confronted by his wife or his brother. By 1977, following the death of his wife, Betty Jean Beckham, of lung cancer, Dederich's behaviour had become increasingly erratic. The Synanon experiment itself ultimately failed, due to the leader's lack of sufficient self-control. A no-smoking rule was implemented and male as well as female members were shaving their heads. Youngsters who had been born in Synanon and did not want to be there like their parents became a problem. Dederich ordered couples to change partners and to be sterilized, and he finally allowed physical violence when dealing with juvenile delinquents who had been referred to Synanon for the first time in 1974.

Synanon declared itself an independent nation and founded an embassy in Washington. Armed Synanon members started to guard the gates of the facilities. The 'snake incident' in 1978 was the beginning of the end. Two residents had put a rattlesnake in the letterbox of a lawyer who was fighting Synanon in a court case. In an infamous broadcast of a game, Dederich had allegedly shouted: 'Don't mess with us...you can get killed dead, physically dead', when this lawyer was mentioned (Mitchell, Mitchell and Ofshe 1980). Dederich was arrested and the tape was subpoenaed. He was convicted and sent to a hospital instead of a prison with a diagnosis of heart problems, obesity and depression (Broekaert 1996). As part of his plea bargaining, he was forced to agree never to have any contact with a drug rehabilitation program again. After he was released on bail he spent the last fifteen years of his life in one of the remaining facilities of Synanon, his daughter having succeeded him as leader. The facilities in Tomales Bay had to be sold.

Synanon collapsed but it gave birth to the stormy development of the therapeutic community for addicts (Deitch and Zweben 1979). From 1981 Synanon named itself a church in order to get tax exemption (Garfield 1978). It is still active in advertising, among other things.

## The self-help therapeutic communities

Ex-residents from Synanon established therapeutic communities which, unlike Synanon, set the resident's return to society as their goal. Some of those self-help programs, such as Delancey Street in San Francisco, founded by ex-Synanon member John Maher, and the X-Calay Community in Canada, managed to survive without any financial support from the government. However, what was more widespread was the application of the model by government-sponsored organizations.

In 1962 a team of four, consisting of Joseph Shelly, head of the Supreme Court Probation Department in New York, Alexander Bassin, psychologist and Director of Research at that department, the criminologist Professor Herbert Bloch and the psychiatrist Daniel Casriel, went on a journey through the United States to study possible solutions to the drug problem. They followed the suggestions of J. L. Moreno, the founder of psychodrama as a method of group psychotherapy, and of Carl Rogers, who had developed his 'Rogerian' psychotherapy and was later to lead and promote encounter group therapy (Rogers 1970), to pay a visit to Synanon. In discussing the Synanon procedures of shouting, criticizing, making judgments, so much unlike the gentle, unconditional acceptance that is at the heart of his own philosophy, Rogers observed that perhaps beneath the cursing and shouting and judging there was a supply of pure undiluted love and concern that none of the residents had ever experienced before (Bassin 1978).

The team was met at the door of the home of Synanon in Santa Monica by Lewis Yablonsky, a sociologist and psychodrama therapist, who had been living for some time in Synanon as a resident. They also recognized some members as addicts they had known in New York, who had come there through Synanon's New York induction centre.

At that time Synanon housed more than one hundred ex-addicts, the majority of them being ex-heroin addicts who apparently were successfully living together without relapsing. Life in this community had little to do with the friendly, understanding approach practised in most professional treatment centres of those days. In the early 1960s this was a unique situation. The team saw how the 'family' demonstrated the 'morning meeting', the 'seminar', both the verbal and real 'hair cuts' and the 'learning experience' of carrying a sign of corrugated cardboard hung around the neck. They were astonished when they experienced the games, which were held three times a week, then also called encounters (Bassin 1978). Casriel asked to stay somewhat longer and got a job in the kitchen. Because he was a good cook they made him 'the Synanon psychiatrist' after a few days and he was present in all group meetings (Casriel 1963).

After Casriel's return to New York, Daytop Lodge was founded in 1963 as a halfway house for addicts referred from prison. 'Daytop' stood for drug addicts treated on probation (Casriel 1971). Of this first intake, all were men, and female addicts were not admitted until the expansion of services in the following year. Unlike Synanon, the goal was to restructure the residents' life in such a way that they would be able to function again in society without a need for drugs (Shelley and Bassin 1965). Although the first year was chaotic due to lack of experienced staff, this changed when, a year later, Casriel brought David Deitch, who had just been expelled from Synanon, to Daytop. Monsignor William O'Brien, who, through his work as a parish priest at St. Patrick's Cathedral in New York had become convinced that drug abuse was behind most of the violence in the city, also became involved at this time.

A non-profit organization, now called Daytop Village, was founded in 1964. Msgr O'Brien became the chairman of the board of governors, and later president. Casriel became the medical director and Deitch became the director of the therapeutic community, located at Staten Island. Daytop expanded and more facilities were opened in old mansions and former hotels. Basic elements in the program's philosophy were self-help and responsible concern: 'You alone can do it, but you cannot do it alone' (Ottenberg 1978).

Five years later the organization went through a crisis, when Deitch began to have grandiose ideas and started putting up pictures of Che Guevara and Mao Tse Tung in the community and threatened to burn the American flag in protest against government policies in Vietnam. He tried to dismiss the board and finally left Daytop, together with hundreds of residents. He later regretted these actions. He went back to study and gained his Ph.D at Stanford University in Palo Alto, California. He helped to start Gateway House in Chicago and much later he worked for some time, first for Phoenix House and again for Daytop, and also as a consultant for therapeutic communities in Sicily and Greece. Daytop survived the crisis and the first resident admitted, Charles Devlin, became the director.

Phoenix House was started, as many other therapeutic community organizations, with support from Daytop. In 1966 the psychiatrist Efren Ramirez was appointed by Mayor Lindsey to establish a program for drug addicts in New York. He was of the opinion that a treatment program should last a minimum of two years and should consist of three phases: induction including detoxification; treatment in a therapeutic community; and a re-entry program. Re-entry residents should assist staff in the therapeutic community and after that in the induction program, before starting to work outside the program (Ramirez 1973). He hired Sam Anglin from Daytop and the psychiatrist Mitchell Rosenthal, who had been working in Synanon projects in California. In that same year, 1966, Phoenix House was founded, financed by the City of New York (Biase and Rosenthal 1969).

In 1967 the psychiatrist Judianne Densen-Gerber became the founder of Odyssey House when she established a therapeutic community with 17 addicts in the Metropolitan Hospital as an alternative to substitution therapy, in response to a growing dissatisfaction with the therapeutic value of methadone. Although Daytop and Phoenix House greatly influenced Odyssey House, unlike these programs, which were staffed almost exclusively by former addicts, in Odyssey House almost half of the staff were professionals.

Daytop Village and Phoenix House were models for a fast growing number of therapeutic communities in North America (Broekaert 1996). Outside the United States, in Montreal in 1973, the Portage program was founded by staff members from Daytop Village with John Devlin as the first director. Staff and a group of residents from Daytop Village had moved to Canada to start this pioneer program, of which the psychologist Peter Vamos later became the director. With the help of Daytop Village, Bob Garon founded Dare in Manila, Phillipines, a therapeutic community which was not dependent on government funds. Modelled after Dare, the Therapeutic Community Pusat Pertolongan was founded in Ipoh, Malaysia in 1973. This therapeutic community also had to survive without any government support under the leadership of a former German priest who became a Muslim, Abdul Rahman Scholer.

In the United States too, a number of self-supporting therapeutic communities were established by ex-Synanon members, such as Delancey Street in San Francisco by John Maher and Habitat in Hawaii by Vincent Marino. Ex-Synanon members were important leaders in the early years of the American therapeutic communities, and included David Deitch and Ron Brancato in Daytop and Frank Natale in Phoenix House. Professionals such as Mitchell Rosenthal, Pauline Kaufmann, George De Leon and Nancy Jainchill in Phoenix House; Judianne Densen Gerber in Odyssey House; Vince Biase in Daytop Village; Harry Sholl and Sherry Holland in Gateway House; and Don Ottenberg, who transformed Eagleville Hospital in Philadelphia from a tuberculosis sanatorium into a therapeutic community for alcoholics and drug addicts, contributed greatly to the scientific evaluation and development of therapeutic communities. The family of the addict was seen as part of the problem, and parents and other relatives were involved in the treatment of therapeutic communities (Kooyman 1993; O'Brien 1983).

Under the leadership of Msgr William O'Brien, who has been the president of the World Federation of Therapeutic Communities for more than two decades, Daytop Village helped to establish many therapeutic communities in Europe and South East Asia. Phoenix House sent a staff member to establish Phoenix House, London, in 1970. Both Daytop and Phoenix House offered professionals from abroad the opportunity to stay as a guest or as a resident in one of their therapeutic communities in order to experience the process for themselves.

A Sydney businessman whose son had died of an overdose in 1976 toured the world seeking a way to help drug addicts. This led to the establishment of Odyssey House, the first Australian therapeutic community, in Sydney in 1977. Other communities quickly followed and in 1986 Joe Lamberti, Executive Director of Odyssey House, Melbourne, organized a national meeting during which the Australian Therapeutic Community Association was founded (Permezel 1989).

## The origins of the therapeutic communities in Europe

As word spread, professionals from Europe visited the United States to see these therapeutic communities for themselves, and returned eager to set up similar centres in their own countries. One of them, Dr Ian Christie, founded Alpha House in 1970 in Portsmouth, England. Some months later Phoenix House, London, was founded by Dr Griffith Edwards. An American ex-addict and graduate of Phoenix House, New York, Denny Yuson, (who later took the Sanyassin name 'Veeresh') became its first director (Kooyman 1978). Also in 1970 the Ley Community was founded in Oxford by Dr Bertram Mandlebrote (Wilson 1978).

In 1972 the 'Emiliehoeve' therapeutic community commenced work in The Hague, the Netherlands. During the first months, the program followed the concepts of the democratic therapeutic communities that had been developed within the psychiatric hospital model of the Henderson Clinic, in which Maxwell Jones had departed from the traditional doctor/patient relationship used within psychiatry. Although there was some knowledge about the American self-help therapeutic communities, those models were seen as too authoritarian and too rigid to be applied in the liberal society of the Netherlands (Kooyman 1975).

The history of the democratic therapeutic communities began in England. During World War II, several psychiatrists worked in the Army Selection Unit, where they were confronted with soldiers returning from the battlefields suffering from mental breakdown. These men were sent to the Northfield Hospital, where each ward was run by a psychiatrist more or less in his own way. One of them, Maxwell Jones, stressed the importance of patients' participation in decision-making. He called this method of working 'democratic therapy'.

The official goal of the treatment was to cure the patients so they could return to the battlefield. The doctors, however, sent their patients home instead. One of the psychiatrists, Bion, was asked to introduce group therapy with the purpose of rehabilitating patients so that they could return to the front, but this initiative met with such resistance that it had to be stopped after six weeks.

The authorities then asked Harold Bridger, an army officer and former teacher, to take over the project. He accepted on condition that he would be responsible for managing the entire hospital. His first action was to empty one ward, call it 'the club' after Bierer's example of social clubs for psychiatric patients, and install his office next to the main room. Bridger waited in his office, suggesting to the patients that they should create a social club in the empty space. After some weeks, a social meeting-place for all patients of the hospital developed (Bridger 1946; Bridger 1985). One of the psychiatrists in the hospital, Tom Main, called it a 'therapeutic community' (Clark 1984). Sometime afterwards, Jones turned a unit of the Belmont Hospital into a therapeutic community with daily meetings of staff and patients, and this became the 'Maxwell Jones' model (Jones 1953).

In the first year of the Emiliehoeve Therapeutic Community, it was found that the democratic principles of the Maxwell Jones model, when applied in the way it had developed in the therapeutic communities for psychiatric patients mainly suffering from neurotic disorders, could become anti-therapeutic. Patients stayed in a regressed state if staff did not apply enough pressure towards making them act responsibly. Staff were surrendering power instead of delegating it, and as the group as a whole was made responsible for everything, individuals avoided their own responsibilities. These difficulties were also encountered in other communities (Schaap 1980).

During the first months of its existence, decisions at the Emiliehoeve therapeutic community were made by staff and residents in consensus, or by a one-man-one-vote system. In making up the plans for the day, the voting usually resulted in going to the beach, to a coffee shop, or staying in bed, but generally not in going to work or having group therapy. Since this behaviour was not challenged within the democratic process, conflicts were avoided. The Emiliehoeve staff had not taken into account the low level of growth or maturity of the residents at that time. As problems were discussed and group sessions were run along psychoanalytical lines, emotions were not dealt with in the group. This resulted in outbursts of violence or other acting-out behaviour (Kooyman 1993).

After those chaotic initial months, the staff decided to take a closer look at the American programs. Two staff members went to an encounter marathon workshop run by the first director of Phoenix House London, Yuson, who had left Phoenix House and had become involved as a therapist in the Human Potential Movement. Encounter groups had been developed from the Synanon games and had become the main therapeutic tool of the American therapeutic communities. Impressed, the two staff members introduced encounter groups in the Emiliehoeve Therapeutic Community immediately after their return from the workshop. At the same time, the importance of the concepts of honesty and openness was emphasized. From that moment on, guilt feelings were treated as a normal mechanism, something that should be talked about openly to get necessary relief, instead of being psychiatrically interpreted as a potential symptom of depression.

Gradually, with the help of staff and ex-staff members of Daytop Village and Phoenix House, a clear and structured program was developed. The staff overcame their initial resistance towards creating residents' departments with a hierarchical structure, and became increasingly aware of the fact that it was important to create conflicts that could be worked out emotionally in the encounter groups where no ranks existed. New residents were now usually seen as unreliable, dishonest, manipulative, egocentric and, emotionally, as children. Staff came to understand, too, that it was of vital importance for the character-disordered resident with his pseudo-adult image that the maturation of this 'child' should take place in a structured therapeutic environment. No longer were residents seen as being on an equal level regardless of the time they had spent in treatment (Kooyman 1993).

## The development of therapeutic communities for addicts in Europe

With the help of the Emiliehoeve staff, several other Dutch therapeutic communities were established in Rotterdam, Utrecht, Amsterdam, Eindhoven and Heerlen. Among these was the Breegweestee, a therapeutic community in Eelde near Groningen, which, in its turn, initiated the transformation of the neighbouring clinic for alcoholics (Hoog Hullen) into a structured therapeutic community (Schaap 1978; Schaap 1980). The Hoog Hullen Therapeutic Community, led by the psychiatrist Tjeerd Jongsma, helped to start other therapeutic communities such as the Oolgaardthuis in Arnhem. Therapeutic communities in Belgium, such as de Sleutel, founded in 1973 by Johan Maertens and Magda Baukeland and de Kiem, established in 1976 by Eric Broekaert, received assistance from the Emiliehoeve program to develop. A number of other similar programs (Choisis, de Spiegel, Trampoline) were also developed in Belgium around this time.

Other therapeutic communities for addicts were established independently in the Netherlands (i.e. Parkweg), as well as in Sweden (Vallmotorp), either by starting from medical clinic models or from the Maxwell Jones model. Step by step, they became more structured as staff realized the importance for residents of learning to deal with limits and frustrations. In Sweden Lars Bremberg, the director of Vallmotorp, a democratic therapeutic community organized as a school, also established a concept-based therapeutic community which he called Daytop Sweden.

In the beginning, the staff of the European therapeutic communities consisted almost exclusively of professionals. One reason for this was that there simply were no ex-addicts available. A further reason was that it took time to convince boards and authorities of the fact that recovered addicts could become reliable staff members. European professionals went to the United States and Canada to learn from the experience of the North American therapeutic communities, and learned the importance of using older residents as role models and introducing encounter and confrontation groups into their programs.

Therapeutic communities developing in Western Europe in the mid-1970s also sent staff to already existing European therapeutic communities. The Emiliehoeve therapeutic community was instrumental in helping the development of many other therapeutic communities in Europe. Staff from a therapeutic community in Bern, Switzerland, called Aebi Hus, visited Emiliehoeve, learned about Synanon and subsequently discovered that Dr

Karl Deissler – a paediatrician once living near Synanon and a doctor there for some time – was living only a few miles away from their community. He was quickly recruited to assist them in restructuring their program.

Staff from an ambulatory program in Rome, the Centro Italiano di Solidarietà (CEIS) visited the Emiliehoeve program in 1976, were put in contact with Daytop Village and initiated their fast-growing movement of therapeutic communities in Italy by organizing the Third World Conference of Therapeutic Communities in 1978. A few months later, at the beginning of 1979, they opened their first therapeutic community (Kooyman 1987). The program, called the 'Progetto Uomo' under the leadership of Don Mario Picchi and Juan Corelli in Rome, helped to establish therapeutic communities in most regions in Italy and also in Spain. At the start of the program in Rome, a training institute was founded where many workers from therapeutic communities in Italy and a number of other countries were trained. Staff members from Daytop Village (Richard Falzone, Anthony Gelormino) and Don Ottenberg have been working as directors of this training institute. Staff from more than 50 therapeutic communities in Italy, more than 40 therapeutic communities in Spain and more than 40 therapeutic communities in South American countries have received their basic training in this institute (van der Straten 1996). The Rome program sent staff to South American countries such as Argentina and Colombia to assist in the establishment of therapeutic programs. In Spain, independent of the 'Proyecto Hombre', numerous therapeutic communities were founded by professionals who did not choose to use ex-addicts as staff members. Also in Italy, some therapeutic communities were founded independent of the programs of the Progetto Uomo. These included therapeutic communities in Syracuse and Caltanisetta in Sicily and the therapeutic community Cascina Verde in Milan, founded in 1974 by the pharmacologist Professor Enzo Gori and his psychiatrist wife.

From the very beginning of this training process, it was believed that the best way to train professional staff was to let them have the experience of a therapeutic community as residents for some weeks, and that in order to avoid role confusion this should take place in a different therapeutic community from the one in which they were going to work. Many staff members from new therapeutic communities in Europe were sent to be trained at the Emiliehoeve therapeutic community. Staff were sent not only from other Dutch programs, but also from programs in Belgium, Sweden, Germany, England, Austria and, at the beginning of the 1980s, Greece. The Greek program, Kethea, founded by the psychiatrist Zafiridis, has developed into a large organization with many different facilities.

In Norway, therapeutic communities developed from psychiatric hospitals, and in 1982 a concept-based therapeutic community (Vexthuset) was established in Oslo under the leadership of the psychiatrist Dag Furuholmen, with the help of Phoenix House, London. Meanwhile, a former member of Alpha House, Anthony Slater, became the director of another concept-based therapeutic community in Norway, Phoenix House Haga. Phoenix House London, under the leadership of David Tomlinson, started a Phoenix House in Germany. This program later joined Daytop Germany to become Phoenix/Daytop. The majority of therapeutic communities in Germany, however, developed independently. Even Daytop Germany, founded by Osterhues, had at its inception not much more in common with the Daytop Village program in New York than its name. In Berlin, Hanover, and in many other areas of Germany, several forms of therapeutic communities were developed by professionals.

Other German-speaking therapeutic communities were established in Switzerland, such as Sonnenbuhle north of Zurich, and Smaragd in Basel. In the French-speaking part of Switzerland, Pierre Rey started the therapeutic community Le Levant near Lausanne. This therapeutic community adopted the concepts of a hierarchical therapeutic community after some training sessions run by staff members from the Emiliehoeve and a therapeutic community attached to the Jellinek Centrum in Amsterdam. Therapeutic communities were also started in Portugal, Finland, Israel and Egypt, and Daytop staff helped to establish Coolemine House in Ireland (Comberton 1986).

In 1977 a treatment facility for drug addicts was set up in Poland within a psychiatric hospital. This therapeutic community was called 'Synanon' and the name was adopted by the program following a visit from a Canadian professional. However, although the group sessions were similar to encounter groups, the staff had never heard of Dederich and the choice of name appears to have been entirely accidental.

Occasionally, successful therapeutic communities have been forced to close down. The most common reason has tended to be lack of financial resources, but in some cases the philosophy has been felt to be controversial, even dangerous. In 1977, during the time of apartheid, a therapeutic community founded in Cape Town by Gerrit van Wijk was ordered to close immediately after a nurse from the psychiatric hospital, which the therapeutic community was part of, reported that she had seen a coloured trainee hugging a white person during a staff training session.

Most of these therapeutic communities were more or less structured according to the Daytop and Phoenix House model. In France and Denmark structured therapeutic communities hardly developed, or only had a short existence. Almost all therapeutic communities that were structured after the concept of the American therapeutic communities described above have been in contact with, and been influenced by, each other.

## Independently developed therapeutic communities

In France, the American therapeutic community model was considered to be incompatible with the democratic principles of most workers in the field. Because the French authorities did not support the development of therapeutic communities, communities of a more or less sectarian character for drug addicts, such as the Patriarch communities, were able to develop. The Patriarch programs spread into Spain and the south of Belgium. They were founded by the charismatic leader Engelmaier, who stressed the importance of traditional values. The residents go through detoxification and work in projects. There is no therapy as such offered, although a great deal of emphasis is given to the development of the creative potentials of the members. Efforts to involve the Patriarch in conferences with other therapeutic communities in Europe have failed, partly due to their negative image. Corrective physical punishment was applied in some situations and there was an outspoken anti-professional attitude among the members. On the other hand, professionals also had strong negative prejudices with regard to the Patriarch programs.

Separate from this movement, therapeutic communities based on a socialistic ideology (the Makarenko model) which considers working together as the main therapeutic element, were developed in Eastern Europe and in Germany. These therapeutic communities did not call their model 'therapy' (Broekaert 1981). Their members worked in projects mostly in agricultural settings. The largest organization of agricultural communities for addicts is the Monar organization in Poland, founded in the 1970s. In Yugoslavia and the former Czechoslovakia, professionals established therapeutic communities for alcoholics with a mutual help ideology.

In Italy, too, many rural therapeutic communities developed where the emphasis was on work and social control. The largest of these, with more than one thousand members, is San Patrignano, founded by the charismatic leader Mucioli. This community became renowned for its racehorses, but in more recent years its image has been tarnished by a series of scandals. In Norway, small collectives were formed in rural areas where residents work in a drug-free environment together with staff.

In several countries the church supported the development of therapeutic communities. In Italy and Spain many therapeutic communities were led by priests. Some programs made religion an integral part of the treatment program, such as the therapeutic community de Hoop in the Netherlands and the Life for the World Trust in England (Wilson 1978).

### International conferences

The conferences of the World Federation of Therapeutic Communities are important in providing opportunities to meet and to exchange ideas and experiences. The first was held in 1975 in Norrköping, Sweden. Maxwell Jones, who had moved to Halifax, USA, was confronted for the first time with a widespread and growing movement of therapeutic communities for addicts, of which he had until then been completely unaware (Jones 1979). Meanwhile, the president of Daytop Village New York, Msgr O'Brien, met with staff of Daytop Germany, an umbrella organization of therapeutic communities for drug addicts as well as alcoholics. Daytop Germany had chosen their name after a visit by their leader Osterhues to the program in New York some years earlier (Osterhues 1990).

The first world conferences were organized by the Therapeutic Community Section of the International Council on Alcohol and Addictions. During the Fifth World Conference of Therapeutic Communities, held in 1980 in Noordwijkerhout, the Netherlands, the World Federation of Therapeutic Communities was founded, followed that same year by the European Federation of Therapeutic Communities.

The first European Conference of Therapeutic Communities was held in 1982 in Eskilstuna, Sweden. The main theme of the Eskilstuna conference was the third generation of therapeutic communities. The second generation of therapeutic communities was established with the help of staff of the first generation, such as Daytop Village and Phoenix House. The third-generation therapeutic communities added new therapeutic elements to the original concepts (Yohai and Winick 1986). These third-generation programs were usually started with the help of second-generation therapeutic communities.

The international conferences were an important forum for international contacts. They led to staff from existing programs assisting others in developing new projects. In this way, drug rehabilitation organizations in Thailand were helped by Bremberg from Sweden and Lutterjohann from Daytop Germany to set up therapeutic communities.

Important too, were the international institutes, such as the First World Institute of Therapeutic Communities held in 1984 in Castel Gandolfo, where many pioneers of therapeutic communities, democratic as well as concept-based, were present (Ottenberg 1985). At the European Institute in Den Haan in 1991 the question of: 'What cannot be changed in a therapeutic community?' was examined to reach a consensus on the basic elements of the therapeutic community (Broekaert, Kooyman and Ottenberg 1991; Broekaert, Kooyman and Ottenberg 1998).

## The present situation

Almost all concept-based therapeutic communities have national and international links with other similar organizations and have been mutually influenced (Comberton 1986). There are, in the year 2000, therapeutic communities in more than fifty countries in all continents.

While most therapeutic communities for addicts outside Europe are highly structured with hierarchical staff and resident structures, many European therapeutic communities use a more egalitarian model. The latter are more like the therapeutic communities in the psychiatric field, having a democratic structure (Jones 1979; Zimmer-Hifler *et al.* 1981). However, therapeutic communities of over twenty-five residents have usually adopted the hierarchical structure of the American programs. European therapeutic communities are now, in their turn, influencing North American therapeutic communities by, for instance, pointing out the importance of introducing creativity into the program. Moreover, they have shown that residents can learn skills such as gardening, farming and printing during their stay in the program. In Europe, as well as in the United States, detoxification centres linked to a therapeutic community have been established, and in some cases day centres and evening programs have been founded, based on the drug-free therapeutic community concept.

Therapeutic communities in Europe have also started to expand into fields of self-destructive behaviours other than drug addiction (Wexler 1986; Ottenberg 1990). The concepts of a hierarchical therapeutic community have been successfully used in the treatment of alcoholics. The therapeutic community Hoog Hullen, originally styled after the Jones model, was transformed in 1974 into a successful hierarchical, structured therapeutic community for alcoholics (Schaap 1978).

However, not all of the picture is so optimistic. In Europe, many therapeutic communities applying the hierarchical structure of the American therapeutic communities have been, and continue to be, faced with strong opposition from professionals as well as politicians. The legacy of World War II has left a deep residual suspicion of the misuse of hierarchical structures, and critics of the therapeutic communities have voiced anxieties regarding the potential abuse of power in the system. There is, indeed, a real risk of abuse of power in a hierarchical, structured therapeutic community (Ottenberg 1984) and it is important to create control systems such as strong boards of management to which the leaders of the therapeutic communities are accountable, to reduce this possibility. Within the programs too, it is important to show that a structure in a therapeutic community is a tool and not an ideology, and that residents are also trained to cope with democratic decision-making in the last phase of the program, the re-entry phase.

Therapeutic communities in most European countries at the turn of the century are having a difficult time surviving. Programs have had to be shortened to the extent that in many cases they cannot achieve their full potential. Politicians and the pharmaceutical industries are actively promoting substitute prescribing as a cheap alternative to intensive, abstinence-based treatment programs. The fear of AIDS has increased the pressure to prescribe methadone or even heroin to all addicts, and prescribing services are generally prioritized by governments concerned about the public health issues for the wider community.

New legislation protecting the rights of patients, while a welcome development, has in some instances made treatment more difficult. In the Netherlands and Sweden, for instance, each resident must have his own bedroom. Changes in tax laws may make it difficult for staff and residents to have lunch together, since free meals may be seen as a taxable benefit. Regionalization of services can be a threat, as not all regions can offer treatment in therapeutic communities and many communities used to work to much wider catchment areas.

The biggest threat, however, is the increasing influence of inexperienced professionals who, in many European countries, have become part of the staff. Incidents like the scandals at San Patrignano have led to legislation in Italy to secure professional input in therapeutic communities. In Spain similar laws have led to the introduction of many young professionals into the staff teams of therapeutic communities. The danger of this development is that these new staff members may be too eager to 'do therapy' with the residents instead of assisting them to solve their conflicts and problems themselves. In this way the concept of self-help may become diluted and the notion that the community itself is the therapy seems in danger of being forgotten in some programs. For some professionals, the emotional interactions which take place in encounter groups can often be inexplicable and frightening. Some therapeutic communities in Spain and Italy have transformed their encounter groups into discussion groups, apparently without recognizing that by doing this, the most powerful instrument of the concept-based therapeutic communities, the emotional confrontation showing angry concern, is removed.

One positive development is that degrading 'learning experiences' in the form of huge signs that had to be worn around residents' necks, have disappeared or been replaced by small badges. Also the measure of shaving one's head is no longer practised in European therapeutic communities.

Practitioners in European therapeutic communities have led the way in adding psychodrama, transactional analysis, primal scream groups, Pesso-motor therapy, bioenergetics groups and New Identity Process or bonding therapy groups to their programs (Martens 1999). Other developments have seen the introduction of family therapy and individual psychotherapy for residents in the re-entry phase of the program. Therapeutic communities with varying structures have been founded, enabling different populations to benefit from a therapeutic community program providing more flexibility in treatment provision. Thus, there are therapeutic communities for adolescents, open communities for day and/or evening treatment, therapeutic communities in prisons, therapeutic communities for women, for homosexuals, for ex-prison inmates, for borderline personalities, programs for mothers and children, short-term (from three to five months) and long-term (from nine to twelve months or longer) therapeutic communities. The Emiliehoeve therapeutic community, for instance, has, under the leadership of the psychiatrist Chris van der Meer, become the centre of a village with several different drug-free treatment modalities. Also, the therapeutic communities De Sleutel in Belgium and Kethea in Greece have become large organizations with several different modalities. The challenge for the future will be to discover which type of therapeutic community model can best be matched to which individual.

Although research has shown that the length of time spent in the program is the main predictor for success, programs have been forced to be shorter. This trend was seen in many countries during the 1990s. In the Netherlands, for instance, the Essenlaan Therapeutic Community in Rotterdam has been changed into a three-month addiction clinic run by professionals. Relatively inexpensive self-help programs are changed into short-term medical model programs. The therapeutic communities of the Jellinek Centrum in Amsterdam have initially become shorter in duration and, more recently, have changed into medical model addiction clinics. Almost all therapeutic communities in Sweden have been closed in recent years.

Methadone programs are seen by politicians and medical doctors (assisted by the pharmaceutical industry) in several countries as being the solution to the drug problem. This is especially the case in Eastern Europe, where the drug problem is on the increase. In some countries in Eastern Europe, however, such as Hungary, Czech Republic, Slovakia, Croatia, Slovenia and, on a small scale, Russia, new drug-free programs were started in the 1990s. Also, new therapeutic communities have been founded in Denmark such as Phoenix House Fyn in 1998.

For the future of therapeutic communities it will be important to prove that their treatment programs are, in the long term, cheaper than lifelong harm reduction programs that keep addicted persons dependent on their services.

## References

Bassin, A. (1978) 'The miracle of the drug-free therapeutic community: from birth to post-partum insanity to full recovery.' In P. Vamos and D. Brown (eds) *Proceedings of the 2nd World Conference of Therapeutic Communities: The Addiction Therapist, Special Edition 2*, 3 and 4, pp. 3–15.

Biase, D. V. and Rosenthal, M. (1969) 'Phoenix House: therapeutic communities for drug addicts.' *Hospital and Community Psychiatry 20*, pp.27–30.

Bridger, H. (1946) 'The Northfield experiemnt.' *Bulletin of the Menninger Clinic 10*, pp. 71–76.

Bridger, H. (1985) 'Groups in open and closed systems.' In D.J. Ottenberg (ed) *The Therapeutic Community Today. A Moment of Reflexion in its Evolution. Proceedings of the 1st World Institute of Therapeutic Communities, Rome*. Contro Italiano do solidarietà, pp. 54–70.

Broekaert, E. (1976) 'De drugvrije therapeutische gemeenschap naar Synanon-model.' *Tijdschr. Alcohol and Drugs 2*, 3, pp. 93–97.

Broekaert, E. (1981) 'Inleiding tot het werk in de therapeutische gemeenschap: Uitg.' *European Federation of Therapeutic Communities*. Ghent: VSW De Kiem.

Broekaert, E. (1996) 'Geschiedenis, filosofie en grondstellingen van de therapeutische gemeenschap.' In E. Broekaert, R. Bracke, D. Calle, G. van der Straten and H. Bradt (eds) *De Nieuwe Therapeutische Gemeenschap*. Leuven: Garant.

Broekaert, E., Kooyman, M. and Ottenberg, D. (1991) *What Cannot be Changed in a Therapeutic Community?* Ghent: Laboratorium voor Orthopedagogiek en Ortoagogiek.

Broekaert, E., Kooyman, M. and Ottenberg, D. (1998) 'The "new" drug-free therapeutic community: challenging encounter of classic and open therapeutic communities.' *Journal of Substance Abuse Treatment 15*, 6, pp. 595–597.

Buchman, F. N. D. (1961) *Remaking the World: The Speeches of Frank N. D. Buchman*. London: Blandford Press.

Casriel, D. (1963) *So Fair a House: The Story of Synanon*. New York: Prentice Hall Inc.

Casriel, D. (1971) 'The Daytop story and the Casriel method.' In L. Blank, G. B. Gottsegen and M. G. Gottsegen (eds) *Confrontation: Encounters in Self and Interpersonal Awareness*. New York: Macmillan.

Clarck, D. M. (1984) 'The therapeutic community over 40 years: some personal reflections.' In *Proceedings of the 8th World Conference of Therapeutic Communities, 1–5 September 1984, Rome*, Vol. 1. Centro Italiano di Solidarietà, 1984, pp. 15–20.

Comberton, J. (1986) 'Origins and development of the therapeutic community or social learning community.' In L. Bremberg (ed) *The 10th World Conference of Therapeutic Communities, Eskilstuna, September 7–12 1986*. Katrineholm: Valmotorp Foundation.

Dederich, C. (1974) Personal communication with the author.

Dederich, C. (1975) *The Circle and the Triangle: The Synanon Social System*. Marchall: Synanon Foundation.

Deitch, D. A. and Zweben, J. E. (1979) 'Synanon: a pioneering response to drug abuse treatment and a signal for caution.' In S. Halpern and B. Levine (eds) *Proceedings of the 4th International Conference on Therapeutic Communities, 16–21 September 1979*. New York: Daytop Village Press.

Endore, G. (1968) *Synanon*. New York: Doubleday and Co.

Garfield, H. M. (1978) *The Synanon Religion: The Survival Morality for the 21st Century*. Marchall: The Synanon Foundation.

Glaser, F. B. (1974) 'Some historical aspects of the drug-free therapeutic communities.' *American Journal of Drug and Alcohol Abuse 1*, pp.37–52.

Glaser, F. B. (1977) 'The origins of the drug-free therapeutic community: a retrospective history.' In P. Vamos and D. Brown (eds) *Proceedings of the 2nd World Conference of Therapeutic Communities: The Addiction Therapist, Special Edition 2*, 3 and 4, pp.3–15.

Glatt, M., Pittman, D., Gillespie, D. and Hills, D. (1967) *The Drug Scene in Great Britain: Journey into Loneliness*. London: Edward Arnold.

Jones, M. (1953) *The Theraputic Community: A New Treatment Method in Psychiatry*. New York: Basic Books.

Jones, M. (1979) 'Therapeutic communities, old and new.' *American Journal of Drug and Alcohol Abuse 6*, 2, pp.137–149.

Kooyman, M. (1975) 'From chaos to a structured therapeutic community: treatment program on Emiliehoeve, a farm for young addicts.' *Bulletin on Narcotics 27*, 1, pp.19–26.

Kooyman, M. (1978) 'The history of the therapeutic community movement in Europe.' In P. Vamos and D. Brown (eds) *Proceedings of the 2nd World Conference of Therapeutic Communities: The Addiction Therapist, Special Edition 2*, 3 and 4, pp.29–32.

Kooyman, M. (1984) 'The drug problem in The Netherlands.' *Journal of Substance Abuse Treatment 1*, pp.125–130.

Kooyman, M. (1987) 'Report on the innovation approach of the Centro Italiano di Solidarietà in Rome to the drug problem in Italy.' In E. Tounge (ed) *Demand Reduction in Practice: A Worldwide Review of Innovative Approaches*. Lausanne: WHO/ICAA.

Kooyman, M. (1993) *The Therapeutic Community for Addicts: Intimacy, Parent Involvement and Treatment Success*. Lisse: Swets and Zeitlinger.

Marcel, G. (1960) *Fresh Hope for the World: Moral Rearmament in Action* (translated from the French by Hardinge). London: Longmans, Green and Co.

Martens, J. (1999) 'Bonding therapy in the therapeutic community.' In *IV European Conference on Rehabilitation and Drug Policy, Marbella, February, 22–26*, PlanMarbella/EFTC, 2000, pp.331–333.

Maslow, A. H. (1967) 'Synanon and eupsychia.' *Journal of Humanistic Psychology 7*, pp.28–35.

Mitchell, D., Mitchell, C. and Ofshe, R. (1980) *The Light on Synanon: How a Country Weekly Exposed a Corporate Cult and Won the Pulitzer Prize*. New York: Seaview Books.

O'Brien, W. B. (1983) 'The family and its interaction with the therapeutic community: a worldwide perspective.' In *Proceedings of the 7th World Conference of Therapeutic Communities, Chicago, 8–13 May 1983*, Gateway House, 1989, pp.19–21.

Osterhues, U. J. (1990) 'Die Behandlung borderline-kranker Suchtpatienten in Therapeutischen Gemeinschaften.' *Drogen-Report-Arbeitsskript Nr. 1/90*, Druck, Rumpel, Nürnberg.

Ottenberg, D. J. (1978) 'Responsible concern.' *The Addiction Therapist 3*, 1, pp.67–68.

Ottenberg, D. J. (1984) 'Therapeutic community and the danger of the cult phenomenon.' In L. Bremberg (ed) *Third Generation of Therapeutic Communities: Proceedings of the 1st European Conference on Milieutherapy, September 1982, Eskilstuna*. Katrineholm: Valmotop Foundation pp. 218–238.

Ottenberg, D. J. (1985) 'The therapeutic community today: a moment of reflection on its evolution.' In *Proceedings of the 1st World Institute of Therapeutic Communities, Castel Gandolfo, 27–31 August, 27–31, 1984* Centro Italiano di Solidarietà.

Ottenberg, D. J. (1990) 'The educational value system of therapeutic communities.' In W. Hellinckx, E. Broekaert, A. Vandenberge and A. Colton (eds) *Innovations in Residential Care.* Leuven: ACCO.

Patton, T. (1973) *The Synanon Philosophy.* Marchall: Synanon Research Institute.

Permezel, I. (1989) 'Present status and future trends of Australian therapeutic communities.' In *Proceedings of the 11th World Conference of Therapeutic Communities, 21–26 February 1988, Bangkok.* National Council on Social Welfare, pp. 96–100.

Ramirez, E. (1973) 'Phoenix House: a therapeutic community program for the treatment of drug abusers and drug addicts.' In *Yearbook of Drug Abuse.* New York: Bril and Harms.

Rogers, C. R. (1970) *Encounter Groups.* Harmondsworth: Pelican Books.

Schaap, G. E. (1978) 'A new Dutch experiment: Hoog Hullen, a drug-free therapeutic community for alcohol addicts.' In P. Vamos and D. Brown (eds) *Proceedings of the 2nd World Conference of Therapeutic Communities: The Addiction Therapist, Special Edition 2,* 3 and 4, pp.170–180.

Schaap, G. E. (1980) 'Democratic and concept based therapeutic communities.' In *Readings of the 5th World Conference of Therapeutic Communities, Samson/Sijthoff, 31 August – 5 September 1980, Alphen a/d Rijn,* pp. 155–165.

Shelley, J. and Bassin, A. (1965) 'Daytop Lodge: a new treatment approach for drug addicts.' *Corrective Psychiatry 11,* pp.186–195.

Spear, B. (1994) 'The early years of the British System in practice.' In J. Strang and M. Gossop (eds) *Heroin Addiction and Drug Policy: The British System.* Oxford: Oxford University Press.

Sugarman, B. (1974) *Daytop Village: A Therapeutic Community.* New York: Holt, Rinehart and Winston.

van der Straten, G. (1996) 'De ontwikkeling van de theraputische gereenschap in Europa.' In E. Broekaert, R. Bracke, D. Calle, G. vander Straten and H. Bradt (eds) *De Nieuwe Theraoutische Gemeenschap.* Leuven: Garant.

Wexler, H. K. (1986) 'Therapeutic communities within prisons.' In G. De Leon and J. Ziegenfuss (eds) *Therapeutic Communities for Addictions.* Springfield: Charles C. Thomas.

Wilson, F. W. (1978) 'Spiritual therapy in the therapeutic community.' In P. Vamos and D. Brown (eds) *Proceedings of the 2nd World Conference of Therapeutic Communities: The Addiction Therapist, Special Edition 2,* 3 and 4, pp.204–205.

Wilson, S. (1978) 'The effect of treatment in a therapeutic community on intravenous drug abuse.' *British Journal of Addiction 73,* 4, pp.407–411.

Yablonsky, L. (1967) *Synanon: The Tunnel Back.* New York: Macmillan.

Yohai, S. J. and Winick, C. (1986) 'AREBA-Casriel Institute: A third-generation therapeutic community.' *Journal of Psychoactive Drugs 18,* 3, pp.231–237.

Zimmer-Hifler, D. and Widmer, A. (1981) 'Democratically or hierarchically structured therapeutic community for heroin addicts.' In *The Therapeutic Community in Various Cultures Worldwide: Proceedings of the 6th World Conference of Therapeutic Communities, 15–20 November 1981, Manila.* DARE Foundation, 1981, pp. 92–98.

# CHAPTER 4

# Therapeutic communities for substance abuse: developments in North America

## George De Leon

## Introduction

In its contemporary form, two major variants of the therapeutic community have emerged. One, in social psychiatry, consists of innovative units and wards designed for the psychological treatment and management of socially deviant psychiatric patients within (and outside of) mental hospital settings (see Jones 1953; Rapaport 1960). The term 'therapeutic community' was first used to describe these psychiatric therapeutic communities. The other form, the therapeutic community for addictions, also termed the concept or drug-free therapeutic community, emerged in North America in the 1960s and has been implemented worldwide. Other than the name, whether or how the British psychiatric therapeutic communities influenced the addiction therapeutic communities of North America is unclear. Distinctions and similarities between the two forms have been outlined in the literature (Broekaert 1998; De Leon 2000; Jones 1986; Sugarman 1986). Contrary to some misperceptions both retain the main elements of community as the primary treatment ingredient (Kennard 1983).

The therapeutic community for addictions is fundamentally a self-help approach which evolved primarily outside of mainstream psychiatry, psychology, and medicine. Brief histories of the therapeutic community for addictions are contained in Broekaert (2000) and De Leon (2000, Chapter 2). Today, however, the therapeutic community for addictions is a sophisticated human services modality which has been implemented worldwide. This chapter reviews the current status of the therapeutic community for addictions in North America, highlighting the diversity of its applications as well as the advances in theory and research.

## The mis-labelling of therapeutic communities

A valid picture of the therapeutic community for addictions requires clarification of issues concerning labels and perception. Not all residential drug treatment programs are therapeutic communities, not all therapeutic communities are in residential settings, and not all programs that call themselves therapeutic communities employ the same social and psychological models of treatment. Indeed, the term therapeutic community is widely used to vaguely represent its distinct approach in almost any setting, including community residences, hospital wards, prisons and homeless shelters. One effect of this labelling has been to cloud understanding of the therapeutic community as a drug treatment approach, how well it works, where it works best, and for which clients it is most appropriate.

Residential treatment is a generic term, describing programs that are extremely diverse with respect to approach, models of treatment, and services delivered. Of special note is the difference between the term 'therapeutic communities' and the often loosely employed label 'residential drug treatment'. There are few common features other than the fact that clients live 24 hours a day in the facility while receiving treatment (De Leon 1995a).

Residential treatment programs are diverse with respect to staffing patterns, philosophy, planned duration of treatment, and clients served. Notably, treatment models are absent, inexplicit or represent complex configurations of medical, mental health, self-help and social psychological elements. Some programs in or connected to institutional settings also call themselves therapeutic communities, although they bear faint resemblance to the traditional therapeutic community program model. Indeed, the term 'community' is rarely defined, much less its therapeutic elements. Nevertheless, these 'therapeutic community' programs are invidiously compared with other treatment modalities as well as traditional long-term therapeutic communities, often yielding misleading conclusions concerning the effectiveness (or non-effectiveness), costs, and general applicability of the therapeutic community model.

The therapeutic community for addictions is a drug-free modality which utilizes a unique social psychological approach to the treatment of drug abuse; its characteristic setting is in a community-based residence. However, therapeutic community programs have been implemented in a variety of other settings, both residential and non-residential, e.g. hospitals, jails, schools, halfway houses, day treatment clinics and ambulatory clinics. Therapeutic communities offer a wide variety of services including social, psychological, educational, medical, legal and social/advocacy. However, these services are co-ordinated in accordance with the traditional residential therapeutic community approach. The latter has proven effectiveness and is the prototype for the current diversity of therapeutic community applications.

## The residential therapeutic community model

Most residential therapeutic community programs are primarily supported by public funding which must be supplemented by additional private and public donations. Thus, there is wide variation in the amount of resources – financial and material – which agencies have at their disposal. The residential capacity of a therapeutic community program varies widely, ranging from 30 in small agencies to 2000 in large agencies that administer separate programs housed in multiple residential facilities. Typically, however, a particular 'house' in a community-based setting will accommodate 40–80 residents.[1]

The 'static capacity' of a therapeutic community is the maximum number of residents it can house at any one time. For instance, a therapeutic community may be a '40-bed' facility, or maintain '40 slots'. Clinical and managerial experience has shown that a static capacity of between 40 and 80 is optimal. A critical mass of residents (about 40) is necessary for shaping the stratified peer structure (e.g. junior, intermediate, and senior residents) and filling all the posts needed in the hierarchical division of labour. This allows for vertical mobility, variations in status, and defined role models – elements considered essential to the therapeutic community model.

The 'dynamic capacity' is the actual number of admissions per year. This is usually about four times higher than the static capacity. Given client turnover – through completion or graduation, client dropout, administrative discharge, etc. – the program may service many more than the '40 beds' over the course of the year.

The size, capacity and funding of therapeutic communities are not unrelated to clinical program issues. Full descriptions of these features and how these relate to the therapeutic community perspective and approach are provided elsewhere (De Leon 2000, Chapter 7).

## Essential elements of the therapeutic community model

The diversity of programs within the therapeutic community modality underscores the need to define, or at least characterize, the essential elements of the therapeutic community perspective and approach. A detailed account of the therapeutic community theory, model and method is provided elsewhere

(De Leon 2000) as are brief versions in other writings (De Leon and Rosenthal 1989).

In the therapeutic community perspective substance abuse is a disorder of the whole person. Recovery is a self-help process of incremental learning toward a stable change in behaviour, attitudes and values of right living which are associated with maintaining abstinence. The quintessential element of the therapeutic community approach may be termed 'community as method' (De Leon 1995a, 1995b, 1997, 2000). What distinguishes the therapeutic community from other treatment approaches (and other communities) is the purposive use of the peer community to facilitate social and psychological change in individuals. Thus, in a therapeutic community all activities are designed to produce therapeutic and educational change in individual participants and all participants are mediators of these therapeutic and educational changes.

The therapeutic community perspective and approach provide the conceptual basis for defining a generic therapeutic community program model in terms of its basic components. Tables 4.1 and 4.2 are abstracted from recent writings on theory and method (De Leon 1995a, 1995b, 2000). They list some essential concepts of community as method, and the program components of a generic therapeutic community model that can be adapted in different ways and in various settings, both residential and non-residential.

| Table 4.1: Community as method: basic elements ||
|---|---|
| **Member roles** | Daily life in the therapeutic community provides learning opportunities through the various social roles individuals assume as participants in the community. Member roles vary in different job functions such as worker, manager and staff person, as well as in interpersonal roles as friend, group member, peer leader, student, tutor, and counsellor.These roles require members to change behaviours, attitudes, emotional management and values as they relate to others. |
| **Membership feedback** | A primary source of instruction and support for individual change is the membership's observations and authentic reactions to the individual. Providing such continual feedback is the shared responsibility of all participants. Whether positive or negative, membership feedback is expressed with responsible concern. |

| Membership as role models | Each participant strives to be a role model of the change process. Along with their responsibility to provide feedback to others as to what they must change, members must also provide examples of how they can change. |
|---|---|
| Relationships | Relationships in the therapeutic community are used to foster recovery and personal growth in various ways. They can facilitate engagement, develop trust, encourage emotional risk-taking and self-learning, and teach interpersonal skills. Relationships developed in treatment often become the basis for the social network needed to sustain recovery beyond treatment. |
| Collective learning formats | The experiences essential to recovery and personal growth unfold through social interactions. Therefore, education, training and therapeutic activities occur in groups, meetings, seminars, job functions and recreation. The individual engages in the process of change primarily with other peers. These collective formats incorporate the empirically demonstrated power of cohorts, teams and groups in enhancing learning and change. |
| Culture and language | The therapeutic community is a culture of change. Thus, celebrations, traditions and rituals are used to enhance community cohesiveness and to reinforce individual progress. In particular, the concepts, beliefs, values, norms and philosophy that guide recovery and right living are expressed in the unique language or argot of the therapeutic community. Thus, learning the therapeutic community vernacular reflects assimilation into the culture of the therapeutic community and a gradual process of identity change. |
| Structure and systems | Job functions, chores, and prescribed procedures maintain the daily operations of the facility. These activities strengthen self-help and are vehicles for teaching self-development. Learning and growth occurs through following procedures and systems and in behaving as a responsible member of the community upon whom others are dependent. The system of privileges and sanctions maintains the order and safety of the community and facilitates individual change through consequential learning. |

| | |
|---|---|
| **Open communication** | The public nature of shared experiences in the community is used for therapeutic purposes for the individual and for others. The private inner life of the individual is a matter of importance in the recovery and change process, not only for the individual but for other members. When and how private issues are publicly shared is always at the discretion of the individual participant. Especially sensitive private issues (child abuse, sexual preference, past crimes, health status) may be initially shared with a close peer or staff counsellor who preserves confidentiality but encourages eventual disclosure in groups. However, private issues relevant to the cardinal and house rules of the community (current drug use, stealing, lending money, criminality, sexual acting out, arson, violence, etc.) *must* be publicly shared to sustain the safety, credibility, and health of the community. |
| **Community and individual balance** | The purpose of the community is to serve the individual, but the relationship between the individual and the community is reciprocal. The needs of the community and of the individual must be balanced to sustain the member's positive perceptions of the community as authentic and credible. This requires that the community has a capacity for self-criticism through continued self-examination of the behaviour and attitudes of staff, as well as residents. The membership itself, staff and residents, has the responsibility to confront, affirm, and correct the community. |

*Source: De Leon, G. (2000)* The Therapeutic Community: Theory, Model and Method. *New York: Springer Publishing Company Inc. Reprinted with permission.*

| Table 4.2: Components of a generic therapeutic community program model | |
|---|---|
| **Community separateness** | Therapeutic community-oriented programs have their own names, often innovated by the clients and housed in a separate space or locale from other agency or institutional programs, units, or generally from the drug-related environment. Residential setting clients remain away from outside influences 24 hours a day for several months before earning short-term day-out privileges. In the non-residential 'day treatment' settings, the individual is in the therapeutic community environment for 4–8 hours, and then monitored by peers and family. Even in the least restrictive outpatient settings, therapeutic community-oriented programs and components are in place. |
| **A community environment** | The inner environment of a therapeutic community facility contains communal space to promote a sense of commonalty and collective activities. Signs state the philosophy of the program, the messages of right living and recovery. Cork boards and blackboards identify all participants by name, seniority level, and job function in the program; daily schedules are posted as well. These visuals display an organizational picture of the program that the individual can relate to. |
| **Community activities** | To be effectively utilized, treatment or educational services must be provided within a context of the peer community. Thus, with the exception of individual counselling, all activities are programmed in collective formats. These include at least one daily meal prepared, served and shared by all members; a daily schedule of groups, meetings, and seminars; team job functions; and organized recreational/leisure time; ceremonies and rituals (e.g., birthdays, phase/progress graduations, etc.). |
| **Staff roles and functions** | The staff are a mix of self-help recovered professionals and other traditional professionals (e.g. nurses, physicians, lawyers, case workers, counsellors) who must be integrated through therapeutic community-grounded training. Professional skills define the function of staff; however, their generic roles are those of community members who, rather than providers and treaters, are rational authorities, facilitators, and guides in the self-help community method. |

| | |
|---|---|
| **Peers as role models** | Members who demonstrate expected behaviours and reflect the community values and teachings are viewed as role models. Indeed, the strength of the community as a context for social learning relates to the number and quality of its role models. Members of the community at all levels and in all situations are expected to be role models to maintain the integrity of the community and assure the spread of social learning effects. |
| **A structured day** | The structure of the program relates to the therapeutic community perspective, particularly the view of the client and recovery. Ordered routine activities counter the characteristically disordered lives of these clients and distract from negative thinking and boredom, factors that predispose drug use. Thus, regardless of its length, the day has a formal schedule of varied therapeutic and educational activities with prescribed formats and routine procedures. |
| **Work as therapy and education** | Consistent with the self-help community method, all clients are responsible for the daily management of the facility (e.g., cleaning activities, meal preparation and service, maintenance, purchasing, security, co-ordinating schedules, preparatory chores for groups, meetings, seminars, activities, etc.). Work roles mediate essential educational and therapeutic effects, strengthen affiliation with the program, provide opportunities for skill development, and foster self-examination and personal growth. The scope and depth of client work functions depend upon the program setting (e.g. institutional vs. free-standing facilities) and client resources (levels of psychological function, social life skills). |
| **Phase format** | The treatment protocol, or plan of therapeutic and educational activities, is organized into phases that reflect a developmental view of the change process. Emphasis is on incremental learning at each phase, which moves the individual to the next stage of recovery. |
| **TC concepts** | A curriculum that is both formal and informal focuses on teaching the therapeutic community perspective, particularly its self-help recovery concepts and view of right living. These concepts get repeated during collective activities and in written materials, public and personal. |

| Peer encounter groups | The main community or therapeutic group is the encounter, although other forms of therapeutic, educational, and support groups are utilized as needed. The minimal objective of the peer encounter is similar in therapeutic community-oriented programs – to heighten individual awareness of specific attitudes or behavioral patterns that should be modified. However, the encounter process may differ in degree of staff direction and intensity, depending on the client subgroups (e.g. adolescents, prison inmates, the dually disordered). |
|---|---|
| Awareness training | All therapeutic and educational interventions involve raising the individual's consciousness of the impact of their conduct/attitudes on themselves and the social environment, and conversely the impact of others' behaviours and attitudes on themselves and the social environment. |
| Emotional growth training | Achieving the goals of personal growth and socialization involves teaching individuals how to identify feelings, express feelings appropriately, and manage feelings constructively through the interpersonal and social demands of communal life. |
| Planned duration of treatment | The optimal length of time for full program involvement must be consistent with therapeutic community goals of recovery and its developmental view of the change process. How long the individual must be program-involved depends on their phase of recovery, although a minimum period of intensive involvement is required to assure internalization of the therapeutic community teachings. |
| Continuity of care | Completion of primary treatment is a stage in the recovery process. Aftercare services are an essential component in the therapeutic community model. Whether implemented within the boundaries of the main program or separately as in residential or non-residential halfway houses or ambulatory settings, the perspective and approach guiding aftercare programming must be continuous with that of primary treatment in the therapeutic community. Thus, the views of right living and self-help recovery and the use of a peer network are essential to enhance the appropriate use of vocational, educational, mental health, social, and other typical aftercare or re-entry services. |

Source: De Leon, G. (1995) 'Therapeutic Communities for Addictions; A Theoretical Framework.' International Journal of the Addictions 30 (20), 1603–1645. Reprinted with permission of Marcel Dekker Inc.

## Developments within the therapeutic community modality

Today, the therapeutic community modality consists of a wide range of programs serving a diversity of clients who use a variety of drugs and present complex social-psychological problems in addition to their chemical abuse. Client differences, as well as clinical requirements and funding realities, have encouraged the development of modified residential therapeutic communities with shorter planned duration of stay (three, six and twelve months) as well as therapeutic community-oriented day treatment and outpatient ambulatory models. Correctional, medical and mental hospitals, community residence and shelter settings, overwhelmed with alcohol and illicit drug abuse problems, have implemented therapeutic community programs within their institutional boundaries. The following sections summarize the main modifications of the therapeutic community approach and applications to special populations.

### Current modifications of the therapeutic community model

Most community-based traditional therapeutic communities have expanded their social services or incorporated new interventions to address the needs of their diverse admissions. In some cases these additions enhance but do not alter the basic therapeutic community regime; in others they significantly modify the therapeutic community model itself.

#### Family services approaches

The participation of families or significant others has been a notable development in therapeutic communities for both adolescents and adults. Some therapeutic communities offer programs in individual and multiple family therapy as components of their adolescent programs, non-residential, and (more recently) short-term residential modalities. Family therapy in traditional therapeutic communities accords with its approach in that the primary target of treatment remains the client in residence rather than the family unit.

Experience has shown that beneficial effects can occur with various forms of significant-other participation other than family therapy. Seminars, support groups, open house, and other special events focus on how significant others can affect the client's stay in treatment; they teach the therapeutic community perspective on recovery and provide a setting for sharing common concerns and strategies for coping with the client's future re-entry into the larger community. Thus, family participation activities enhance the therapeutic community's rehabilitative process for the residential client by establishing an alliance between significant others and the program.

### Primary health care and medical services

Although funding for health care services remains insufficient for therapeutic communities, these agencies have expanded services for the growing number of residential clients with sexually transmitted and immune-compromising conditions, including HIV sero-positivity, AIDS, syphilis, Hepatitis B and C (Barton 1994; McCusker and Sorenson 1994). Screening, treatment and increased health education have been sophisticated, both on site and through linkages with community primary health care agencies.

### Aftercare services

Currently, most long-term therapeutic communities have linkages with other service providers and 12-Step groups for their graduates. However, therapeutic communities with shorter term residential components have instituted well-defined aftercare programs both within their systems and through linkages with other agencies. There are limits and issues in these aftercare efforts concerning discontinuities between the perspectives of the therapeutic community and other service agencies. These are discussed in other writings (De Leon 1990–91).

### Relapse prevention training (RPT)

Based on its approach to recovery, the traditional therapeutic community has always focused on the key issues of relapse prevention. The 24-hour therapeutic community communal life fosters a process of learning how to resist drug-taking and negative behaviour. In its social learning setting the individual engages many of the social, emotional and circumstantial cues for, and influences upon, drug use that exist in the larger macro society. This broad context of social learning essentially provides a continual relapse prevention training.

Currently, however, a number of therapeutic communities include special workshops on relapse prevention training (RPT) utilizing the curriculum, expert trainers and formats developed outside the therapeutic community area (Marlatt 1985). These workshops are offered as formal additions to the existing therapeutic community protocol, usually in the re-entry stage of treatment. However, some programs incorporate RPT workshops in earlier treatment stages, and in a few others RPT is central to the primary treatment protocol (Lewis et al. 1993). Clinical impressions supported by preliminary data of the efficacy of RPT within the therapeutic community setting are favorable (McCusker et al. 1995).

*'12-Step' components*

Historically, therapeutic community graduates were not easily integrated into Alcoholics Anonymous (AA) meetings for a variety of reasons (De Leon 1990–91). In recent years, however, there has been a gradual integration of AA/ Narcotics Annoymous (NA)/ Cocaine Annoymous (CA) meetings during and following therapeutic community treatment, given the wide social and demographic diversity of users and the prominence of alcohol use regardless of the primary drug. The common genealogical roots found in North American therapeutic communities and the 12-Step groups are evident to most participants of these, and the similarities in the self-help view of recovery far outweigh the differences in specific orientation. Today, 12-Step groups may be introduced at any stage in residential therapeutic communities, but are considered mandatory in the re-entry stages of treatment, and in the aftercare or continuance stages of recovery after leaving residential setting.

*Mental health services*

Among those seeking admission to therapeutic communities, increasing numbers reveal documented psychiatric histories (Carroll and McGinley 1998; De Leon 1993; Jainchill 1994; Jainchill and De Leon 1992). Certain subgroups of these clients are treated within the traditional therapeutic community model and regimen, requiring some modification in services and staffing. For example, psychopharmacological adjuncts and individual psychotherapy are utilized for selected clients at appropriate stages in treatment (Carroll and McGinley 1998). Nevertheless, the traditional community-based therapeutic community models still cannot accommodate the substance abuser with serious psychiatric disorder. As described below in the section on mentally ill chemical abusers, the primary psychiatric substance abuser requires specially adapted forms of the therapeutic community model.

*The multi-modal therapeutic community and client-treatment matching*

Many therapeutic community agencies are multi-modality treatment centres that offer services in their residential and non-residential programs, depending upon the clinical status and situation needs of the individual. Modalities include short (under 90 days), medium (6–12 months), and long-term (1–2 years) residential components, drug-free outpatient services (6–12 months). Some operate drug-free day treatment and methadone maintenance programs. For example, managed care pressures have prompted the therapeutic community to develop short-term residential and ambulatory models for employed, more socialized clients. Admission criteria and assessment protocols attempt to match clients to the appropriate modality within the agency. However, the feasibility and efficacy of these matching strategies are still under evaluation.[2]

## Current applications of residential therapeutic communities for special populations

The evolution of the therapeutic community is most evident in its application to special populations and special settings. In the main examples of these the mutual self-help focus is retained, along with basic elements of the community approach, i.e. meetings, groups, work structure, and perspective on recovery and right living. This section highlights some of the key applications of the therapeutic community treatment approach for client populations in different settings (De Leon 1997).

### Therapeutic communities for adolescents

The prominence of youth drug abuse and the unique needs of the adolescent has led to adaptations of the traditional therapeutic community approach that appear more appropriate for these clients. These include age-segregated facilities with considerable emphasis on management and supervision, educational needs, family involvement and individual counselling. More extensive accounts of the treatment of adolescents in therapeutic communities and its effectiveness is contained in other writings (De Leon and Deitch 1985; Jainchill, Battacharya and Yagelka 1995; Jainchill 1997; Jainchill et al. in press; Pompi 1994).

### Addicted mothers and children

Several therapeutic communities have adapted the model for chemically dependent mothers with their children. The profile of the addicted mother in residence is generally not different from that of other abusers, although it reflects more social disadvantage, poor socialization and a predominance of crack/cocaine abuse. Most evident is that these women need a lifestyle change and an opportunity for personal maturation. Thus, within the context of the basic therapeutic community regime, additional services and modifications are provided which address their specific needs and those of their recovery. These include family unit housing for mothers and children, medical and psychological care, parental training and child-care. Further accounts of clinical issues in therapeutic community programs for females in general and addicted mothers in particular are contained in the literature

(Coletti 1989; De Leon and Jainchill 1991; Egelko 1996; Galanter *et al.* 1993; Stevens, Arbiter and Glider 1989; Stevens and Glider 1994).

*Therapeutic communities for substance abusers in prison settings*

In recent years therapeutic community models have been adapted for substance abusers in prison settings. Currently several thousand substance abusers in prisons are engaged in modified therapeutic community programs (Lipton 1999). This development has been fostered by overcrowded prisons, the influx of drug offenders, and the documented success of an early therapeutic community prison model in reducing recidivism to crime and relapse to drug use (Wexler and Williams 1986).

Modifications of the therapeutic community model are shaped by the unique features of the correctional institution, e.g. its focus on security, its goal of early release, its limited physical and social space, and the prison culture itself. Nevertheless, a peer-managed community for social learning is established for inmates who volunteer for the program. A prominent feature of the modified prison model is the mutual involvement of correctional officers and prison administrators, mental health and therapeutic community treatment para-professionals. For inmates who leave these prison therapeutic communities, models for continuance of recovery have recently been established outside the walls in therapeutic community-oriented residences (Knight, Simpson and Hiller 1999; Lockwood *et al.* 1997; Martin *et al.* 1999; Wexler *et al.* 1999).

*Therapeutic communities for mentally ill chemical abusers*

Special therapeutic community-adapted models have been developed to exclusively treat more seriously disturbed mentally ill chemical abuser (MICA) clients. Several of these have been developed by community-based therapeutic community agencies as special programs in separate facilities, or as separate tracks in a mainstream therapeutic community (Carroll and McGinley 1998). Others have been implemented as innovative research demonstration projects in the mental hospital (Silberstein, Metzger and Galanter 1997) and in community residence settings for the homeless mentally ill chemical abuser (Sacks *et al.* 1997: De Leon *et al.* 1999, 2000; Rahav *et al.* 1995; Egelko *et al.* in press).

In these models for the dually disordered, the basic peer orientation and elements of the daily regime are retained, although there is more focus on individual differences, evident in a greater flexibility in planned duration of stay, the structure and phase format. Specific modifications include the use of standard psychotropic medications, moderated intensity of groups, a less demanding work structure, significant use of individual psychotherapy, case management, and skills training.

In summary, successful adaptations of the therapeutic community adhere to the perspective on recovery and right living and to the fundamental approach – community as method. They retain basic components of the generic model including its social organization, work structure, daily schedule of meetings, groups, seminars and recreational activities and program phases. The variety of staff needed in these adaptations are integrated conceptually in the therapeutic community perspective and approach through intensive and continuous cross-training. Modifications in practices and in program elements for special populations and settings centre upon the treatment goals and planned duration of treatment, the flexibility of the program structure to accommodate individual differences, and the intensity of peer interactions. Special services and interventions are integrated into the program as supplemental to the primary therapeutic community treatment. Successful implementation of therapeutic community program models within special settings requires accommodation to the goals, procedures, personnel, general practices and restrictions of these settings. Research related to these adaptations of the therapeutic community are summarized in the following section.

## Research and evaluation

Research on the therapeutic community for addictions dates back some 30 years. Studies have involved both single programs and multi-programs, and have been conducted by program-based and independent investigative teams. Virtually all of the research on therapeutic communities in North America has been federally funded, primarily by the National Institute on Drug Abuse (NIDA).

Obviously, this literature cannot be adequately reviewed within the purview of the present chapter. However, the main conclusions can be summarized in key areas of inquiry: treatment effectiveness, retention in treatment, and client predictors of success. More recently, investigation has shifted toward evaluating the efficacy of modified therapeutic community programs for special populations and settings, economic analyses of therapeutic community treatment, illuminating treatment process and improving treatment.

### Treatment effectiveness

A substantial evaluation literature documents the effectiveness of the therapeutic community approach in rehabilitating drug-abusing individuals (De

Leon 1984, 1985; Hubbard and Condelli 1994; Hubbard *et al.* 1984; Institute on Medicine 1990; Simpson and Sells 1982; Tims, De Leon and Jainchill 1994; Tims and Ludford 1984). The findings on short- and long-term post-treatment follow-up status from single program and multi-program studies are summarized briefly.

Significant improvements occur on separate outcome variables (i.e. drug use, criminality and employment) and on composite indices for measuring individual success. Maximum to moderately favourable outcomes (which are based on opioid, non-opioid, and alcohol use; arrest rates; re-treatment; employment) occur for more than half of the sample of completed patients and dropouts (De Leon 1984; Simpson 1979; Simpson and Sells 1982).

There is a consistent, positive relationship between time spent in residential treatment and post-treatment outcome status. For example, in long-term therapeutic communities, success rates (on composite indices of no drug use and no criminality) at two years post-treatment approximate 90%, 50%, and 25% respectively for graduates/completers, dropouts who remain more than one year, and dropouts who remain less than one year in residential treatment. Improvement rates over pre-treatment status approximate 100%, 70%, and 40%, respectively (De Leon, Jainchill and Wexler 1982).

In a few studies that investigated psychological outcomes, results uniformly showed significant improvement at follow-up (Biase, Sullivan and Wheeler *et al.* 1986; De Leon 1984; Holland 1983). A direct relationship has been demonstrated between post-treatment behavioral success and psychological adjustment (De Leon 1984; De Leon and Jainchill 1981–1982).

The outcome studies reported were completed on an earlier generation of chemical-abusing individuals, primarily opioid-addicted individuals. Since the early 1980s, however, most admissions to residential therapeutic communities have been multiple-drug-abusing individuals, involving cocaine, crack and alcohol, with relatively fewer primary heroin users. The emerging findings of several large-scale federally funded evaluation efforts all document the effectiveness of therapeutic communities for the changing population of substance abusers. These include the National Treatment Improvement Evaluation Study (NTIES 1996), the Drug Abuse Treatment Outcome Study (Hubbard *et al.* 1997) and the multi-site program of research carried out in the Center for Therapeutic Community Research (see 1996, 1997 Newsletters).

*Retention*

Dropout is the rule for all drug treatment modalities. For therapeutic communities, retention is of particular importance because research has established a firm relationship between time spent in treatment and successful outcome. However, most admissions to therapeutic community programs leave residency, many before treatment influences are presumed to be effectively rendered.

Research on retention in therapeutic communities has been increasing in recent years. Reviews of the therapeutic community retention research are contained in the literature (De Leon 1985, 1991; Lewis and Ross 1994). Studies focus on several questions: retention rates, patient predictors of dropout, and attempts to enhance retention in treatment. The key findings from these are briefly summarized below.

### Retention rates

Dropout is highest (30–40%) in the first 30 days of admission but declines sharply thereafter (De Leon and Schwartz 1984). This temporal pattern of dropout is uniform across therapeutic community programs (and other modalities). In long-term residential therapeutic communities, completion rates range from 10–25% of all admissions. One-year retention rates range from 20–35%, although more recent trends suggest gradual increases in annual retention.

### Predictors of dropout

There are no reliable patient characteristics that predict retention, with the exception of severe criminality and/or severe psychopathology, which are correlated with earlier dropout. Recent studies point to the importance of dynamic factors in predicting retention in treatment, such as perceived legal pressure, motivation, and readiness for treatment (Condelli and De Leon 1993; Condelli and Dunteman 1993; De Leon 1988; De Leon, Melnick, Kressel and Jainchill 1994; Hiller et al. 1998; Hubbard et al. 1988; Joe, Simpson and Broome, 1998).

### Enhancing retention in therapeutic communities

Some experimental attempts to enhance retention in therapeutic communities have used improved orientation to treatment by experienced staff 'senior professors' to reduce early dropout (De Leon, Hawke and Jainchill 2000). Other efforts provide special facilities and programming for mothers and children (Coletti et al. 1992; Stevens, Arbiter and McGrath 1997) and curriculum-based relapse prevention methods (Lewis et al. 1993) to sustain retention throughout residential treatment. The results from these efforts are promising, showing increased retention leading to higher proportion of favourable outcomes.

Although a legitimate concern, retention should not be confused with treatment effectiveness. Therapeutic communities are effective for those who remain long enough for therapeutic influences to occur. Obviously, however, a critical issue for therapeutic communities is maximizing holding power to benefit more patients.

*Treatment process*

Recent developments have facilitated empirical studies into the hitherto under-investigated area of treatment process. A comprehensive theoretical framework of the therapeutic community for addictions has been elaborated in the literature (De Leon 2000). This formulates the essential elements of the therapeutic community approach, a conceptualization of the treatment process and the stages of recovery in the therapeutic community (De Leon 1996, 2000). Developing research based upon these formulations illuminates some active ingredients in the treatment process (Melnick and De Leon 1997). A special emphasis is upon the role of motivation and readiness in seeking and remaining in treatment as well as in the treatment process itself (De Leon *et al.* 1994; De Leon, Melnick and Hawke 2000; Joe, Simpson and Broome 1998; Simpson *et al.* 1997).

*The effectiveness of modified therapeutic communities*

The effectiveness of the various applications of the therapeutic community has been documented. Although the evaluation research is still developing, the main findings for different populations are briefly summarized. Multi-site studies of adolescents in various adaptations of the community-based therapeutic community have documented positive outcomes at one year (Jainchill 1997; Jainchill, Battacharya and Yagelka 1995; Jainchill *et al.* 2000) while five-year studies are nearing completion.

A number of studies have documented the effectiveness of modified therapeutic communities for inmates in prison (Knight, Simpson and Hiller 1999; Martin *et al.* 1999; Wexler *et al.* 1999; Wexler, Melnick, Peters and Lowe 1999). These studies emphasize the importance of post-release aftercare in the stability of outcomes.

Similarly, evaluations demonstrate the effectiveness and cost-effectiveness of modified therapeutic community models for homeless substance abusers in shelters (Liberty *et al.* 1998); for homeless mentally ill chemical abusers in community-based residences (De Leon *et al.* in press; French *et al.* 1999); addicted mothers with their children (Coletti *et al.* 1992; Stevens,

Arbiter and McGrath 1997); and though not described, methadone clients in a day treatment therapeutic community model (De Leon *et al.* 1995).

## Developmental initiatives

The wide diversity of its applications, the insistent pressures to reduce costs, the influx of staff from the traditional health and human services, are some of the factors which threaten the integrity of the therapeutic community's unique self-help approach. In response to this challenge several initiatives are underway or are urgently needed. Though discussed more fully in other writings (De Leon 1997, Chapters 1 and 17; De Leon 2000, Chapter 25), these initiatives may be briefly summarized under the broad theme of applying theory and research to practice.

### *Theory and practice*

As noted earlier, a comprehensive theoretical framework of the therapeutic community for addictions has been formulated which can guide clinical practice, research and policy (De Leon 2000). In this framework the essential components of a generic therapeutic community model offer general guidelines for adapting and modifying the therapeutic community for special settings, special populations and funding limits. Theory, practice and research also provide the basis for codification of principles and practices of the therapeutic community into explicit standards to maintain the integrity of the program model and method. These have been developed specifically for prison-based therapeutic community programs (Therapeutic Communities in Correctional Settings 1999) and generically for community-based therapeutic community agencies (TCA Newsletter 1998).

### *Research for practice*

Various strategies have been implemented to advance therapeutic community training and technical assistance grounded in theory and research. Funded mainly by the National Institute on Drug Abuse (NIDA) and the Center for Substance Abuse Treatment (CSAT), these are designed to sustain the fidelity of therapeutic community practices and to improve treatment in general. Federal grants are awarded for evaluating technology transfer methods, and conferences are staged with the express goal of strengthening the alliance between researchers and practitioners in drug treatment, including therapeutic communities. The Addiction Technology and Training Centers (ATTCs) represent a CSAT-funded system of regionally based centres for improving treatment based upon research and best practices (Talboy 1998).

Manuals are available for program development and training in modified therapeutic communities for mentally ill chemical abusers (Sacks *et al.* 1998), for prison-based therapeutic communities (Talboy 1998). Other training material utilizing research findings has been independently developed (Carroll and Sobel 1986; Deitch and Solit 1993). An initiative currently in the planning stage is to launch a large-scale training capability based upon clinical and research experience (e.g. a national therapeutic community academy). This effort incorporates and co-ordinates the key staff training components of a uniform curriculum, a faculty of skilled trainers, and an appropriate, didactic and experiential training format (CTCR Newsletter July 1999).

In conclusion, the evolution of the contemporary therapeutic community for addictions over the past 30 years in North America may be characterized as a movement from the marginal to the mainstream of substance-abuse treatment and human services. Although risky, the current stage of this evolution is perhaps the most exciting, challenging the therapeutic community to retain its unique identity while effectively adapting and modifying its approach.

## Notes

1. In recent years, some larger agencies operate residential facilities with a static capacity of 200–300 in community-based settings and even larger numbers in prison settings. Formative evaluations suggest that these capacities are feasible if managed as smaller units of 50–100 residents (Corcoran prison in California). Conversely, modified TC programs in shelters and mental health settings are smaller 'houses' of 30–50 residents (De Leon 1997; Liberty *et al.* 1998). Increasingly, issues such as resident capacity, staff to client ratios, and number of programming hours are under regulatory influences (California Department of Corrections, 1998).

2. Comparative studies of inpatient and outpatient alcohol and cocaine treatment indicate no differences in outcomes (Alterman *et al.* 1993). However, these do not refer to therapeutic community oriented residential treatment programs.

## References

Alterman, A. I., O'Brien, C. P. and Droba, M. (1993) 'Day treatment vs. inpatient rehabilitation of cocaine abusers: an interim report.' In F. M. Tims and C. G. Leukefeld (eds) *Cocaine Treatment: Research and Clinical Perspectives, NIDA Research Monograph Number 135*, NIH Publication No. 93–3639, pp. 150–162. Rockville, MD: National Institute on Drug Abuse.

Barton, E. (1994) 'Nature and nurture: the adaptation of the therapeutic community to HIV/AIDS.' In *Proceedings of the Therapeutic Communities of America 1992 Planning Conference, Paradigms: Past, Present and Future.* December, Chantilly, Virginia. Providence, RI: Manisses Communications Group.

Biase, D. V., Sullivan, A. P. and Wheeler, B. (1986) 'Daytop Miniversity – Phase 2 college training in a therapeutic community: development of self-concept among drug-free addict/abusers.' In G. De Leon and J. T. Ziegenfuss (eds) *Therapeutic Communities for Addictions* pp. 121–130. Springfield, IL: Charles C. Thomas.

Broekaert, E., Vanderplasschen, W., Temmerman, I., Ottenberg, D. J. and Kaplan, C. (2000) 'Retrospective study of similarities and relations between the American drug-free and the European therapeutic communities for children and adults.' *Journal of Psychoactive Drugs 32*, 4, 407–417.

Carroll, J. F. X. and McGinley, J. J. (1998) 'Managing MICA clients in a modified therapeutic community with enhanced staffing.' *Journal of Substance Abuse Treatment 15*, 6, pp.565–577.

Carroll, J. F. X., and Sobel, B. S. (1986) 'Integrating mental health personnel and practices into a therapeutic community.' In G. De Leon and J. T. Ziegenfuss (eds) *Therapeutic Communities for Addictions: Readings in Theory, Research and Practice* pp. 209–226. Springfield, IL: Charles C. Thomas.

Center for Therapeutic Community Research (Winter 1996). *Communications 1*, 1.

Center for Therapeutic Community Research (December 1997). *Communications 2*, 1.

Center for Therapeutic Community Research (July 1999). *Communications 3*, 1.

Coletti, D. S. (1989) 'Eliminating barriers: residential treatment of addicted mothers with their infants.' Findings from NIDA Grant Number R18 DA06369–01, awarded to PAR, Inc. St. Petersburg, FL.

Coletti, S. D., Hughes, P. H., Landress, H. J., Neri, R. L., Sicilian, D. M., Williams, K. M., Urmann, C. F. and Anthony, J. C. (1992) 'PAR village: specialized intervention for cocaine abusing women and their children.' *Journal of the Florida Medical Association 79*, pp.701–705.

Condelli, W. S. and De Leon, G. (1993) 'Fixed and dynamic predictors of retention in therapeutic communities for substance abusers.' *Journal of Substance Abuse Treatment 10*, pp.11–16.

Condelli, W. S. and Dunteman, G. H. (1993) 'Issues to consider when predicting retention in therapeutic communities.' *Journal of Psychoactive Drugs 25*, pp.239–244.

Deitch, D. A. and Solit, R. (1993) 'Training drug abuse workers in a therapeutic community.' *Psychotherapy: Theory, Research and Practice 30*, 12, pp.305–316.

De Leon, G. (1984) 'The therapeutic community: study of effectiveness.' *National Institute on Drug Abuse Treatment Research Monograph Series* (ADM 84–1286). Washington, DC: Superintendent of Documents, US Government Printing Office.

De Leon, G. (1985) 'The therapeutic community: status and evolution.' *International Journal of Addictions 20*, 6–7, pp.823–844.

De Leon, G. (1988) 'Legal pressure in therapeutic communities.' In C. G. Leukefeld and F. M. Tims (eds) *Compulsory Treatment of Drug Abuse: Research and Clinical Practice, NIDA Research Monograph 86* (DHHS Publication Number Adm 88–1578, pp. 160–177). Rockville, MD: National Institute on Drug Abuse.

De Leon, G. (1990–91) 'Aftercare in therapeutic communities.' *International Journal of Addictions 25*, pp.1229–1241.

De Leon, G. (1991) 'Retention in drug-free therapeutic communities.' In R. W. Pickens, C. G. Leukefeld and C. R. Schuster (eds) *Improving Drug Abuse Treatment, NIDA Research Monograph 106*, pp. 218–244. Rockville, MD: National Institute on Drug Abuse.

De Leon, G. (1993) 'Cocaine abusers in therapeutic community treatment.' In F. M. Tims and C. G. Leukefeld (eds) *Cocaine Treatment: Research and Clinical Perspectives, NIDA Research Monograph*

*135* (NIH Publication No. 93–3639, pp. 163–189). Washington, DC: Superintendent of Documents, US Government Printing Office.

De Leon, G. (1995a) 'Residential therapeutic communities in the mainstream: diversity and issues.' *Journal of Psychoactive Drugs 27,* 1(Jan–Mar), pp.3–15.

De Leon, G. (1995b) 'Therapeutic communities for addictions: a theoretical framework.' *International Journal of the Addictions 30,* 12, pp.1603–1645.

De Leon, G. (1996) 'Integrative recovery: a stage paradigm.' *Substance Abuse 17,* 1, pp.51–63.

De Leon, G. (ed) (1997) *Community as Method: Therapeutic Communities for Special Populations and Special Settings.* Westport, CT: Greenwood Publishing Group, Inc.

De Leon, G. (2000) *The Therapeutic Community: Theory, Model, and Method.* New York, NY: Springer Publishing Company, Inc.

De Leon, G. and Deitch, D. (1985) 'Treatment of the adolescent substance abuser in a therapeutic community.' In A. Friedman and G. Beschner (eds) *Treatment Services for Adolescent Substance Abusers* (DHHS Publication No. [ADM] 85–1342, pp. 216–230). Rockville MD: National Institute of Drug Abuse.

De Leon, G., Hawke, J., and Jainchill, N. (2000) 'Therapeutic communities: enhancing retention in treatment using "Senior Professor" staff.' *Journal of Substance Abuse Treatment 19,* 4, 375–382.

De Leon, G. and Jainchill, N. (1981–82) 'Male and female drug abusers: social and psychological status two years after treatment in a therapeutic community.' *American Journal of Drug and Alcohol Abuse 8,* 4, pp.465–497.

De Leon, G. and Jainchill, N. (1991) 'Residential therapeutic communities for female substance abusers.' *Bulletin of the New York Academy of Medicine 67,* 3 (May/June), pp.277–290.

De Leon, G., Jainchill, N. and Wexler, H. (1982) 'Success and improvement rates five years after treatment in a therapeutic community.' *International Journal of Addictions 17,* 4, pp.703–747.

De Leon, G., Melnick, G. and Hawke, J. (2000) 'The motivation-readiness factor in drug treatment: implications for research and policy.' *Advances in Medical Sociology 7,* pp.103–129.

De Leon, G., Melnick, G., Kressel, D. and Jainchill, N. (1994) 'Circumstances, motivation, readiness and suitability (the CMRS scales): predicting retention in therapeutic community treatment.' *American Journal of Drug and Alcohol Abuse 20,* 4, pp.495–515.

De Leon, G. and Rosenthal, M. S. (1989) 'Treatment in residential therapeutic communities.' In *Treatments of Psychiatric Disorders: A Task Force Report of the American Psychiatric Association* Vol 2, pp. 1379–1397. Washington, DC: American Psychiatric Association.

De Leon, G., Sacks, S. and McKendrick, K. (1999) 'Modified therapeutic communities for homeless mentally ill chemical abusers; emerging subtypes.' *American Journal of Drug and Alcohol Abuse 25,* 3, 493–513.

De Leon, G., Sacks, S. and McKendrick, K. (2000) 'Modified therapeutic communities for homeless mentally ill chemical abusers: treatment outcomes.' *American Journal of Drug and Alcohol Abuse 26,* 3, 461–480.

De Leon, G. and Schwartz, S. (1984) 'The therapeutic community: what are the retention rates?' *American Journal of Drug and Alcohol Abuse 10,* 2, pp.267–284.

De Leon, G., Staines, G. L., Perlis, T. E., Sacks, S., McKendrick, K., Hilton, R. and Brady, R. (1995) 'Therapeutic community methods in methadone maintenance (Passages): an open clinical trial.' *Journal of Drug and Alcohol Dependence 37,* pp.45–57.

Egelko, S., Galanter, M., Dermatis, H., Jurewicz, E., Jamison, A., Dingle, S. and De Leon, G. (in press) 'Improved psychological status in a modified therapeutic community for homeless MICA men.' *Journal of Addictive Diseases.*

Egelko, S., Galanter, M., Edwards, H. and Marinelli, K. (1996) 'Treatment of perinatal cocaine addiction: use of the modified theraputic community.' *American Journal of Drug and Alcohol Abuse 22*, pp.185–202.

French, M. T., Sacks, S., De Leon, G., Staines, G. and McKendrick, K. (1999) 'Modified therapeutic community for mentally ill chemical abusers: outcomes and costs.' *Evaluation and the Health Professions 22*, 1, pp.60–85.

Galanter, M., Egelko, S., De Leon, G. and Rohrs, C. (1993) 'A general hospital day program combining peer-led and professional treatment of cocaine abusers.' *Hospital and Community Psychiatry 44*, 7, pp.644–649.

Hiller, M. L., Knight, K., Broome, K. M. and Simpson, D. D. (1998) 'Legal pressure and retention in a national sample of long-term residential programs.' *Criminal Justice and Behavior 25*, 4, pp.463–481.

Holland, S. (1983) 'Evaluating community-based treatment programs: a model for strengthening inferences about effectiveness.' *International Journal of Therapeutic Communities 4*, 4, pp.285–306.

Hubbard, R. L., Collins, J. J., Valley Rachal, J., *et al.* (1988) 'The criminal justice client in drug abuse treatment.' In C. G. Leukefel and F. M. Tims (eds) *Compulsory Treatment of Drug Abuse: Research and Clinical Practice. NIDA Research Monograph Number 86* (DHHS Publication No. [ADM] 88–1578, pp. 57–80). Rockville, MD: National Institute on Drug Abuse.

Hubbard, R. L. and Condelli, W. (1994) 'Client outcomes from therapeutic communities.' In F. M. Tims and G. De Leon (eds) *Therapeutic Community Research and Evaluation.* National Institute on Drug Abuse Monograph. Rockville, MD: National Institute on Drug Abuse.

Hubbard, R. L., Craddock. S. G., Flynn, P. M., Anderson, J. and Etheridge, R. M. (1997) 'Overview of one-year follow-up outcomes in the drug abuse treatment outcome study (DATOS).' *Psychology of Addictive Behaviors: Special Issue: Drug Abuse Treatment Outcome Study (DATOS) 11*, 4, pp.261–278.

Hubbard, R. L., Valley Rachal, J., Craddock, S. G. and Cavanaugh, E. R. (1984) 'Treatment outcome prospective study (TOPS): client characteristics and behaviors before, during, and after treatment.' In F. M. Tims and J. P. Ludford (eds) *Drug Abuse Treatment Evaluation: Strategies, Progress, and Prospects. NIDA Research Monograph Number 51* (DHHS Publication No. [ADM] 84–1329; pp. 42–68). Rockville, MD: National Institute on Drug Abuse.

Institute on Medicine (1990) 'Treating drug problems: a study of the evolution, effectiveness, and financing of public and private drug treatment systems.' Report by the Institute of Medicine Committee for the Substance Abuse Coverage Study, Division of Health Care Services. Washington, DC: National Academy Press.

Jainchill, N. (1994) 'Co-morbidity and therapeutic community treatment.' In F. M. Tims, G. De Leon and N. Jainchill (eds) *Therapeutic Community: Advances in Research and Application, NIDA Research Monograph 144*, NIH Publication Number 94–3633, pp. 209–231. Rockville, MD: National Institute on Drug Abuse.

Jainchill, N. (1997) 'Therapeutic communities for adolescents: the same and not the same.' In G. De Leon (ed) *Community as Method: Therapeutic Communities for Special Populations and Special Settings*, pp. 161–177. Westport, CT: Greenwood Publishing Group, Inc.

Jainchill, N., Battacharya, G. and Yagelka, J. (1995) 'Therapeutic communities for adolescents.' In E. Rahdert and D. Czechowicz (eds) *Adolescent Drug Abuse: Clinical Assessment and Therapeutic Interventions, NIDA Research Monograph 156*, pp. 190–217. Rockville, MD: National Institute on Drug Abuse.

Jainchill, N. and De Leon, G. (1992) 'Therapeutic community research: recent studies of psychopathology and retention.' In G. Buhringer, J. J. Platt and F. L. Malabar (eds) *Drug Abuse*

*Treatment Research: German and American Perspectives*, pp. 367–388. Malabar, Fl: Krieger Publishing.

Jainchill, N., Hawke, J., De Leon, G. and Yagelka, J. (2000) 'Adolescents in therapeutic communities: one-year post-treatment outcomes.' *Journal of Psychoactive Drugs 32*, 1, 81–94.

Joe, G. W., Simpson, D. D. and Broome, K. M. (1998) 'Effects of readiness for drug abuse treatment on client retention and assessment of process.' *Addiction 93*, 8, pp.1177–1190.

Jones, M. (1953) *The Therapeutic Community: A New Treatment Method in Psychiatry.* New York: Basic Books.

Jones, M. (1986) 'Democratic therapeutic communities (DTCs) or programmatic therapeutic communities or both?' In G. De Leon and J. T. Ziegenfuss, Jr. (eds) *Therapeutic Communities for Addictions,* pp. 19–28. Springfield, IL: Charles C. Thomas.

Kennard, D. (1983) *An Introduction to Therapeutic Communities.* London: Routledge and Kegan Paul.

Knight, K., Simpson, D. and Hiller, M. (1999) 'Three-year reincarceration outcomes for in-prison therapeutic community treatment in Texas.' *The Prison Journal 79*, 3, pp.337–351.

Lewis, B. F., McCusker, J., Hindin, R., Frost, R. and Garfield, F. (1993) 'Four residential drug treatment programs: project IMPACT.' In J. A. Inciardi, F. M. Tims and B. W. Fletcher (eds) *Innovative Approaches in the Treatment of Drug Abuse: Program Models and Strategies,* pp. 45–60. Westport, CT: Greenwood Press.

Lewis, B. F. and Ross, R. (1994) 'Retention in therapeutic communities: challenges for the Nineties.' In F. M. Tims, G. De Leon and N. Jainchill (eds) *Therapeutic Community: Advances in Research and Applications. NIDA Research Monograph Number 144.* NIH Publication Number 94–3633. Rockville, MD: Superintendent of Documents, US Printing Office.

Liberty, H. J., Johnson, B. D., Jainchill, N., Ryder, J., Messina, M., Reynolds, S. and Hossain, M. (1998) 'Dynamic recovery: comparative study of therapeutic communities in homeless shelters for men.' *Journal of Substance Abuse Treatment 15*, 5, pp.401–423.

Lipton, D. S. (1999) 'Therapeutic community treatment programming in corrections.' In C. R. Hollin (ed) *Handbook of Offender Assessment and Treatment.* London: John Wiley and Sons Ltd.

Lockwood, D., Inciardi, J. A., Butzin, C. A. and Hooper, R. M. (1997) 'The therapeutic community continuum in corrections.' In G. De Leon (ed) *Community as Method: Therapeutic Communities for Special Populations and Special Settings,* pp. 87–96. Westport, CT: Greenwood Publishing Group, Inc.

Marlatt, G. A. (1985) 'Relapse prevention: theoretical rationale and overview of the model.' In G. A. Marlatt and J. R. Gordon (eds) *Relapse Prevention: Maintenance Strategies in the Treatment of Addictive Behaviors.* New York: Guilford Press.

Martin, S., Butzin, C., Saum, C. and Inciardi, J. A. (1999) 'Three-year outcomes of therapeutic community treatment for drug involved offenders in Delaware: from prison to work release to aftercare.' *The Prison Journal 79*, 3, pp.294–320.

McCusker, J. and Sorensen, J. L. (1994) 'HIV and therapeutic communities.' In F. M. Tims, G. De Leon and N. Jainchill (eds) *Therapeutic Community: Advances in Research and Application, NIDA Research Monograph 144* (NIH Publication No. 94–3633, pp. 232–258). Rockville, MD: National Institute on Drug Abuse.

McCusker, J., Vickers-Lahti, M., Stoddard, A., Hindin, R., Bigelow, C., Zorn, M., Garfield, F., Frost, R., Love, C. and Lewis, B. (1995) 'The effectiveness of alternative planned durations of residential drug abuse treatment.' *American Journal of Public Health 85*, pp.1426–1429.

Melnick, G. and De Leon, G. (1997) 'Clarifying the nature of therapeutic community treatment.' *Journal of Substance Abuse Treatment 16*, 4, pp.307–313.

National Treatment Improvement Evaluation Study (NTIES). (September 1996) 'Preliminary report: The persistent effects of substance abuse treatment – one year later.' Rockville, MD:

US Dept. of Health and Human Services, Substance Abuse and Mental Health Services Administration, Center for Substance Abuse Treatment (CSAT).

Pompi, K. F. (1994) 'Adolescents in therapeutic communities: retention and posttreatment outcome.' In F. M. Tims, G. De Leon and N. Jainchill (eds) *Therapeutic Community: Advances in Research and Application, NIDA Research Monograph 144* (NIH Publication No 94–3633, pp. 128–161). Rockville, MD: National Institute on Drug Abuse.

Rahav, M., Rivera, J. J., Nuttbrock, L., *et al.* (1995) 'Characteristics and treatment of homeless, mentally ill, chemical-abusing men.' *Journal of Psychoactive Drugs 27*, pp.93–103.

Rapaport, R. N. (1960) *Community as Doctor.* London: Tavistock Publications.

Sacks, S., De Leon, G., Bernhardt, A. I. and Sacks, J. (1996, revised 1998) *Modied Therapeutic Community for Homeless MICA Individuals: A Treatment Manual.* Center for Mental Health Services (CMHS)/Center for Substance Abuse Treatment (CSAT) Grant #1UD3 SM/TI51558–01. New York: NDRI/CTCR.

Sacks, D., De Leon, G., Bernhardt, A. I. and Sacks, J. Y. (1997) 'a modified therapeutic community for homeless mentally ill chemical abusers.' In G. De Leon (ed) *Community as Method: Therapeutic Communities for Special Populations and Special Settings,* pp. 19–37. Westport, CT: Greenwood Publishing Group, Inc.

Silberstein, C. H., Metzger, E. J. and Galanter, M. (1997) 'The Greenhouse: A modified therapeutic community for mentally ill homeless addicts at New York University.' In G. De Leon (ed) *Community as Method: Therapeutic Communities for Special Populations and Special Settings,* pp. 53–65. Westport, CT: Greenwood Publishing Group, Inc.

Simpson, D. D. (1979) 'The relation of time spent in drug abuse treatment to post-treatment outcome.' *American Journal of Psychiatry 136,* pp.1449–1453.

Simpson, D. D. (1986) '12-year follow-up: outcomes of opioid addicts treated in therapeutic communities.' In G. De Leon and J. T. Ziegenfuss (eds) *Therapeutic Communities for Addictions: Readings in Theory, Research and Practice.* Springfield, IL: Charles C. Thomas.

Simpson, D. D., Joe, G. W., Rowan-Szal, G. A. and Greener, J. M. (1997) 'Drug abuse treatment process components that improve retention.' *Journal of Substance Abuse Treatment 14,* pp.565–572.

Simpson, D. D. and Sells, S. B. (1982) 'Effectiveness of treatment for drug abuse: an overview of the DARP research program.' *Advances in Alcohol and Substance Abuse 2,* pp.7–29.

Stevens, S. J., Arbiter, N. and McGrath, R. (1997) 'Women and children: therapeutic community substance abuse treatment.' In G. De Leon (ed) *Community as Method: Therapeutic Communities for Special Populations and Special Settings,* pp. 129–142. Westport, CT: Greenwood Publishing Group, Inc.

Stevens, S., Arbiter, N. and Glider, P. (1989) 'Women residents: expanding their role to increase treatment effectiveness in substance abuse programs.' *International Journal of the Addictions 24,* 5, pp.425–434.

Stevens, S. J. and Glider, P. (1994) 'Therapeutic communities: substance abuse treatment for women.' In F. M. Tims, G. De Leon and N. Jainchill (eds) *Therapeutic Community: Advances in Research and Application, NIDA Research Monograph 144* (NIH Publication No 94–3633, pp. 162–180). Rockville, MA: National Institute on Drug Abuse.

Sugarman, B. (1986) 'Structure, variations, and context: a sociological view of the therapeutic community.' In G. De Leon and J. T. Ziegenfuss (eds) *Therapeutic Communities for Addictions: Readings in Theory, Research and Practice,* pp. 65–82. Springfield, IL: Charles C. Thomas.

Talboy, E. S. (1998) *Therapeutic Community Experiential Training: Facilitator Guide.* Kansas City, MO: University of Missouri-Kansas City, Mid-America Addiction Technology Transfer Center (ATTC).

Theraputic Communities of America (TCA) Criminal Justice Committee (1999) *Therapeutic Communities in Correctional Settings: The Prison-Based Therapeutic Community Standards Development Project, Final Report of Phase II.* (Prepared for the White House Office of National Drug Control Policy [ONDCP]). Washington, DC: National Drug Clearinghouse, 1–800–666–3332 [NCJ179365]. Or available at http://www.whitehousedrugpolicy.gov

Therapeutic Communities of America (TCA) Newsletter (winter 1999).

Tims, F. M., De Leon, G. and Jainchill, N. (eds) (1994) *Advances in Therapeutic Community Research and Practice, National Institute on Drug Abuse Research Monograph Series No.144.* Rockville, MD: National Institute on Drug Abuse.

Tims F. M. and Ludford, J. P. (eds) (1984) *Drug Abuse Treatment Evaluation: Strategies, Progress and Prospects. NIDA Research Monograph Number 51,* RAUS, Special Issue on Research Analysis and Utilization System. Rockville, MD: National Institute on Drug Abuse.

Wexler, H. K., De Leon, G., Thomas, G., Kressel, D. and Peters, J. (1999) 'The Amity prison therapeutic community evaluation: reincarceration outcomes.' *Criminal Justice and Behavior 26,* 2, pp.144–167.

Wexler, H. K., Melnick, G., Lowe, L. and Peters, J. (1999) 'Three-year reincarceration outcomes for Amity in-prison therapeutic community and aftercare in California.' *The Prison Journal 79,* 3, pp.321–336.

Wexler, H. and Williams, R. (1986) 'The Stay'n Out therapeutic community: prison treatment for substance abusers.' *Journal of Psychoactive Drugs 18,* pp.221–230.

# CHAPTER 5

# Therapeutic communities for the treatment of addictions in Australia

*Clive F. Lloyd and Frances V. O'Callaghan*

## General overview and context

As Australia enters the new millennium it is becoming increasingly apparent that the federal government's 'tough on drugs' strategy has had little impact on the nation's substance abuse crisis. The Howard government's policy of 'tough on drugs' was introduced in 1997. Two years later, the Alcohol and other Drugs Council of Australia (ADCA) reported that drug use and drug-related deaths have both increased, while the age of first use has decreased. With the exception of cocaine, Australians have higher rates of abuse than Americans across all illicit drugs (ADCA 1997). Despite this, the federal government allocates only $35 million (less than $2 per person) to the activities of the National Drug Strategy. In contrast, the USA spends $28 per person in the areas of drug education and treatment research alone.

The government's emphasis on being 'tough on drugs' has resulted in annual funding of $450 million allocated to the enforcement of illicit drug laws. This has led to a greater number of arrests and incarcerations for drug-related crimes, placing an extra burden on already over-populated prisons (ADCA 1997). Around 75% of prisoners in Australian jails are incarcerated due to drug-related offences at an annual cost per person of approximately $50,000 (ADCA 1997). Meanwhile, provisions for the treatment and rehabilitation of substance abusers are much less liberal. Whereas in the past, treatment agencies were often successful in obtaining funds without documenting evidence of the success of their programs, it is increasingly the case that in order to receive any level of government support, treatment agencies are required to provide empirical evidence with regard to program content and treatment outcomes.

Against this backdrop of economic rationalism, Australian therapeutic communities are in the process of adapting to meet an overwhelming demand for places while under severe financial restraint. The Australasian Therapeutic Communities Association estimates that 70% of residential beds in Australia are provided by therapeutic communities; however, few are fully funded by state or federal government monies (ATCA 1999).

Almost all Australian therapeutic communities are non-government agencies and rely on funding from a variety of sources. As a result of reductions in state and federal government grants, increasingly therapeutic communities have been required to cultivate relationships with the corporate community. Residents are expected to contribute towards their accommodation and treatment costs. These contributions are often based on a proportion of clients' welfare benefits. However, many clients prefer (and have the financial means) to pay the full fees independently. Therapeutic communities are one of the few modalities in addiction treatment where such a 'user pays' system has been adopted, with up to 25% of total revenue being raised through client contributions.

Despite fluctuations in government policies and funding, Australian therapeutic communities have not only survived, but flourished in the past two decades. Moreover, this treatment modality has been increasingly recognized as an effective means of rehabilitating chronic substance abusers (De Leon 1995). Unfortunately, a lack of sound empirical outcome data in Australia has provided detractors of the therapeutic community model with ample material for criticism. This lack of research may serve to maintain the erratic nature of government support and, if not addressed, threatens to dilute the successes so evident to those who have witnessed the change process in therapeutic communities.

The ATCA comprises 30 agencies representing a variety of programs from all states and territories in Australia and New Zealand. The aim of this chapter is to provide an overview of the history and development of therapeutic communities in Australia, and an outline of the current issues facing this treatment modality. Also included is a comprehensive description of an influential therapeutic community specializing in the treatment of dually-diagnosed substance-dependent adolescents, and a brief overview of therapeutic communities in Australian prisons.

## History and development

Naming Australia's first therapeutic community is a contentious issue. The Kuitpo community in South Australia established a rehabilitation centre for alcoholic men as early as 1945, pre-dating Synanon by a decade. However, Kuitpo's approach was crude (even by Synanon's standards) and unlikely to fall within the boundaries of what traditionally defines a therapeutic community. While several residential addiction treatment agencies began operating in the early 1970s, the South Australian organization We Help Ourselves (WHOs) generally claims the title of Australia's first therapeutic community for chemical dependency. Established in 1972, WHOs' early years, not unlike those of its American counterpart, attracted publicity for unorthodox 'therapeutic' methods. However, the program's long evolution has seen WHOs become and remain a highly influential member of the ATCA (ATCA 1999).

The next major development was the direct importation of the Odyssey House model by Walter McGrath in 1977. McGrath (whose son had died from a heroin overdose) wanted to provide services for others with drug problems. Receiving a small grant from the New South Wales (NSW) Health Department, McGrath travelled to North America to investigate various treatment programs and therapeutic community models. He finally decided the Odyssey House model was the most appropriate to Australian culture and set up the first Australian Odyssey House in Campbelltown, NSW (Toumbourou *et al.* 1988).

Thus, the early influences on Australian therapeutic communities were based on the hierarchical Synanon model. The highly structured confrontational approach advocated by hierarchical therapeutic communities was the source of much criticism. Perhaps as a result of this bad press, funding agencies were initially unenthusiastic about funding replicas of Odyssey House, preferring to cope with the growing demand for drug treatment by supporting more democratic Christian-based programs such as the Buttery.

The Buttery was originally a service assisting itinerant youth at the end of the 'hippie' movement. Between 1972 and 1977 it operated as a Christian community, caring for many young people with drug problems. Rewarding this good work, the program received government funding in 1975. Further funding from the NSW Drug and Alcohol Authority saw the Buttery expand and change direction toward the hierarchical end of the continuum. The Buttery has continued to evolve, and today is one of the most highly regarded therapeutic communities in the country. Indeed, the Buttery has influenced the formation of many subsequent therapeutic communities (ATCA 1999).

During the early 1980s, funds from the National Campaign Against Drug Abuse tended to favour shorter-term residential treatment, allowing the formation and expansion of several therapeutic communities. However, funding for the longer-term, hierarchical agencies such as Odyssey House was downgraded after 1985 after several studies (e.g. Rosenthal 1984; Simpson and Sells 1982) indicated little difference in treatment outcomes between modalities. Long-term, inpatient treatment was, therefore, viewed as not cost effective. With the traditional therapeutic communities struggling for funding, respectability and acceptance, it became clear that there was a need for a national organization that could represent the Australian therapeutic community movement. This need was met by the formation of the ATCA.

Affiliated with the World Federation of Therapeutic Communities (WFTC), the ATCA is a non-profit organization dedicated to promoting the therapeutic community movement and establishing mechanisms to maintain and improve standards of treatment. One of the most significant achievements of the ATCA has been the implementation of a quality assurance peer review system that requires a therapeutic community to undergo initial and further periodical visits by ATCA representatives in order to gain and maintain ATCA accreditation. The peer review essentially seeks to ensure quality service provision and sound ethical treatment approaches.

The ATCA has also promoted the independent evaluation of member therapeutic communities by the Quality Improvement Council Limited (1999). The aim of the standards is to improve drug-related services by providing a framework for ongoing evaluation and review in order to maintain high-quality and effective services. The underlying approach is that of harm minimization and the manual contains guidelines on the following topics:

1. Assessment, treatment and care
2. Early identification and intervention
3. Health promotion and harm prevention
4. Community liaison and participation
5. Rights and responsibilities of consumers
6. Client and program records
7. Education, training and development
8. Planning, quality improvement and evaluation
9. Management
10. Work and its environment.

Each topic includes a set of standards and their associated indicators so that service providers can achieve consistency in evaluating their performance. Services that undergo a successful review receive accreditation for one, two or three years, with an agreement being made for further development in relation to the standards.

As well as being encouraged to participate in such rigorous program evaluations, all member therapeutic communities must now incorporate an ATCA-endorsed staff code of ethics and client bill of rights into their programs. Having a national representative organization has resulted in a wide variety of programs all functioning within the framework of a basic therapeutic community model.

Currently, ATCA member communities vary in size from 10 to 100 beds, with program lengths varying from 3 months to 18 months. The majority of programs, however, are between 6 and 12 months. Agencies also vary in terms of program content and structure, some emphasizing 12-step fellowship philosophy, while others focus on family therapy and/or cognitive-behavioural models (ATCA 1999).

Despite this variety, a recent ATCA conference demonstrated the unanimous acceptance of an overall model of therapeutic community treatment outlined by De Leon (1995). Responding to items from the therapeutic community Scale of Essential Elements Questionnaire (SEEQ) few delegates expressed significant deviations from the program components and philosophies which De Leon and Melnick (1992) use to define a therapeutic community. Such consistency may serve the therapeutic community movement by making research findings more generalizable. However, the historical reliance on American research, and lack of empirical data from Australian studies, continue to inhibit the widespread acceptance of the model by funding authorities.

## Outcome studies

The lack of Australian research into therapeutic communities becomes more salient with the observation that local agencies generally cite American studies as a rationale for treatment protocol or evidence of treatment effectiveness. Currently only four therapeutic communities in Australia have participated in research projects. Moreover, research of a publishable standard has been even more scarce.

The ATCA cites a lack of resources as the main barrier to research, and emphasizes that all member therapeutic communities welcome the opportunity to participate in program outcome evaluations by independent agencies. While the difficulties associated with maintaining adequate funding have resulted in the current need for independent evaluation, in previous years there seems to have been a mutual disregard between researchers and therapeutic communities. In their early years, therapeutic communities actively excluded the input of professionals and, to some degree, this anti-academic streak has remained a part of therapeutic community culture. Similarly, professional researchers have been reticent regarding studies of a treatment modality perceived as unprofessional and lacking any theoretical framework.

Interestingly, most of the published Australian research findings are from studies conducted on one particular model of therapeutic community treatment, that of Odyssey House (Powell 1984; Toumbourou and Hamilton 1993; Toumbourou et al. 1998). It may be the case that the researchers selected a model of treatment that is well established and researched in North America. However, focusing exclusively on such 'safe' models is likely to inhibit the evaluation of short-term, specialist or innovative therapeutic communities. It is hoped that the increasing professionalism and sophistication of Australian therapeutic communities will result in increased activities by research bodies. To date, the published Australian studies have focused on predictors of client attrition (Powell 1984) and treatment outcomes (Toumbourou and Hamilton 1993; Toumbourou et al. 1998). Overall, findings are consistent with those cited by De Leon (1995).

Time spent in treatment was shown to be a consistent predictor of successful treatment (Toumbourou and Hamilton 1993). However, more recent research (Toumbourou et al. 1998) has cast doubt on the widespread assumption that time spent in treatment best predicts positive outcomes. Rather, treatment progress (i.e. stage of treatment achieved) was found to predict improved functioning better than time in treatment. Indeed, a prolonged stay in any level of treatment provided no significant advantage to treatment outcomes. This finding emphasizes the need for further studies evaluating the effectiveness of short-term therapeutic community treatment. Moreover, in recent years many therapeutic communities have started to cater for specialized groups such as adolescents, women with young children, and addicts in prisons. More research is required to evaluate the effectiveness of therapeutic communities specializing in the treatment of specific populations. One such therapeutic community, Mirikai, while operating within the overall framework of the therapeutic community model, has adapted its program to cater for a particularly challenging population – adolescent substance abusers with co-morbid psychiatric conditions. The therapeutic community is comprehensively described below.

## Portrait of an Australian therapeutic community: Mirikai

*Mirikai* is an Aboriginal word meaning 'place of peace'. The therapeutic community began operating in 1971 with the establishment of the Gold Coast Drug Council in Queensland. The Council operates two discrete but interrelated program areas: the Mirikai residential program, and a community program. The residential program caters for up to 34 young people with complex problems associated with their drug use. The broad aim of the program is to enhance the capacity and commitment of clients to achieve and maintain an optimal level of personal and social functioning free from harmful drug use. Approximately 70% of the residents are aged between 14 and 25 years and the remainder from 25 to 29 years. In 1998–1999, 175 new residents were admitted to Mirikai. With 34 in residence, this brought the population for the year to a total of 209. Of those, 149 graduated from various treatment stages.

The staff and residents of Mirikai have had an active role in establishing various community programs such as youth shelters and needle exchange programs. Information and referral services are also provided.

### Staff

Mirikai currently employs eleven paid staff (including psychologists, nurses and a social worker), and approximately forty volunteers, including ex-residents and community members who undertake duties related to administration, maintenance and supervision of the residential program. A psychiatrist visits four times per week to assess and treat psychiatric co-morbidity and participate in case-management activities.

### The community program

This program involves two ten-week drug awareness courses involving a two-hour information evening each week, presented by a range of specialists working in various aspects of the drug field. There is also an annual community event called Drug Awareness Month. The aim of the program is to improve community knowledge and awareness of drug issues and to facilitate the development and implementation of strategies to reduce drug-related personal harms and social costs within the wider community.

### The Mirikai residential program

The residential program consists of five phases:

1. Orientation and assessment

2. Safety Net

3. Transition

4. Pretreatment

5. Treatment.

Before admission to the program there is an assessment of the client's stage of change, based on Prochaska and DiClemente's (1984) transtheoretical model. Other variables assessed include:

o history (family, legal and criminal, drug use, medical, psychological, educational and social)

o mental health (e.g., suicidal ideation/risk)

o prior reports and points of contact

o referral to additional internal or external assessment resources (e.g., psychiatric services, family services, case managers etc.)

and other standardized psychometric tests.

Because there is a waiting list for Mirikai, the final decision regarding entry to the program also involves an assessment of each individual's needs, together with a consideration of the current mix in the residential community so that an optimal therapeutic environment may be achieved.

## Phase 1: Orientation

This is a two-week period when new clients have an opportunity to decide whether, or not, Mirikai is a suitable program for their needs. Residents are assigned a 'buddy' to assist them as well as a staff member to provide counselling as required. Residents attend a weekly induction group covering the community's Bill of Rights, code of ethics, rules, and program details. Detoxification and medical appointments are organized as required. All residents also visit a sexual health clinic and approximately 85% are given a full psychiatric assessment.

The main focus during this period is on the following:

o observation and evaluation of clients' suitability for the therapeutic community program

o assessment of those considered to have a dual diagnosis or dual diagnosis-related issues

o advocating and brokering existing or needed external resources and services

o consultation between medical, welfare, counselling and psychiatric staff, in addition to outside supports

○ reinforcement of client strengths and the encouragement of the notion of a partnership between the client and staff in relation to problem solving needs.

If clients decide to remain at Mirikai, they enter the Safety Net Program.

## Phase 2: Safety Net program

This is a six- to eight-week program which includes education modules on:

○ anger management
○ self-esteem
○ relapse prevention
○ goal setting
○ assertion training
○ communication
○ literacy
○ stress management
○ relaxation
○ health
○ identifying feelings.

Residents in the safety net phase also undergo three two-hour group therapy sessions per week, a daily debriefing group (known as 'huddle') where each resident can discuss the day's events without any staff present, a weekly huddle with the whole community (again, without staff present), exercise/sporting activities (e.g. surfing and touch football teams), weekly attendance at self-help support groups (e.g. Alcoholics Anonymous and Narcotics Anonymous), weekly individual counselling, life skills activities such as cooking, creative activities (e.g. art and live theatre visits), and weekly outings such as bush-walking and museum visits. Music appreciation and drama groups are also popular elements of the program. There is a weekly literacy update that includes creative writing, and individual tuition to develop literacy skills. Drug urinalysis screenings are also performed three times each week and randomly if necessary.

## Phase 3: Transition

This is a two-week period which gives the residents who are graduating from the Safety Net program an opportunity to catch up on the individual didactic modules they may have missed through, for example, illness or appointments. It also gives them the opportunity to role-model the behaviours they have already learnt and to make a decision as to whether they are ready to leave Mirikai and return to the wider community or, alternatively, to prepare for the intensive treatment program.

### Phase 4: Pretreatment

This is a one-week period for those residents who have made the decision to undertake the treatment program. During this time, residents reflect upon which therapeutic issues they might need to deal with in the context of preventing relapse. This culminates in the production of a document titled 'My Life Story'.This is a reflective time to consider unresolved problems or behaviours that contributed to drug misuse, and events that may be helpful in generating treatment goals.

### Phase 5: Treatment Program

This is a three- to five-month program focusing on two key components: therapy and responsibility.

#### Therapy

The therapy program includes the following:

- group therapy (three two-hour sessions per week)
- assertion training
- stress management
- relaxation
- gender group
- extended relapse prevention (three hours per week)
- literacy
- split group – a small, more intensive therapy group which gives residents the opportunity of working through some of their more complex issues (e.g. family dynamics, relationship dynamics and abuse)
- attendance at self-help groups
- huddles (twice per week)
- community huddle (weekly)

- o stage application meetings – weekly meetings at which the progress of all residents who have applied for movement through the program is discussed
- o business meetings, where treatment residents elect individuals to take on various work positions, food positions, and attending to rosters and routines
- o an exercise program.

The therapy component also includes a consequence group. This is a weekly group session for residents, without staff present. The group is designed as a behaviour modification group that underpins the order in the community. All the residents are made aware of any house rules that they have broken during the week and the consequences that will apply (e.g. one hour in the garden and an essay for each rule infringement). Any resident with more than five consequences is denied their day out on Sunday.

A further aspect of the therapy component is the objections panel. This is a weekly event facilitated by one staff member, the house co-ordinator (a person nominated by staff to oversee various aspects of the community) and two residents from the treatment stage. The panel considers formal objections by any residents who feel they have been unfairly dealt with as a result of the consequence group. If the issue is not resolved, it is the panel's responsibility to inform the residents of their rights and to facilitate the organization's formal grievance procedure.

Finally, residents are given individual therapy and follow-up psychiatric care. Individual therapy allows the residents some time to explore unresolved issues such as sexual abuse, and assists them in developing a new framework for unwanted protective mechanisms and behaviours. Treatment of dual diagnosis is a major aspect of the care provided at Mirikai. Approximately 85% of clients have a dual diagnosis, and complex case management is provided, with ongoing psychiatric evaluation, medication and planned, regular treatment. This is the case for clients in the treatment phase as well as those in aftercare. Aftercare for dual diagnosis clients includes co-case management with state psychiatric services.

*Responsibility*

The second key aspect of the treatment program is responsibility. Residents are responsible for the maintenance of the therapeutic communities. Various people are elected each week to assume a range of housekeeping roles which are written in the form of job descriptions. During this process, residents are expected to use all of the skills they have learnt in the Safety Net program. A six-week job skills training module is included in the treatment stage to assist residents in areas such as interview techniques, resumé writing, grooming, education and training pathways, and volunteer programs.

### Re-entry program

This is a time of giving back to the community, practising newly acquired psychosocial skills and preparing for departure. The major responsibility of the residents in this phase is to monitor the emotional needs of all the residents in the Safety Net and treatment programs. It is their responsibility to implement the buddy system, to maintain optimal harmony within the community by regularly reporting any concerns about individual residents, and to ensure that huddles and all other parts of the program are attended. The house co-ordinator assists residents with this responsibility. The house co-ordinator has clearly designated roles and responsibilities and attends daily debriefing sessions with staff. The house co-ordinator can call any of the following three groups at any time, without staff in attendance:

- Red Group – to deal with anger that may arise
- Blue Group – a care and concern group
- Green Group – a house function group. If the house coordinator has difficulty in resolving any concerns, staff or volunteers are immediately informed.

Other aspects of this phase involve attending business meetings to assist treatment residents with the functioning of the house; negotiating individual programs which include outside networking, job searches and some free time; and developing a departure plan and timetable that clearly outlines all reintegration elements, which may or may not include moving to the aftercare houses and programs.

### Reintegration

There are three supervised aftercare (halfway) houses currently available, each housing up to five residents. The residents may or may not choose to enter this accommodation.

### Aftercare program

This consists of a weekly two-hour support group which is available to all ex-residents of the Mirikai residential program. Individual counselling is available to all residents. Regular social activities are also organized. Volunteer work is an important part of this program until residents enter employment or education/training courses.

*Early Birds group*

This is a weekly harm reduction group offered to people who are on the Mirikai waiting list or members of the community who need assistance with drug use. This may include those who have dropped out of the residential program, or any other person from the wider community who has made a commitment to reduce consumption and minimize the harm associated with drug use.

*Community activities*

Residents of Mirikai become involved in a range of activities within the wider community, including participation in annual events such as World Aids Day, as well as local environmental projects. Adventure-based activities such as high ropes courses, survival skills and camping also play an important role within the activities of the community because they are particularly appealing to the youthful age group for whom Mirikai caters.

Currently Mirikai has no published outcome studies to demonstrate the efficacy of its programs. However, the therapeutic community is participating in a large-scale study of retention rates and treatment efficacy. Pilot data (as well as qualitative observations by the researchers) indicate retention rates comparable to or greater than those cited in the literature (e.g. De Leon 1995). Moreover, Mirikai's clients show significant post-treatment improvement on a range of quantitative measures such as psychological symptoms, self-esteem, self-efficacy and confidence in resisting drug-use.

Such success with a highly challenging population demonstrates the effectiveness of the therapeutic community approach, and illustrates the ability of the model to adapt to suit particular client groups. Another example of this flexibility is the relatively recent appearance of therapeutic communities in the correctional services.

## Therapeutic communities in prisons

There are two therapeutic communities currently operating in Australian prisons – in Victoria (currently in Bendigo Community Prison) and South Australia (at Cadell). A third therapeutic community is being established in NSW (at Long Bay Jail in Sydney) and is expected to commence operations in mid-2000. The programs offered range from three to four months and accommodate approximately 20 inmates, who enter the therapeutic community in the final stage of their sentences.

Prison therapeutic communities incorporate standard phases that are characteristic of therapeutic communities in the community. Being only a recent development, little evaluation of such therapeutic communities has been undertaken. A preliminary evaluation undertaken in Victoria, however, found that one year after completing the program, graduates' recidivism rates were approximately 25% lower than before undertaking the program (Pead 1996). Approximately 62% of graduates had not reoffended during this period. Positive urine tests and assaults also showed a dramatic decline, while the prisoners' coping strategies improved from below average to average in a range of areas. After the therapeutic community was moved to a different location, results of a further evaluation showed similar reductions in both drug use and assaults (Morison *et al.* 1997). Other key outcomes reported by inmates were that the atmosphere of the prison changed from tense to relaxed, that the prison reinforced personal and community responsibility, and that the program could reduce the use of drugs and alcohol. While preliminary, such findings suggest merit in the further implementation of therapeutic community philosophies within Australian prisons.

## Current issues facing therapeutic communities in Australia

It remains clear, at least to those who have witnessed the change process in a therapeutic community, that the model is the treatment of choice for individuals with severe dependence on substances. The challenge, however, is to be able to demonstrate the mechanisms of change empirically. Given the emphasis on economic rationalism and the resurgence of the medical model into the addiction treatment arena, therapeutic communities must adapt and attempt to reconcile a drug-free philosophy with an increasing need to rehabilitate clients who are on methadone or naltrexone regimes, or medication for co-morbid psychiatric conditions.

It is ironic that the initial development of therapeutic communities was largely a reaction against the inability of the dominant medical paradigm to deal effectively with addicted individuals. However, with increasing pressure to provide short-term, cost-effective and empirically sound interventions, therapeutic communities are required to move closer to the very model they once actively sought to exclude.

Spiritual development has always been a strong component of the therapeutic community model, and remains a key factor in many programs, particularly those adopting a 12-step approach. Indeed, a spiritual awakening is seen by many as the most robust aspect of ongoing recovery. Unfortunately, the move towards a more rational, empirically based model is likely to dilute this important aspect of treatment. Academics and proponents of the medical model have traditionally been less than enthusiastic about studying such intangible topics as spirituality. Perhaps the greatest challenge for the therapeutic community model in Australia, then, is to be able to fulfil the requirements of the economic rationalists, while preserving the holistic philosophies so integral to the successful rehabilitation of clients.

This issue has not escaped Andrew Biven, a key figure in the Australian therapeutic community movement for over two decades and a valued contributor to this chapter. In a recent communication to the authors, Biven, while conceding the need for continued research, soulfully outlines his concerns as follows:

> ...funding and the search for respectability and acceptance by the drug and alcohol field has brought stability, and has no doubt improved some programs and provided protection for clients. However, some of that spark of creativity has been lost I feel. When they started, therapeutic communities were often run by young people, not many years removed from their problem pasts. We have grown older and more comfortable, and the rules have changed to exclude the very people we once were. I guess what I'm saying is that professionalism is all very well, but, like economic rationalism, it can tend to rip the guts out of the soul of a community.

## References

Alcohol and Other Drugs Council of Australia (1997) *Drug Matters: The ADCA Perspective.* Canberra: ADCA.

Australasian Therapeutic Communities Association (1999) *Terrigal Conference Proceedings.* Palm Beach, Qld: P and G Lynch and Associates Pty Ltd.

De Leon, G. (1995) 'Residential therapeutic communities in the mainstream: diversity and issues.' *Journal of Psychoactive Drugs 27*, 1, pp.3–15.

De Leon, G. and Melnick, G. (1992) *Theraputic Community Scale of Essential Elements Questionnaire (SEEQ).* New York: Center for Theraputic Community Research.

Morison, Kershaw, Happell and Smith (1997) paper presented at ATCA National Conference: *Research, Rehabilitation and Reality.* 5–7 November, Perth, W.A.

Pead, J. (1996) *New Directions in Drug Treatment. An Evaluation of the Drug Treatment Unit Metropolitan Reception Prison.* Department of Justice: Victoria.

Powell, J. (1984) 'Attrition during the pretreatment stage of a drug-free therapeutic community.' *Australian Psychologist 19*, 2, pp.217–228.

Prochaska, J. O. and DiClemente, C. C. (1984) *The Transtheoretical Approach: Crossing Traditional Boundaries of Change.* Homewood, IL: Dorsey Press.

Quality Improvement Council Limited (1999) *Australian Health and Community Services Standards: Alcohol, Tobacco and Other Drug Services Module.* Bundoora, Vic: Australian Institute for Primary Care.

Rosenthal, M. S. (1984) 'Therapeutic communities: a treatment alternative for many but not all.' *Journal of Substance Abuse Treatment 1*, pp.55–58.

Simpson, D. D. and Sells, S. B. (1982) 'Effectiveness of treatment for drug abuse: an overview of the DARP research program.' *Advances in Alcohol and Substance Abuse 2*, pp.7–29.

Toumbourou, J. W. and Hamilton, M. (1993) 'Perceived client and program moderators of successful therapeutic community treatment for drug addiction.' *The International Journal of the Addictions 28*, 11, pp.1127–1146.

Toumbourou, J. W., Hamilton, M. and Fallon, B. (1998) 'Treatment level, progress, and time spent in treatment in the prediction of outcomes following drug-free therapeutic community treatment.' *Addiction 93,* 7, pp.1051–1064.

Part 3

# Life in the Therapeutic Community

# CHAPTER 6

# The staff member in the therapeutic community

## Alan Woodhams

## Introduction

In recent times there has been a resurgence of interest in therapeutic communities, and this paper has been written in the context of the revitalized and changing face that therapeutic communities present to their residents, the staff, and outside agencies. The purpose of this paper is to give some idea of what a therapeutic community staff member's role is, and how the role is managed. To do this there needs to be some idea of the environment the staff member works in.

This paper will begin by looking at the idea of 'community as method' and go on to describe briefly what a therapeutic community is, and look at its views of the *disorder, the person, recovery* and *right living*. This first part will also look at some of the concepts and tools that are used in the community, since these form the treatment environment which the staff wants both to create, and work within. The paper will then attempt to describe how staff members attempt to facilitate residents' development, and what kinds of problems and challenges this may create for them.

## Concepts and tools

George De Leon, who for many years has researched therapeutic communities in the USA, particularly Phoenix House, New York, provides the following definition of what makes the therapeutic community different from other treatment environments. He calls this 'community as method'.

The quintessential element of the therapeutic community is community. What distinguishes the therapeutic community from other treatment approaches (and other communities) is the purposive use of the community as the primary method for facilitating social and psychological change in individuals.

Community as method means integrating people and practices under a common perspective and purpose, to teach individuals to learn about and change themselves.

Thus all activities are designed to produce therapeutic and educational change in the individual participants, and all participants are mediators of these therapeutic and educational changes. (De Leon 1997)

'Community as method' means that the community and not the staff are the means by which treatment is delivered. The residents are seen as responsible for both themselves and their peers. This gives them a sense of ownership of their own treatment program. This requires an investment in mutual self-help, with the accompanying need for responsibility and accountability. These are prime influences in their social learning and their internalization of positive attitudes and behaviour.

### What is a therapeutic community?

A therapeutic community is a society in miniature where attitudes and behaviours, thoughts and feelings, relatedness and unrelatedness are viewed as if under a magnifying glass. It is there to do just this: to enable individual members to view themselves from other perspectives, and in roles different to the ones they have carved out for themselves. Each person is everyone else's mirror, reflecting the positive and negative back to one other in a supportive and caring way.

The culture in a therapeutic community is defined, by both the residents and the staff, through their adoption of the concepts and the view of 'right living'. The residents are the culture itself, ever changing, ever developing. The view of right living is handed down through the generations of therapeutic community residents, and is constantly reinforced by senior residents as they take on and internalize the therapeutic community concepts and philosophy. Thus the therapeutic community culture is developed.

It is the staff role to facilitate the maintenance of this view, which they do by utilizing, and making transparent to the community, their own use of the therapeutic community concepts and philosophy in their decision-making processes. Both residents and staff share common beliefs. These are:

### The view of the disorder

The problem is centred within the person, and any symptoms are secondary.

### The view of the person

People have more similarities than differences. There are shared characteristics, such as low self-esteem, lack of impulse control, low tolerance for frustration, inability to cope with feelings, dishonesty, poor interpersonal skills, immaturity and feelings of being a victim. These and other characteristics vary in degree and intensity. Although the program works with all these areas, treatment plans within it are individually tailored.

### The view of recovery

Individuals can only make a successful recovery through fundamental changes in their feelings and behaviour. Recovery is brought about through two main vehicles of change: the encounter group, and the social structure of the therapeutic community.

Encounter groups provide feedback from the community to a resident about his or her negative attitude and behaviour, and create social pressure on the resident to change.

The structure enables residents to learn experientially through their interactions with each other, rather than being 'taught' in classroom style.

### The view of right living

This view is a philosophy consisting of moral and ethical beliefs that are supportive of the views held by mainstream society. They are also diametrically opposed to the negative, self-serving views of the various subcultures that the residents may previously have been subsumed into.

All residents are expected to conform to the program, and to actively make the changes to their feelings and behaviours through the program. It is this sense of ownership of their own feelings and behaviours that enables residents to internalize the pro-social view of 'right living'. Any resident with needs that cannot be met by the program would be actively encouraged either to join the program at a later date, or to deal with these specific needs after the program, if it did not interfere with their treatment.

These views give staff and residents a framework on which to base their interactions with individual residents, and the community, and themselves. A number of concepts and tools are used in the community to support these views. These include:

*Rational authority*

Decisions made by staff need to be objective and transparent, and consistent with the community philosophy. They need to be supportive of the community views of right living.

*Role modelling*

Staff members should conduct themselves in a way that does not inflict their own views on residents. Role modelling accounts for much human learning, and staff should behave in ways that are a positive reinforcement of the therapeutic community perspective.

*Act as if*

This describes a process: Act as if = think as if = feel as if = be.

This means: 'If I act in a positive way, even if it is uncomfortable for me, I will eventually think, and then feel in that way.' This is a tool to enables individuals to manage and change their behaviours.

*Responsible concern*

This is a rejection of the negative and selfish 'street' codes of drugs and crime. These are replaced with care and concern for peers, expressed by residents' confronting each other's negative behaviour through genuine human concern.

*I am my brother's keeper*

This means mutual self-help: 'I am responsible for my peers' well-being, as this will have an effect on my own. If I do not challenge their attitudes and standards of behaviour, then I am saying that it is all right for them and me to behave in those ways. If I challenge them, then I am also challenging those attitudes and behaviours within myself.'

*What goes around comes around*

'If I behave towards others in negative ways, they will behave towards me in ways that reflect those negative behaviours.'

*Honesty*

The underpinning concept: 'Be honest with others, but most importantly be honest with your inner self about your motivations, intentions and fears.'

This is not an exhaustive list. As communities develop they also develop slightly different systems and concepts. The above, however, would be considered 'core' concepts.

## How staff run a concept-based therapeutic community
### Administration

Staff have organizational responsibilities in terms of record-keeping, monitoring, through-care planning, statistics, case notes, etc. The welfare of the community can be dependent on information provided to funders, and government bodies. Part of a staff member's workload is to ensure that this information is accurately recorded, and used to help the community to develop. Delivery of the program is monitored by statistics collected daily, often by the residents' administration department, and these are validated by staff. The significance of this monitoring, in terms of funding, etc., is openly conveyed to the residents, who have real responsibilities in the continuing survival of the program. The statistics are usually around group attendance, sanctions, residents moving through the program phases, and other internal community activities. They provide a measure of the aspects of the program that are being delivered, and can be used to evaluate the effectiveness of the various interventions. The monitoring process is an important tool in helping residents and staff measure the community's effectiveness in changing attitudes and behaviour, and is constantly updated by community and staff feedback processes. Staff can feel burdened by the amount of paperwork involved, and feel that it detracts from what they perceive as their primary task, that of therapist, but the welfare of the community needs to come first, and the monitoring ensures the community's future.

Staff also monitor the individuals they have responsibilities for, by a casework or keywork system. This may be in the form of meetings with the resident, where goals and objectives are formally made and progress monitored, or by impromptu conversations in more of a social context 'on the floor' or at mealtimes, where conversation is less formal.

Notes are made in residents' files regarding attitude, behaviour, issues being worked on, progress, needs, and plans for the future, both in the program and after graduation. Information is obtained from the resident, other residents and staff, and the caseworker's own observations. Most information is centred on the resident's progress through the program. This information can then be passed on to social workers, probation services and other outside agencies.

*Staff structure and hierarchy*

There is a line management structure with decision-making meetings at different levels, e.g. policy meetings, team meetings and senior team meetings. The staff are expected to adhere to and support the decisions made when they are on the 'floor', and not to undermine the staff team decision-making processes.

It is equally important that all decisions made and acted upon are subject to review and revision, thereby promoting the community concept of 'rational authority'.

Staff, through their daily observations and facilitation, are aware of and subject to the general 'feel' or atmosphere in the community. As with all people, there is the need for a sense of order or control, so that the environment does not feel too threatening, or out of control. Part of therapeutic community living is centred around the thoughts, feelings and behaviours that arise when crises occur, and it is at these times that staff need to get residents to focus on their own functioning, so as to enable them to understand themselves better. This is experiential learning, and it is where residents can begin to develop the insights that will enable them to internalize positive approaches to themselves and others. The staff need to have strong personal boundaries as well as good coping mechanisms, in order to function effectively in these situations.

A staff member who is struggling in the work may have a personal crisis in their lives, or they may be worn down by the constant demands made on them by their role. Their line manager or the supervisor needs to be able to recognize the situation and respond appropriately, and be empowered to meet the individual's needs.

*Structure of activities*

The therapeutic community day is made up of work, encounter group, and social activities, including meaningful work experience with set start and finish times, standards of work which can be evaluated and monitored and an ongoing work ethic which actively reflects the view of right living. All these need to be planned and monitored. The role of the staff is to monitor these activities and the processes of the structure within them. To do this, the staff work closely with the residents' hierarchy on the therapeutic community, enabling and empowering the residents in higher positions to develop their potential and to work through the issues that they bring with them. Residents develop through their application of the ethos and concepts of the therapeutic community. It is the job of staff to enable this process to happen. To carry this enabling work out effectively, staff need to focus on three different levels of operation: the community level, the individual resident's level, and the internal level of emotions and feelings.

*Community level*

The underlying philosophy in a concept-based therapeutic community is that the community itself is the most effective means of delivering treatment. The therapeutic community has a work ethic, encounter groups and a structure and hierarchy to do this. At this level, the main function of staff is to monitor, assess and evaluate the effectiveness of the community as a healing process. As all interactions which take place within the therapeutic community are regarded as having a therapeutic value, a further part of the staff role is to bring into focus the processes residents utilize within the community.

Staff work on the periphery of the structure, maintaining the boundaries between the community and the external world, as well as facilitating the residents in the hierarchy to develop the community's therapeutic and environmental standards.

There are many facets to the staff role. These reflect elements of the community structure – for instance:

o being the liaison with a particular work group

o providing appropriate one-to-one input with residents

o facilitating groups

o delivering seminars

o working with residents on community issues

o developing aspects of the community

o working with drama, art and other therapeutic tools.

Staff are there as role models and rational authority, advocating, in the way they respond to the crises and dilemmas that arise on the therapeutic community, the view of right living.

Staff also need to examine the standard of their work. There can be a mirroring quality between the resident and staff structures. If the staff are under pressure and stretched, they can become less effective in maintaining community boundaries. Then the residents' structure may come to reflect this, standards may drop, and acting out and drug use may increase.

Staff are expected to use the community structure when dealing with individual residents. Rather than respond immediately and directly to a resident's complaint, for example, the staff member will tell the resident to 'use your structure'. This means that the complaint should be made to the resident's immediate senior in the hierarchy, who will deal with it or pass it up higher. Responses from the staff, similarly, go back down through the structure to the resident. One aspect of the therapeutic value of this is to deny the resident's immediate gratification – a common feature of drug-abusing and criminal lifestyles. The difficulty is that staff need to recognize that denial of themselves to a resident may have a therapeutic benefit. This can be difficult for staff trained in the caring professions, as it can seem contrary to their duty of care. A benefit for the resident, however, could be the increased ability to self-manage uncomfortable feelings.

Thus, if staff are asked to intervene in community situations, the first response needs to be 'use your structure'. When the situation persists and an individual is in need of support, they should be advised to seek support from their peers. This can be very difficult for newer and less experienced staff members, as their background training and life experience can drive them to want to help solve the individual's problems, rather than trusting them to find their own solutions.

In residents' meetings such as the department managers' meeting, staff will model concepts like rational authority and responsible concern by interacting with residents in a respectful and enabling way, offering supportive suggestions, and providing clarity about issues like standards or responsibilities. So, rather than being directive about what residents should be doing, staff will facilitate the processes that are used to arrive at these decisions, all the while utilizing the therapeutic community concepts. These situations provide staff with the opportunity to evaluate an individual's progress in dealing with their own issues such as low self-esteem, giving or receiving directions or acting assertively.

### Individual resident's level

Although the staff generally work through the senior residents, and maintain more of a distance from the more junior residents, the staff team still needs to be aware of all the people in the program, and to keep up-to-date with their behaviour, problems and progress.

With the drug-culture client group come their past behaviours and motivations, values and belief systems. These are often acted out in a therapeutic community by the engineering of situations, e.g. taking drugs or causing a fight in order to get thrown off. There can be much acting out in the form of self-mutilation and property damage, and the projection of residents' fantasies onto other residents or staff. Staff need to be aware of these and other behaviours that may manifest themselves in the community, and at the same time need to acknowledge the residents who are positively engaged in the community. Staff have the responsibility of ensuring that they are involved with all residents and do not focus on the most verbal, or on those residents who 'act out', as this can reinforce negative behaviours.

If the community can deal with the situation, then the staff team needs to let it keep the responsibility to do so. If it is beyond the bounds of the community, then the staff may need to intervene. In taking this step, staff need to be transparent and show rational authority. An instance of this may be where a drug user brings heroin into the community, and, through peer pressure and abuse of his or her position, involves newer and less experienced residents in drug use that binds them in a negative and collusive relationship, where they cannot challenge the negative behaviours of others because of their own negativity. This can lead to a situation where the collusion spirals and involves more and more residents, and it can become almost impossible for positive residents to challenge the growing negative culture. Staff need at some point to intervene. This may mean directly challenging the residents involved, taking urine tests, or holding a special community meeting where these issues are highlighted. At all times, throughout this type of intervention, staff need to be aware that their interventions disempower the community, and that at the earliest opportunity they need to be giving the power back.

Staff develop relationships with residents which change throughout the duration of their time in treatment. Initially they could be very directive with residents, getting them to conform to the therapeutic community rules and protocols. The relationship then becomes more of a supporting one, facilitating and motivating, with the residents doing more, and taking more upon themselves.

When a major incident occurs, it may be that half of the upper echelons of the structure are demoted overnight, and other residents promoted in their places. This can be difficult for the staff member who has had time away from the community and comes back to find radical changes, but it is a necessary aspect of the therapeutic process in community life. It puts real pressure on residents to cope with upheaval and change, and highlights issues that residents can work on, as well as giving staff the opportunity to view how residents cope with difficult and demanding situations.

*Internal level*

Staff working in a therapeutic community need to have sufficient understanding of their own processes to self-analyse and to use the appropriate staff support processes to maintain their own boundaries.

Working in a therapeutic community involves working with an individual's internal and external conflict and confrontation. A staff member is in the position of navigating through the turbulence of community life and continually monitoring their own boundaries, as well as dealing with the emotional pain that is released by residents who are engaged in the therapeutic community processes. The staff team in a therapeutic community is the main purveyor of the rational authority concept, and the main example of the 'act as if' principle.

One of the key factors that enables a staff member to function safely in a therapeutic community is to remember that the presenting problem is not necessarily the issue, and that the underlying emotional beliefs are what need to be challenged. These beliefs are born of the residents' past experiences. They may have experienced trauma or a particular form of environmental conditioning through being institutionalized in the care system as children, or through having parents who themselves have dependency issues. They may be emotionally disabled as a result of physical, sexual, psychological or emotional abuse. These issues can result in various symptoms such as self-harm, drug abuse, depression, emotional immaturity and a host of other symptoms that can manifest themselves as negative behaviours. If the staff member only focuses on what is presented, the underlying belief systems which drive the resident will never be challenged or changed. The ability to communicate this sort of information to defensive and vulnerable residents is a skill that can only be learned through experience and practice, and not taught.

Everything that occurs in a therapeutic community can be utilized as a 'learning experience' and the residents' attitude, behaviour and feelings are examined by themselves and their peers as they progress through the structure. The learning is then experienced in the form of the residents working through their own difficulties with issues such as low self-esteem, delayed gratification, association with antisocial attitudes, manipulation or being a victim. Thus they learn for themselves rather than being taught by professionals who 'know'. Learning is thus more likely to be assimilated and internalized, as it can be part of an individual's experience and can be 'owned'.

When staff confront their own fears and feelings of vulnerability, they can gain an insight into how difficult it can be for a resident to confront and change him- or herself. The staff are then able to show a high degree of honesty and openness towards community members. Presented with this role model of self-knowledge and personal honesty, the rest of the community is enabled to learn the true meaning of responsible concern.

## Staff support, supervision and training

The value of staff support and training cannot be over emphasized. In working in what is referred to as a therapeutic milieu, it is easy for an individual to lose direction, or to be pressurized by the needs of residents and the community. When this happens, they should be able to access the appropriate support. Without appropriate training and supervision it is all too easy to feel deskilled, disempowered and demotivated. Unlike other therapeutic interventions, where contact with clients is restricted to one- or two-hour sessions, therapeutic communities can be an almost constant interaction between staff and residents. When staff members lose their objectivity, they can begin to internalize the daily problems that beset a therapeutic community and find it very difficult to function congruently.

Where there are no procedures in place for support and supervision, staff can be subject to many confusing pressures. If this situation is not addressed, 'burnout' can occur. This is where the staff members' internal responses and ability to deal with the situations around them reach a critical level, and they are unable to function appropriately. The reality in many TCs is that there is rarely sufficient time or money to provide constant and appropriate training and support. While staff sometimes get outside supervision partly funded by the organization, usually it will done in house. This can lead to difficulties for staff who feel they should be able to manage better, and are concerned about telling their manager that they feel they cannot cope. Supervision falls into two main categories. There are feedback sessions from encounter and other groups, and a more formalized supervision process, which separates and recognizes individual and organizational needs and responsibilities.

Training in working on TCs is usually experiential. For the new staff member, it can be like working in another country where there is a different language and approach to daily living. The local customs dictate that when a person is upset by someone, they will 'pull them up' and confront them in a very ritualistic way. When someone does something that seriously offends the individual or community, they will be 'encountered' by their peers in a group that has its own rituals and processes. If a resident should want something or someone they have to 'use the structure', and how much of this they use depends on where they are in the hierarchy. There is a great emphasis laid on a person's 'commitment' and on the 'issues' they are working on. All this is integral to the therapeutic community way of working and living, and it can only be learned through experience.

The staff structure needs to ensure that appropriate training is available in the principles and ethos of the therapeutic community. Such training should be experimental, didactic and ongoing. There needs to be training in group work and individual skills, for instance, group dynamics, motivational interviewing and facilitation skills. As well as training and updating in the structural and group processes of the community, staff may also need to develop specific skills, such as presentation skills for delivering seminars to residents, visitors and other external, interested parties.

Different therapeutic communities have developed different ways of doing things, so it is very difficult to specify what the training needs for staff should be. This may be why experiential training, along with a taught basic understanding of a therapeutic community's philosophy and ethos, has become the norm.

### Staff members and personal development

The most important resource staff members bring to the community is themselves. This creates the most challenging aspect of working on a therapeutic community. A staff member is expected to respond positively to, and challenge, residents and other staff, as well as themselves, in respect of their behaviour and attitudes. At the same time they should be looking reflectively upon their own functioning in terms of the community.

For the staff member, the time spent working in a therapeutic community can be extremely productive in terms of personal growth and the development of group-working and one-to-one skills. Staff who bring their own experience and views to a therapeutic community, and view it as an opportunity for personal development, are much more likely to benefit from the experience, as the challenges it throws up for them will be placed in a much more constructive framework.

A staff member's views will be challenged by the residents and by other members of the staff team. Since therapeutic community teams are multidisciplinary and also can consist of ex-users as well as professionally trained staff, there will naturally be a conflict in their approaches. The common ground they have, though, is the therapeutic community approach, and when things work well, the differences they have in working with clients can be productively applied under the therapeutic community ethos. This can lead to stimulating debate and argument, providing staff are prepared to develop their professionalisms. However, where staff feel subject to their original training and beliefs they can experience extreme difficulties, as the demands of the therapeutic community environment can lead them into conflict with their own strongly-held views.

### A more personal view

To an extent these are the best of times, and these are the worst of times. To explain, therapeutic communities are at present more supported as a method than in previous times, and more supported financially by funders. However, there are also much greater expectations of them in terms of research evaluative studies and evidence of outcomes.

The pressure is on the staff to provide this evidence through the record-keeping and monitoring demanded of them by their funders. Some would say that too much attention to this detracts from the delivery. Others see it as a blessing because it acts as a foil to those staff who could lose their objectivity by their over-involvement with residents. Staff can regain a necessary degree of objectivity by writing reports, for example, for other agencies, as this enables them to take a more 'meta' view of their work.

Over time it has become generally accepted that it takes one year to become acclimatized to a therapeutic community and another year to start to work effectively. Thus the new member of staff does not become a fully functioning staff member until the third year. The effective life of a staff member is then dependent on the supports in place and their own ability to cope with the challenges the environment produces.

Whenever I have worked in a therapeutic community there has been a mixture of staff, from varying professions and with varying experiences of life. They have come from backgrounds as diverse as education, ex-substance misuse, person-centred and psychodynamic counselling, gestalt therapy, the arts and drama and nursing.

On the other side come the residents, with their expectations of one-to-one counselling or miracle cures and their view of the expert employed by the therapeutic community to heal them. Some already believe that only they can change themselves, but have previously lacked the guidance of others.

All have differing views and expectations of what a therapeutic community should be delivering and what they themselves should be doing in the therapeutic community. It is a complex business, and truly reflective of life, albeit a little more concentrated and polarized. In essence the therapeutic community is both a cross-section of society, and a society in miniature.

In the therapeutic community, we all vie and jockey for position in the hope of finding a niche or something stable to hold on to. Being a staff member is about accepting that in this environment the change process itself is speeded up and that it is impossible to keep up with it. It is also about trying at the same time to hold on to our own internal values and beliefs, hoping to be respected and liked, being supportive, or confrontational when we feel affronted, and feeling vulnerable in being ourselves in an environment which dares to question our motives and feelings.

In a therapeutic community it is said that if you are not part of the cure you are part of the problem. As staff, we are under the microscope to be part of the cure and our own individuality is put under question. Our own motivations and abilities come under scrutiny as we become more involved in the political and social life of the therapeutic community. Do we really believe in what we practise? Or is it just a job? Difficult questions to answer within ourselves, especially when decisions are made by the staff team as a whole that we individually disagree with.

Residents often say they are there as a result of circumstances, not all of which were in their control. In essence their very being there can justify any errant behaviour they display. This is a luxury staff do not have. We made a choice to work there. We are respected citizens doing our bit for society, and living pro-social lives. It follows that we know the 'right way to live', but do we?

Working in a therapeutic community has changed my life. I trained as a person-centred counsellor and practised as an alcohol counsellor working in the learning disabilities field. I have been used to having control in my life, and having the time and energy to acknowledge and process my thoughts and feelings. The clients I used to treat never really questioned my ability or qualifications, and indeed, they do not overtly question them in a therapeutic community. But the culture does, and frequently staff feel similar pressures to the residents. To do their job in this environment, staff need to have quality supervision in terms of the aims of the project and their job in relation to the aims, and support in terms of their own internal functioning, their locus of evaluation, and their emotional well-being. This support needs to be meta and objective and grounded in the world outside the therapeutic community, the kind that enables you to leave the emotional baggage of others behind, and clear yourself of the projections neuroses and politics of the work you do.

Support in therapeutic communities has been sporadic, poorly thought out and compromised by financial restrictions. In other therapies, where there is less client contact, there is a higher supervision contract, i.e. counselling with one hour of supervision to every four client hours while in training, and one hour of supervision to every eight client hours on completion of training, although this can vary depending on the organization and an individual's experience. Staff in a therapeutic community can have 20 to 35 hours a week contact with their clients. Now that the increased interest in therapeutic communities has increased their status, the staff who work in this extremely exposed and pressurized environment need to ensure that their needs, like those of any other professional in the caring professions, are met by appropriate support and supervision.

The therapeutic community can provide growth and development out of the chaos and fear that people's lives have become. It does this by being a small society with a view of how life should be lived. It challenges and confronts those who do not accept its philosophy and ethos. It is both challenging and rewarding to work there.

## References

De Leon, G. (ed) (1997) *Community as Method: Therapeutic Communities for Special Populations and Special Settings.* Westport, CT: Greenwood Publishing Group, Inc.

# CHAPTER 7

# Self-help or sink-or-swim? The experience of residents in a UK concept-based therapeutic community

## Keith Burnett

This chapter is based upon research carried out at Phoenix House, Tyneside while training as a social worker at the University of Durham.

### Introduction

Allen observed that 'There seems to be an unspoken assumption by its adherents that the therapeutic community must be a good thing [and to] question whether it follows any guiding principles of empowerment – let alone whether it rehabilitates clients – is a topic close to heresy!' (Allen 1992, p.254). Although Allen was writing about a mental health project, this could equally well apply to a concept-based therapeutic community. Literature searches produce few recent published texts involving qualitative research in hierarchical 'concept-house' therapeutic communities for recovering drug/alcohol users, perhaps reflecting the anti-intellectual roots of the hierarchical therapeutic community movement (Manning 1989, p.37). This anti-intellectual bent is perhaps partly a result of the tough approach adopted by some hierarchical therapeutic communities designed to counteract what is seen as the obfuscating web of defensive attitudes and deceit presented by many drug users. However, many of the residents interviewed for this study used the opportunity to voice opinions or feelings that they did not believe would be taken seriously in the house; one twenty-year-old resident, when asked what would make her feel more involved, suggested:

'Ask us what *we* think of things – like this [interview].'

For the newcomer, whether client or worker, a hierarchical therapeutic community is initially a very disorientating environment. This is particularly because, contrary to many other forms of modern social work or therapy, residents are initially deliberately *dis*empowered, albeit with the long-term aim of fuller empowerment and constructive participation in society. If we are genuinely concerned with empowerment – and I firmly believe we should be – it would perhaps seem an obvious step to ensure that service users have a voice, but the majority of published research on hierarchical therapeutic communities is still based largely upon the observations of professionals. A notable exception is Ravndal and Vaglum's (1994) research into the causes of high dropout rates in Phoenix House, Oslo (Norway), which used both participant observation and qualitative interviews. To this author's knowledge there are no previous published studies of residents' perceptions of a concept-based therapeutic community in Britain, where therapeutic community research has been scarce and ad-hoc in nature (Broekaert *et al.* 1999).

The research which forms the basis of this chapter, intended as a contribution to redressing this deficit, took place during a six-month placement as a member of staff at Phoenix House Tyneside (north east England), which was preceded by a two-week period of participant observation as a resident.

## Methodology

Participant observation, a creditable approach in therapeutic community research from Rapoport (1960) onwards, and also a major factor in a number of studies of concept-based therapeutic communities (Bloor *et al.* 1988; Mello *et al.* 1997; Weppner 1983; Yablonsky 1965, 1989) was useful in giving an experience of what it *felt* like to enter the community as a resident. The frustrations voiced by many of my fellow 'induction' residents (e.g. not feeling as if they were listened to) highlighted a number of questions for qualitative research, as did Ravndal and Vaglum's (*op.cit.*) commentary on attachment and Poulopoulos and Tsibouki's (1998) identification of key problems in a concept-based therapeutic community.

These semi-structured qualitative interviews took place over a two-week period in early 1999 with eighteen residents in total, selected randomly from each program phase (see below), although attempting to account for the gender balance of the project. For reasons of space, not all of the areas covered by the original research (Burnett 1999) are discussed here.

At the time of the interviews the main house had a population of up to 39, with around a quarter female. Most stay in the main house for six months, after which they may move to the 're-entry' (resettlement) project, which is

## Table 6.1: The program phases (after Ravndal and Vaglum 1994)

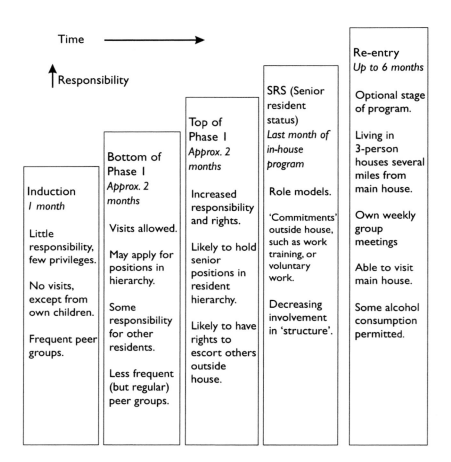

seen as an extension of the main-house program. Ages range from the late teens to early forties, with most residents being in their twenties or early thirties. All of the residents at the time of the interviews were white.

## Findings and discussion

### Adjusting to the environment

Many of the residents in this study had come to a therapeutic community because community-based (i.e. non-residential) treatments or other residential approaches had been unsuccessful:

'I tried detoxing on my own but always relapsed' (male resident, 25, top of Phase One).

Perhaps partly as a result of this, there was general acceptance that a challenging but supportive regime was necessary. As one resident observed of the process of regaining a routine in his lifestyle:

'You don't enjoy it, even though you need to do it' (male resident, 25, Induction).

For many of the residents in this study the most significant challenges came after detoxification, which was generally felt to be a supportive experience by those who had survived it without leaving:

'Valium didn't help but my rattle [withdrawal symptoms] was easier because I had people around who'd done it and could support you' (male resident, 25, bottom of Phase One).

Residents generally felt they had been supported by their peers and 'people further up the house' (male resident, 23, bottom of Phase One), but there were exceptions:

'There wasn't any [support] to be honest – I supported myself' (male resident, 24, bottom of Phase One).

Some suggested that previous experience of a concept-based therapeutic community, even if abortive, was useful at this point:

'I have done a program before so I know how to use support' (male resident, 25, Induction).

This raises the question of whether, when a resident has to be admitted two or three times before they can progress through the early phases of the program, this is really because of individuals not being 'ready' (as is often assumed), or whether this indicates deficiencies in service delivery, particularly in terms of induction and pre-admission contact.

Most respondents had considered leaving during the induction period, often due to the difficulty of adjusting to the demanding regime:

'I found the program harder than I expected and it was a shock to the system' (male resident, 32, Induction).

'I couldn't get my head round the place' (female resident, 20, top of Phase One).

'I didn't like the environment, it reminded me of being back in care' (male resident, 25, top of Phase One).

Induction was almost universally felt to be a confusing and/or frustrating time, but residents in all phases commented upon:

'The care and support from everyone in the house... There was no real pressure on me' (male resident, 23, bottom of Phase One).

Most had also appreciated the more lenient regime applied to very new residents, particularly those undergoing detoxification:

'It was understood that things will go wrong at this point' (female resident, 20, top of Phase One).

Groupwork, group activity and group membership are all central to this concept-based project's program, but these are areas many residents have difficulty adjusting to. In the interviews for this study it was noticeable that newer residents tended to complain about the number of group sessions (which is higher in the induction phase than subsequently), whereas more senior residents tended to be broadly positive about the usefulness of groupwork to their recovery.

Even among experienced residents, however, not all groups were considered to be useful or constructive. The perception of 'community groups', often the most outwardly confrontational group sessions with visible traces of Synanon 'attack therapy' encounter groups, varied considerably among respondents (and apparently among sessions too):

'You can always pull people in a community group' (female resident, 24, bottom of Phase One). [To 'pull someone up' is to point out to them, often bluntly, that they have broken the rules.]

but they 'can go off on a tangent' (male resident, 24, bottom of Phase One), or they can become '*degrading*' (male resident, 25, Induction).

Among this client group it appears that it may take up to two or three months to generate and use mutual support in the therapeutic community effectively. However, on the smaller scale of the peer group (rather than the whole community) respondents indicated having developed a sense of group identity very early; one resident felt the best part of Induction was:

'Bonding with peers drug-free – an intense, close-knit group' (male resident, 34, Re-entry).

In peer groups participants are able to take risks and increasingly control the functioning of the group, staff intervention decreasing during the course of the program to the point that SRS (senior resident status – the final phase of the in-house program) peer groups do not always have a worker present.

Peer groups were highly valued by respondents, and this seems to have been through a combination of feelings of safety and ownership:

'…you can share problems with others and see how others have coped' (male resident, 25, top of Phase One).

Change in thought processes and behaviour is not limited to formal groupwork or counselling, of course. One respondent, for instance, felt that the most important form of groupwork in terms of changing behaviour was:

'Talking to room-mates after follow-up (i.e. after staff rounds to check that all were in their rooms)' (male resident, 31, top of Phase One).

The degree of adjustment necessary to benefit from the program seems to generate risks in terms of residents having difficulty enduring the induction period, and again in readjusting to the 'normal' world upon leaving. By the later stages of the program, however, residents saw the therapeutic community as an alternative to, rather than another type of, institutional treatment:

'The normal world's always led back into institutions before' (male resident, 33, Re-entry).

Poulopoulos and Tsibouki (1998) identified the formation of a utopian culture with a false 'we' as potentially problematic aspects of the concept-based approach. While it would arguably be fairer to describe the approach of the project studied as idealistic rather than utopian, these seemed particularly pertinent issues towards the end of the program in the period of *re*adjusting to 'normal' life. One resident found it a challenge having to adjust to:

'going [to college] for *me*, not just for the prestige in the house' (male resident, 34, Re-entry).

However, Poulopoulos and Tsibouki (1998) also discussed cultural shock upon entering the community as a key area of concern, and indeed, it seems that the culture of this therapeutic community is more of a challenge to new residents than established ones. Those who have reached the later stages of the program will (perhaps by definition) generally have benefited from the regime or at least absorbed to some degree the concepts of accepting criticism ('taking it on') and modelling behaviour ('acting as if'). The danger is that newer residents with genuine concerns or grievances may have their input 'discounted…as further signs of pathology, rather than complaints to be taken seriously' (Barbara Rawlings, personal communication). This could be seen as an illustration of those at the top of the hierarchy – staff, and some experienced residents – having adjusted fully to the hierarchical therapeutic community culture (based on the Synanon concepts), whereas most residents find themselves located somewhere between this 'ideal' and prison/drug culture. The gap between the actual culture of many residents and the culture the concept-based approach aims for was often illustrated in attitudes to sanctions.

### Sanctions

This therapeutic community employs a variety of sanctions to respond to aberrant behaviour in a way intended to make the resident think about their behaviour and its causes. Everyday sanctions include community pull-ups and personal pull-ups (the 'up' is often omitted when referred to in practice), where groups or individuals whose behaviour is felt to be unacceptable are verbally admonished by another (usually relatively senior) resident. Minor infractions such as smoking while on any form of work duty or being late for a meeting result in an 'outcome' – these can be set by staff or residents in positions of responsibility, and commonly include tasks such as a 'dishpan' (washing-up for the whole community after dinner) or an 'A4 seminar' (a written exercise to be read to the community by the offender). More serious interpersonal tensions or support needs may be addressed through a 'family group', essentially a confrontational/encounter group focused upon one person (or perhaps more, such as when responding to in-house sexual rela- tionships); these can be called by a member of staff, fellow resident, or indeed, the resident who is to be the subject of the group (in which case it is referred to as a support group). Major breaches of the house rules such as drug use, leaving without permission, or threats of violence usually lead to work contracts determined by staff, such as the 'time-out' contract, which for a set time limits social contact with fellow residents and aims to encourage sober reflection through a combination of solo manual work, written work and 'co-counsels' with selected residents. Repeated serious breaches or actual violence can and do result in notice to leave, or in some cases immediate expulsion on the authority of management-level staff.

In the early stages of the program, interview responses indicated simple behaviour modification as a result of basic sanctions, for instance, having to wake up fellow residents for three mornings in a row as a result of failing to do so on time once:

> '...it didn't really bother me but I didn't do it again' (female resident, 24, bottom of Phase One).

Respondents in early phases often referred to sanctions not 'bothering' them, by which we can interpret that at this stage they were sometimes making them act differently, but not resulting in a change in thinking patterns. As a participant observer I became aware of a samizdat trade in recycled 'A4 seminars' (short pieces of written work to be read to the whole community as a sanction). According to Goffman (1961) this kind of phenomenon can be seen as a 'secondary adjustment' to institutionalization. It betrays either a failure to understand or accept the purpose of a sanction or a belief that since the sanctions are being administered unfairly, there is no harm in not carrying them out properly. Within the organisation it may be argued that the latter reason is an excuse to obscure the former. However, several residents felt that the 'outcome' system (which allows residents to comment upon the behaviour of others and request sanctions) was open to abuse:

'...you get punished for personal reasons' (male resident, 24, bottom of Phase One).

Residents in later phases of the program indicated that sanctions had enabled them to gain greater insight into the causes of their behaviour, with written work often referred to as the most helpful element:

'...written work helped me by highlighting issues' (male resident, 22, top of Phase One).

The general feeling from more senior residents was that written work and other tasks set as part of 'time-out' contracts were particularly beneficial. Here a resident over half-way through his first admission to a concept-based therapeutic community describes the effect of two such sanctions:

'I got a time-out for drinking – I benefited from that as they kicked my arse. Its inevitable that Induction [residents] [make mistakes], but I was able to use it. 'Time-out for using cannabis kicked my arse and made me realize where I was and how I was risking it' (male resident, 31, top of Phase One).

This resident is not, of course, suggesting that he was physically punished, but signifying that the experience of working his time-out contract was (perhaps necessarily) uncomfortable, but effective.

As a worker it seemed to me frequently to be the case that residents who, as in the case above, accepted their allotted sanction (however grudgingly) and did not deny to themselves the effect it had upon them were able to benefit from the experience, whereas those who claimed that sanctions had no effect upon them were often those who left the program early with an apparently low likelihood of establishing a drug-free lifestyle. However, conclusions should perhaps be tempered here by the awareness that there is considerable pressure upon residents (and indeed staff) in a concept-based therapeutic community to accept the belief that such planned forms of sanction are always beneficial. The Phoenix House 'philosophy' is recited by all residents every morning; to compare this to a religious community's morning prayer would certainly be an exaggeration, but there is perhaps a secular form of dogma at work. Those higher in the hierarchy are presented as knowledgeable and right, and while most are skilled in explaining *why* they are right, opposition is not tolerated. There is a genuine justification for this. There is a widely observed tendency for drug users in the early stages of recovery to be manipulative, even devious, in finding ways to blame others (including staff) for their predicament. It takes them time to 'take it on', i.e. to accept that their behaviour is their own responsibility and to accept the full scale of the work required to change. The pressure to accept this, and to act on it, leaves residents with three choices: genuinely to do so; to convincingly *appear* to do so (although this is difficult to sustain indefinitely); or to leave. It is the difficulty in distinguishing between the comments of residents who have genuinely accepted the 'concepts' and those who can explain them but do not (at least yet) genuinely embrace them that makes this area of research so fraught with the danger of misinterpretation.

*Power*

The hierarchical ordering of this community invests considerable power on a day-to-day basis in the hands of senior residents, especially those entrusted with house management or 'desk' duties. It is worth noting that despite their nominal seniority these residents will have been admitted only four-and-a-half to six months previously, and often have much progress to make before becoming ready for independence. Residents interviewed recognized this power distribution, although with the proviso that ultimate power rested with the staff:

> 'House managers and residents [have power]. Obviously staff have more power though' (male resident, 24, top of Phase One).

On a practical level this can empower residents and accustom them to gradually taking more responsibility for their own lives and accepting duties towards others, which is seen by residents as useful preparation for a drug-free lifestyle upon completing the program. For instance, a female induction resident felt that work on 'departments':

> '...keeps you busy, and gets you into a routine for when you move on' (female resident, 20, Induction).

However, there is obviously potential for the power held by residents to be abused, and the interview responses from many, such as this re-entry resident, indicated considerable resentment of the frequency with which this happens:

'The wrong person getting power can be manipulative and abuse power' (male resident, 33, Re-entry).

As 'jumping structure' – approaching staff without seeking permission to do so through the resident hierarchy – is an offence attracting sanctions, attempting to complain quickly to workers about perceived power abuse by more senior residents can be a discouraging prospect. The degree of anger that abuse of power generates was palpable in the interviews, but the feeling seemed to be that this was either ignored or that residents receiving 'outcomes' of dubious validity were told to simply 'take it on' (accept it):

'Power-trippers do my head in' (male resident, 23, bottom of Phase One).

The staff mix may have a bearing on this. Ex-addict staff are seen as essential as positive role models and because of their immunity to 'the persuasive deceits and rationalizations that addicts use with professional helpers' (Kennard 1998, p.95). But 'graduate' (i.e. ex-resident) staff may too easily dismiss external criticism or complaints from residents with the response that they have been through the program, it worked for them and they are best placed to dictate how the community should be run. This arguably ignores the likelihood that these staff were, as residents, those who 'took it on', 'acted as if' and found the concept-based therapeutic community approach well-suited to them. They are perhaps less well-placed to speak for those who struggle just to remain in the community.

## Why do people leave?

Artificial indicators of success or failure, and to a large extent actual effectiveness (which may be impossible to measure), seem to hinge upon time. Entering a therapeutic community as a resident, even without drug use issues, can bend one's perceptions of time considerably – I was warned before embarking on a short period as a resident participant observer that 'two weeks will feel like two months', and indeed it did, not through any lack of support and consideration from fellow residents but because the experience was so radically different from the outside world and there was so much to take in, understand and adjust to. Not surprisingly, the Induction phase produces many 'splitters', those who leave without completing their program, or without the symbolic permission of the house.

Much of the published concept-house literature is concerned with the optimum length of treatment to balance effectiveness with cost (Bleiberg *et al.* 1994; McCusker *et al.* 1997; Toumbourou *et al.* 1993, 1998). As this study did not follow up former residents, it is not possible to comment here upon treatment outcomes. What *could* be observed was the development of respondents' thinking and behaviour at different stages of the program. For instance, respondents often indicated an understanding (or at least an awareness of the stated purpose) of the concept of 'feedback' (informing staff about residents using drugs or having other difficulties), but an unwillingness or perceived inability to use it until around the middle of Phase One, which seems in line with experience in the project:

'I still see it as grassing' (male resident, 23, bottom of Phase One).

It has previously been suggested that the therapeutic community approach may be best suited to service-users who have not been treated successfully by other means (Schimmel 1997). The responses from residents interviewed were certainly in line with this proposition:

'A community detox would be no use as I didn't have enough will-power' (male resident, 33, Re-entry).

'I'd been in one before and knew I couldn't survive independence straight away' (male resident, 22, top of Phase One).

These two quotes perhaps illustrate two of the model's strengths – a safe place from which to start recovery and a gradual move towards independence. However, they also touch upon one of the areas of potential weakness in the current application of the model, which is the high degree of motivation needed to stabilize drug use and minimize offending during the wait (typically several months in the UK) for a funded place in therapeutic community. Although much of a typical concept-based approach will function to build and maintain motivation to 'stay clean', once members of the therapeutic community, this highlights the considerable motivation – 'will-power' – required at the pre-admission stage and the difficulties of maintaining this without support.

As well as insufficient or unclear motivation, another possible key factor in failing to complete a program of treatment lies in the difficulty in forming attachments to the community and fellow residents, as identified by Ravndal and Vaglum's (1994) research (which also suggested failure to master an adult role, power abuse, and sexual relationships inside and outside the house, as factors).

Because of the resource limitations of this study, the responses from residents who left are limited to those who either returned immediately or were subsequently re-admitted. Of those who had left, attachment to the community (or lack of it) was relevant:

'People were leaving, I wasn't getting on with a few people and I felt out of place' (male resident, 29, Re-entry).

For those who considered leaving but did not, contact with family/partners, cravings for drugs, and difficulty accepting sanctions were all factors, as had been the case with the residents who left in Ravndal and Vaglum's study.

Some voiced frustration with the demanding nature and gradual pace of the program, and:

'...the lack of freedom' (male resident, 30, SRS – senior resident).

Many also indicated that lack of contact with partners or family had been a factor, but this is offset to a degree by the importance many attached to the project being at some distance from their home area, in choosing to apply for a place:

'I couldn't have done it nearer home' (male resident, 22, SRS – senior resident).

It seems to have become the norm in British social work (rightly, I believe) to act on the principle that while client groups often have common experiences, the life and needs of each individual client – including drug users – are unique. This is usually the approach that new residents in a therapeutic community have come to expect, but is quite at odds with the concept-based approach which dictates that new residents should stop asserting their rights to individuality and independence (since they have abused them), listen, take direction (act upon orders from senior residents and staff), and learn. The cognitive dissonance this gives rise to may be one of the important factors in high dropout rates; I often heard in groups what one interview respondent told me about why he considered leaving:

'I was not getting classed as an individual, and was frustrated with the pace of the program' (male resident, 24, top of Phase One).

It is worth considering, too, that it may not be appropriate to assume that those residents who choose to leave before their allotted treatment period is over all act in ignorance or error – some of them may genuinely be ready to move on sooner than some concept-house cultures are willing to countenance.


## Conclusion

The particular therapeutic community at the heart of this study emerges as a solid example of a 'living-learning environment' (Hawkins 1989; Jones 1968) which is valued by residents. It has coherently adapted a radical approach to function in line with modern practice. The results – socially included adults who could often otherwise have expected death or long-term incarceration – to an extent speak for themselves, although continued qualitative and quantitative research appears crucial in maintaining good practice and economic viability.

However, challenges to the effectiveness of this project also emerged, perhaps not so much from the model as from its application. The most serious of these were those that threatened residents' willingness to stay the course or their ability to make constructive use of the experience rather than using it merely as a 'jail blag'. (Several residents accepted referral to the therapeutic community as a direct alternative to a custodial sentence.) Considering the question of how far practice adhered to the treatment ideology, many of the weaker areas of practice could best be summed up as a (conscious or unconscious) deviation from 'self-help' towards 'sink-or-swim'.

Concept-based therapeutic communities can evolve, and certainly have done – there is little likelihood that a project operating exactly like Synanon would receive referrals and funding from state social services now, and yet those concept-houses that survive in the UK are predominantly kept alive in just this manner. But this admittedly limited study suggests that there may be a need for further progress from the 'service-led' model (where the workers always know best) to the 'needs-led' model that is coming to dominate many other forms of social provision that drug users will have come into contact with. This would not necessarily entail a dilution of the fundamental concepts of the hierarchical therapeutic community approach, or indeed the atmosphere of a community. The format has already changed a great deal since 1958, leaders increasingly relying upon training and professional experience rather than charisma and personal experience, and some sanctions becoming symbolic rather than aggressively punitive. Nevertheless, the new professionalism of concept-based therapeutic communities has not removed the familiarity that will be felt by readers of Yablonsky's (1965) account of Synanon, if visiting a project such as Phoenix House Tyneside.

## Some lessons for practice

The following points highlight ways in which interviews with residents suggested that the quality of work in this and other such projects may be improved and the 'enduring problem of high dropout rates' (Barbara Rawlings, personal communication) addressed:

- Many residents 'didn't know what to expect' (male resident, 25, bottom of Phase One) upon admission, and this element of culture-shock seems to have been relevant to those who thought about leaving the community. Providing more information before arriving, perhaps even through some form of pre-admission group (as written information is unlikely to be absorbed while one is continuing a chaotic, addict lifestyle) may be part of the answer. There may be scope to incorporate such an information-giving role with work on a potential resident's motivation for entering a concept-house through the increasingly accepted approach of motivational interviewing (Miller and Rollnick 1991).

○ Futile or highly repetitive manual work can create genuine resentment among residents, and may inhibit the development of a sense of attachment to the community, so increasing the risk of premature withdrawal from the program. A positive response may be for staff to be alert to this and if necessary use targeted interventions from their position at the top of the hierarchy to ensure that manual work is of genuine use to the community itself or the neighbourhood the project is sited in.

○ Previous failed attempts at recovery from drug addiction outside a concept-based therapeutic community may be a predictor of success for residents, although research with a larger sample would be necessary to support this. However, the effect of previous failed programs in a concept-house is less clear.

○ Feedback and sanctions systems are open to abuse. Such abuse, when it occurs, is keenly felt by residents and may be a contributory factor to dropout, particularly for a resident already suffering from culture shock and/or withdrawal symptoms. The hierarchy itself may offer the means to reduce the incidence of power abuse if those in positions of seniority are vigilant.

Perhaps the most important lesson, however, is that, given the insights that could result into the recurring questions of long-term effectiveness, treatment length, and dropout rates, further qualitative research would appear to be highly worthwhile, as well as having practical value at a global level in 'counter[ing] the charges that there is not a proven case that therapeutic communities are effective' (Lees and Rawlings 1997). A challenge for researchers is that in many cases they may continue to have to first overcome the perception of research as 'an external and potentially destructive force' (Broekaert et al. 1999) among some concept-based therapeutic community programs. My experience, though, was that residents enthusiastically took the opportunity to voice their feelings and concerns openly, many expressing the desire for further such consultation; there is much to be gained from ensuring they have it.

## Acknowledgements

I am grateful for the assistance and advice of (in no particular order) Craig Fees and the Planned Environment Therapy Trust, Di Barnes, Jeff Watson, Barbara Rawlings and, of course, the residents of Phoenix House Tyneside.

## References

Allen, P. (1992) 'User involvement in a therapeutic community.' *Therapeutic Communities 13*, 4, pp. 253–263

Bleiberg, J. L., Devlin, P., Croan, J. and Briscoe, R. (1994) 'Relationship between treatment length and outcome in a therapeutic community.' *International Journal of the Addictions 29*, 6, pp.729–740.

Bloor, M., McKeganey, N. and Fonkert, D. (1988) *One Foot in Eden: A Sociological Study of the Range of Therapeutic Practice.* London: Routledge.

Broekaert, E., Raes, V., Kaplan, D. K. and Coletti, M. (1999) 'The design and effectiveness of therapeutic community research in Europe: an overview.' *European Addiction Research 5*, pp.21–35.

Burnett, K. (1999) *How do Service Users Perceive the Experience of Drug/Alcohol Rehabilitation in a Therapeutic Community?* University of Durham DipSW/MA thesis (unpublished).

Goffman, E. (1961) *Asylums.* London: Penguin.

Hawkins, P. (1989) 'The social learning approach to residential and day care.' In A. Brown, R. Clough (eds) *Groups and Groupings: Life and Work in Day and Residential Centres.* London: Routledge.

Jones, M. (1968) *Social Psychiatry in Practice.* Harmondsworth: Penguin.

Kennard, D. (1998) *An Introduction to Therapeutic Communities.* London: Jessica Kingsley Publishers.

Lees, J. and Rawlings, B. (1997) *An International Review of Therapeutic Communities and Their Outcomes.* Papers of the 1998 Association of Therapeutic Communities Windsor conference; unpublished.

Manning, N. (1989) *The Therapeutic Community Movement: Charisma and Routinization.* London: Routledge.

McCusker, J., Bigelow, C., Vickers-Lahti, M., Spotts, D., Garfield, F. and Frost, R. (1997) 'Planned duration of residential drug abuse treatment: efficacy versus effectiveness.' *Addiction 92*, 11, pp.1467–1478.

Mello, C., Pechansky, F., Inciardi, J. and Surratt, H. (1997) 'Participant observation of a therapeutic community model for offenders in drug treatment.' *Journal of Drug Issues 27*, 2, pp.299–314.

Miller, W. R. and Rollnick, S. (1991) *Motivational Interviewing: Preparing People to Change Addictive Behavior.* New York: The Guilford Press.

Poulopoulos, C. and Tsibouki, A. (1998) 'The origins and evolution of Greek therapeutic communities for drug addicts.' *Social Work in Europe 5*, 2, pp.29–33.

Rapoport, R. (1960) *Community as Doctor.* London: Tavistock Publication.

Ravndal, E. and Vaglum, P. (1994) 'Why do drug-abusers leave the therapeutic community – problems with attachment and identification in a hierarchical treatment community.' *Nordic Journal of Psychiatry 48*, Supplement 33.

Schimmel, P. (1997) 'Swimming against the tide? A review of the theraputic community.' *Australia and New Zealand Journal of Psychiatry, Feb. 1997.*

Toumbourou, J. and Hamilton, M. (1993) 'Perceived client and program moderators of successful therapeutic community treatment for drug addiction.' *International Journal of the Addictions 28*, 11, pp.1127–1146.

Toumbourou, J., Hamilton, M. and Fallon, B. (1998) 'Treatment level progress and time spent in the prediction of outcomes following drug-free theraputic community treatment.' *Addiction 93*, pp.1051–1064.

Weppner, R. (1983) *The Untherapeutic Community.* London: University of Nebraska Press.

Yablonsky, L. (1965) *The Tunnel Back: Synanon.* New York: Macmillan.

Yablonsky, L. (1989) *The Therapeutic Community: A Successful Approach For Treating Substance Abusers.* New York: Gardner Press.

# CHAPTER 8

# The ex-resident experience of working as a staff member in a therapeutic community

## *Staff from the Ley Community, Oxford*

## Introduction

> I felt that I had so much to offer after actually participating in the program myself, that I really wanted to be involved in helping other people with their problems. It was about turning a negative experience into a positive experience, where I was able to give back most things that I had learnt to other residents. (Neil Dickson, Key Worker)

A significant feature of the concept house programs has been the role ex-residents play as members of the staff team. The role of the ex-resident staff member can be traced back to the earliest days of concept houses where 'graduates' from the program would remain in the community and take on increasing responsibilities, ultimately evolving into a change in status in becoming a member of staff.

The experience for residents in participating in a concept house program is profoundly powerful. The successful graduate resident feels that by offering the opportunity of a future without drugs, the program has literally changed his or her life. This is a powerful motivation to go back as a staff member. In the language of the therapeutic community, it is not surprising that residents on a self-help program frequently decide that they would like to 'put something back' into the program that they feel has been so central to their survival.

> I think that my experience of being an ex-user and ex-resident puts me in a unique position of being of some use, some value to the people that

come to the Ley for rehabilitation. I know how they felt when they were using or drinking alcohol, and I know what it is like to be a resident.

I have to try and remember what I was like when I arrived at the doors of the Ley, looking like Charles Manson, and how frightened I became when my images or defences were challenged and stripped away from me. I also remember when staff gave me a hug and showed me that they cared about me, and how much that meant to me at the time. As a result, I try to encourage and pass on my experience to the people that come to the Ley with the hope and the determination to change their lifestyle, behaviour and attitude.

When residents know you've been there, I think you capture their confidence. I know that when I was a resident I really looked up to the staff and senior residents. They were my role models. They seemed to know how to live and enjoy life, and I desperately wanted to know the secret. I know it now, and hope that I can pass it on to others. (Lawrence Everett, Care Worker)

The concept house program depends on residents taking responsibility for both themselves and each other. Within the hierarchy of the program, senior residents take a crucial role in 'passing down' the culture from one generation of residents to the next. Staff have the role of keeping their hand on the tiller to ensure that the process of 'handing down' is carried out effectively.

What qualifications should members of staff have to qualify them to work in a concept house? This question is frequently asked by professional visitors who expect that staff involved in overseeing a therapeutic program would, and should, have professional qualifications to equip them to undertake the work. This, of course, misses the point that the program is first and foremost a self-help program. The status of 'ex-resident' is in itself an important qualification for a staff member, but not in isolation from other qualities and attributes.

The label of 'ex-resident' hangs around for quite a while, and still being treated as though you were in the program was an obstacle. I think that sometimes this drags on – 'once a junkie, always a junkie' – particularly by non ex-resident staff. I don't know whether that comes down to paranoid feelings, but I know that it's not something that only I have felt. I think that it's a consistent thought – that ex-resident staff are there for some other game rather than simply trying to help people achieve. (Steve Walker, Programme Director)

An effective concept house staff team needs to be a balanced team. The balance needs to address a range of issues – including gender and race – and in addition a range of previous experience and qualifications. The ex-addict staff member has a great deal to offer to the 'professional staff', but also much to gain from them in making the transition from 'ex-addict' to professional drugs worker.

When does this transition take place?

> I still find myself in a situation where I don't feel I'm on an equal par with other people – always feeling that someone, somewhere, still sees me as an ex-addict, although it has been some 20 years since I have used. The question I face is: when does a person stop being an ex-addict, and become a person within their own rights? (Steve Walker, Programme Director)

In attempting to answer this question, it is helpful to step back and review the hierarchy of relationships that lie at the heart of the therapeutic community structure. Two specific strands flow through the structure that directly impact on the role of ex-resident staff: the significance of 'role modelling' and the importance of 'auxiliary staff'.

Everyone living and working within a therapeutic community experiences a combination of vested and personal authority. The resident structure constructs a hierarchy of positions which allows residents to experiment in managing their behaviour within the vested authority denoted by their position. The staff structure imposes a further hierarchy on top of the residents' structure, and a frequent refrain within community life is to remind residents not to 'jump structure' to get a decision they want from either a staff member or a resident higher up the structure than the level where the decision should be made.

An important component of the community hierarchy is 'auxiliary staff'. The great majority of the staff team work Monday to Friday, 9.00am to 5.00pm. This is the time for the core therapeutic program to run, which staff closely oversee. During the rest of the week, the community is covered by a small rota of three care workers, frequently with only one care worker on duty at a time. The reason why the Social Services Inspectorate[1] has been able to approve such a low level of staff cover for a residential establishment with up to sixty residents is the role taken on by senior residents in the capacity of 'auxiliary staff'.

'Auxiliary staff' are senior residents in Stage 5 of the program, who are in full-time employment and living in one of the three Ley Community self-contained houses. During Stage 4 of the program, residents undertake training to equip them to work as an 'auxiliary staff' member. During Stage 5, they are required to attend a compulsory weekly group and work set shifts as an auxiliary staff member during weekday evenings and at weekends. The auxiliary staff member on duty works with, and in support of, the care worker on the shift. In effect, senior residents are expected to 'put back' into the community some of the learning they have achieved on the program, and act as role models for residents following after them. Of course, some residents find the responsibilities and demands of the auxiliary staff role more difficult than others, and issues that emerge from the way that they manage the role are taken up by the staff members responsible for facilitating the Stage 5 group.

Thus the principle of senior residents taking on responsibilities as 'staff members' – albeit auxiliary staff members – is intrinsically built into the program. The importance to newly arrived residents of close contact with people who have recently been through the program, and who can speak with authority about the positive impact it has had on them, underlines the significance of the role models' contribution within the structure. Ex-residents who have completed the program are encouraged to continue to visit the community after they have left, in part for themselves, but also to demonstrate to current residents that they too can rebuild a life for themselves if they continue to stick stubbornly with the program, even when it gets unbearably difficult.

Of course, a balance has to be struck between providing encouragement, and overcompensating in a desire to demonstrate progress. A recent concern has been ex-residents coming up to the community and displaying flash images with mobile phones and fast cars. We have to remember that the process of re-establishing oneself in the wider community after an intense residential experience is complex, and the potential for overcompensation is huge and needs to be monitored and kept in check.

The Ley Community has developed a policy that ex-residents will not be employed as permanent staff members until they have been out of the program for at least three years. Ex-resident staff members need to have separated clearly from their own experience in treatment prior to coming back to the community in a different role. The first two years following completion of the program is often a fairly turbulent time for many ex-residents, as they progressively put into practice the learning that has been accumulated while in treatment. An ex-resident needs to have had an opportunity to successfully make the transition away from the community before taking up employment within it, and be sure that returning to work as a staff member is the right move for them professionally, rather than a return to an environment which feels safe and familiar.

For the ex-resident returning as a staff member, the familiar environment can seem suddenly strange:

> You see a different side of the staff team. When you are a resident, the staff are on pedestals. When you join the staff, you see that they are really no different to anyone else, and that there is still the internal wrangling, and the gossip and everything else that goes on in a work environment. That

was quite a difficult thing to get used to. It took me a long time really to find my own niche and to be able to stand up for myself and actually be confident that what I was doing, I was doing for the right reasons – and that I was actually good at what I did. (Sara Lewis, Admissions Officer)

The advantage for the program of employing ex-residents in key staff posts is immediately apparent. Anyone who has had close involvement with a therapeutic community will be only too aware that a community develops its own language and understandings, which can be quite bewildering to the outsider. The learning curve for a new member of staff who has not previously worked in, or been a resident in, a therapeutic community, is huge. The ex-resident has no such problem. The way that the program runs will be deeply ingrained through their own experience, and while they will need to integrate the changes which will have occurred since they graduated from the program, the basic principles will be clear.

Not only will new ex-resident staff members have a huge advantage in getting to grips quickly with their responsibilities, but they also have a head start in gaining the trust and respect of residents. There can be no doubt that the ex-resident can short-circuit the 'testing process' which residents, understandably, put all new staff members through. They can speak with authority and from personal experience, and personify what can be achieved through successfully completing the program.

However, it will be clear from a number of the extracts quoted above from ex-resident staff that while the potential advantages can be articulated, many ex-resident staff still struggle with fully internalizing the transition. Perhaps the following quote succinctly sums up this contradiction:

Inevitably staff will be affected by some of the issues residents go through, whether ex-addict or not. Some staff detach themselves totally by avoiding the resident that brings up the unpleasant feelings – others get unhealthily engrossed. (Jane Brogan, Resettlement Officer)

The material brought up by residents in the program is frequently both powerful and painful. The extent to which the individual ex-resident staff member has integrated their own material will inevitably affect the way in which they are able to respond to material in others. The challenge for the staff team, and in particular for line managers and external supervisors, is to be able to help individual staff members separate out their own material from that of the people with whom they are working.

To return to the question asked earlier: when does a person stop being an ex-addict and become a 'professional' in their own right? The answer, of course, will vary between individuals. The Ley Community 'three-year rule' before eligibility for employment was established to provide a gap, a space between living and working in the community and coping for a period in the 'real world'. For some, three years is too short, for others it might well be possible to offer employment sooner without detriment to either the new staff member or the community.

What does become clear, however, is that once on the staff team, ex-resident staff members go through a process of establishing themselves fully in their new staff role. This process will, of course, vary depending on the personality of the individual concerned, and involves both an internal and an external dimension.

Internally, it takes time for any new staff member to feel fully integrated into any new staff team. The ex-resident new staff member has both the advantages and corresponding disadvantages of having known many of the staff team during their time in the program. Staff will have experienced their struggles and vulnerabilities, and the new ex-resident staff member will have experienced staff previously in a different capacity. The time that it will take to really feel a full and equal colleague cannot be prescribed: it is a process which will essentially be determined by the characteristics of the individual, and the extent to which the issues they confronted during their program have been resolved.

Externally, as far as residents are concerned, the new ex-resident staff member has fewer hurdles to overcome than new staff members who have not been through the program. Their credibility is bound up with their achievement, with the immediate vested status as 'role model'. There are dangers, however, that other staff will make assumptions of knowledge about the program that may well have developed since the new ex-resident staff member left the program, and the need for a full induction program should not be short-circuited.

It would be hard to overstate the significance of a staff training and development strategy in bridging the gap between 'ex-resident' and 'staff member'. The setting of national standards for drug workers (Quality in Alcohol and Drug Services (QuADS): competencies for specialist drug workers) will go a long way to providing a benchmark for all drug workers to demonstrate that they meet the standard – ex-addict or not. The introduction of on-site training in the form of National Vocational Training (NVQ) has also provided a mechanism for staff to gain a recognized professional qualification by demonstrating competence in carrying out their duties in the workplace. Formal recognition of competence will go some way to reinforce the self-belief that the transition from ex-addict to staff member has been completed.

> I knew what it was like to be an addict. I knew what it was like to walk up
> the drive and for the first time in my life to get honest. I also knew the

struggles that people face going into a program. I felt equipped to do the job.

I was disappointed at times when some staff could only see the ex-addict. But I think that the bottom line for me is that it's a privilege. It felt like a privilege to work with residents and to have them open up to me and take direction from me. It felt that in 1988, and it feels the same privilege now in 2000. (Vivienne Young, Key Worker)

## Notes

1. In England and Wales, local Social Services Inspectorates are responsible for registering and monitoring care establishments in their area. They have the power to insist that particular standards of physical, social and adminstrative care are met.

Part 4

# Modifications to the Therapeutic Community Model

# CHAPTER 9

# Therapeutic communities for drug-misusing offenders in prison

*Peter Mason, Diana Mason and Nadia Brookes*

## Introduction

The proportion of people in the criminal justice system who are drug misusers has grown in recent years, and rehabilitation and treatment offered to prisoners across England and Wales has been inconsistent. This chapter will look at a number of themes, including the background to the introduction of pilot drug services in prison, the prison setting, and the reasons for the introduction of the first prison-based therapeutic communities for drug users. It will focus on those therapeutic communities set up as part of the implementation of the prison service drug strategy, evaluated and monitored by the authors since 1996. Drawing on observation and findings from this evaluation, the therapeutic communities and their early progress in treating prisoners will be described.

## Background

The British prison system is one of the largest in Europe. In England and Wales this consists of approximately 136 institutions, mostly built over 100 years ago. Currently, approximately 65,000 prisoners are incarcerated and over 160,000 pass through the system each year. (Home Office 2000). A major expansion program is currently being undertaken, utilizing both state and private sector services. As well as the adult male population there are facilities for women (who represent about 14% of the prison population) and young offenders aged between 17 and 21 years old.

There are essentially two systems within prisons: a remand system for those people who are charged with an offence and awaiting trial, and a sentenced system for those who are convicted. Prisons operate on four levels of security from maximum to low level, and prisoners are allocated to institutions on that basis.

Research has indicated a relationship between drug misuse and crime, although there are differing views about the nature of the causal process (Chaiken and Chaiken 1990, Hammersley *et al.* 1989). It has been well documented that there are increasing numbers of drug users in the prison population. Maden *et al.* (1992) found that 11% of men and 23% of women in the adult convicted prison population were dependent drug users prior to imprisonment in 1989. Evidence from the National Treatment Outcome Research Study (Gossop *et al.* 1995) indicated that 1,100 drug misusers had committed 70,000 crimes in the three months before they entered treatment.

With the increase in drug-related crime there has been a growing interest in the effects of treatment in reducing drug misuse and associated crime. Debate continues regarding the effectiveness of treatment in reducing recidivism and drug misuse, but opinion is no longer as pessimistic as the 'nothing works' viewpoint of the 1970s. Evaluation studies hold out more hope that treatment can yield positive results. There has also been a gradual shift in attitude within parts of the criminal justice system. This is most evident among the police, who previously tended to see securing a conviction and imprisonment as the main means of reducing demand.

The prison service was forced to acknowledge that drug misuse did occur in prison, despite efforts to stop drugs from entering the prison system. There was increasing evidence of injecting drug use and needle-sharing, with the associated risks of HIV and hepatitis infection. Reportedly, heroin and cannabis use was almost routine in some prisons, and the violence and intimidation associated with drug dealing and extortion was placing a strain on many prisoners and the prison system (HMSO 1996).

In April 1995 the prison service produced the strategy document 'Drug Misuse in Prison' (HMSO 1995). This strategy document committed increased resources to 'provide help to prisoners who misuse, have misused or are at risk of misusing drugs'. The vehicle for achieving a reduced level of drug misuse was local drug strategies that would focus on:

o measures to reduce the supply of drugs

o measures to reduce the demand for drugs

o provision of treatment

o measures to reduce the potential for damage to the health of prisoners, staff and the wider community arising from drug misuse.

The drug strategy also introduced some firm measures to reduce the supply of drugs in prison settings. A key strategy was the introduction of mandatory drug urine testing of prisoners. Each prison was required to test prisoners randomly by laboratory urine analysis; refusal to test and positive results led to adjudication and days being added to sentences.

There is evidence from the United States to suggest that therapeutic communities in the community for drug users have been relatively successful and that reduced crime and drug use and increased employment were related to the amount of time spent in treatment. This provided the rationale behind establishing prison-based therapeutic communities in the United States. Before 1980 there had been relatively few studies of therapeutic communities for drug-using offenders in prison settings. Since then, evaluative studies have shown some positive results. The following are examples of some of the large-scale evaluations conducted:

- the Cornerstone therapeutic community program in Oregon, established in 1975, was evaluated twice and similar results were produced both times. The first evaluation followed prisoners for three years to find out whether they had returned to prison; graduates of the therapeutic community were found to be more successful than those who had dropped out of the program, and a sample of those on parole. The second evaluation found that the re-arrest, conviction and imprisonment rates were lower for therapeutic community graduates than for each comparison group (Field 1984,1989).

- the Stay'n Out prison-based therapeutic community program in New York was established in 1977 by former drug misusers who were ex-offenders. This provided a model for a number of other prison-based therapeutic communities which were subsequently set up. It was evaluated in 1984 (Wexler, Falkin and Lipton 1990) to assess the 'time in treatment' theory. It was expected that the prison environment would lead to a lower dropout rate than the community-based therapeutic communities. The central conclusion was that drug misusers who remained in the therapeutic community longer were much more likely to succeed than those who left earlier. Graduates from the therapeutic community had a significantly lower re-arrest rate than those who received no treatment and those who received all other forms of treatment.

- Amity Prison in California established a therapeutic community in 1989 modelled on Stay'n Out. It consisted of three phases lasting twelve months in total: observation, assessment and orientation.

Aftercare in a community-based therapeutic community was offered upon release. Outcomes were examined for therapeutic community graduates one year after release, and it was found that participants re-entered prison less than dropouts or the control group (Wexler *et al.* 1995). The imprisonment rates of those who completed both aftercare and the prison-based therapeutic community were lower than for graduates of the prison-based therapeutic community alone.

In the United States there has been a marked increase in drug treatment in prisons. 30% of prisoners with moderate to severe drug problems are treated in 34 residential therapeutic communities (Lipton 1995). The Federal Bureau of Prisons provides for continuity of treatment when prisoners are released either to supervision or to a halfway house.

In 1996, during the early stages of the implementation of the prison service drug strategy, Michael Howard, then Home Secretary, visited drug treatment therapeutic communities and boot camps in the United States. On his return Mr. Howard was keen that the structured therapeutic community models he had seen were adopted by the prison service in England and Wales.

As part of the prison service strategy, between September 1995 and January 1997 21 drug treatment and rehabilitation pilot programs were established in 19 prisons in England and Wales. A range of service modalities with different philosophies and varying levels of intensity were piloted, including three therapeutic communities. The therapeutic communities were the first to be introduced for drug-misusing offenders by the prison service in England.

The prison system is very overcrowded and Britain has one of the highest prison rates among European Community member states. The introduction of prison drug treatment programs took place at a time when the prison population had grown to record levels, alongside a renewed emphasis on security. During 1996 the average prison population was 55,300; in May 1997 the actual prison population was 61,100, greater than in any previous year (Home Office 1998).

## The therapeutic community models

A therapeutic community is a community of individuals who are totally 'immersed' in the program; that is, it is a 24-hour program. The therapeutic community model views drug use as a symptom of a larger problem of personality and socialization for the individual. The aim of the therapeutic community is to change virtually every aspect of a person, with the primary goal of helping him/her to mature into a drug-free and socially responsible individual. A hierarchical structure with a social contract instils individual accountability and responsibility. Applying the principles of personal responsibility, caring, concern and community values enables the therapeutic community residents to learn new ways of looking at themselves and their lives and a new way to operate in society.

The therapeutic community philosophy is strictly 'drug-free'. The primary mechanism for change is mutual self-help; the residents address their problems together and support each other. The key elements are: job functions, progress through stages of treatment, rewards and sanctions, community meetings, peer confrontation groups and tutorials. Residents take from six to twelve months to complete the program.

The three establishments to house the therapeutic communities were two adult male medium-security prisons and one closed young offender institution. The two adult male therapeutic communities could accommodate 84 and 65 prisoners respectively and were located on wings separated from the main prison. The therapeutic community for young offenders could house 72 prisoners and was in a self-contained unit isolated from the other accommodation blocks. Residents were recruited from within the prisons where they were located, and the intention was that individuals from other prisons could apply to the therapeutic community. A mixture of outside staff and prison officers generally staffed the therapeutic communities.

The therapeutic community specification was based on the Phoenix House USA model run in several prisons in New York state. However, the philosophy employed by the service provider in one of the adult prisons differed from the American generic therapeutic community model in a number of ways:

- there were no menial tasks and there was negotiation and flexibility within given boundaries, as it was felt that therapeutic communities could become too ritualistic

- drug use was seen as multi-factorial rather than a result of individual pathology

- the prime objectives of the therapeutic community were to improve social functioning and employability

- an association was made between status in the hierarchy and clinical progress. This was believed to be an artificial distinction. The principles were 'order, routine, meaningful occupation and hope for the future'.

The therapeutic community at the young offenders institution (YOI) conformed to much of the generic drug therapeutic community specification developed by Phoenix House USA. It had also developed features from other therapeutic community providers in the community (one Christian-based), as well as adapting to cater for young offenders.

There were differences in aspects of the programs provided by the therapeutic communities, but they included some or all of the components described. The therapeutic communities had three phases of treatment and offered at least three community meetings every day. There were morning meetings with activities planned by residents, where information was shared and announcements made. There were also house meetings where announcements were made about rewards and sanctions for residents, and administrative matters were dealt with. The third type of meeting was educational or informational in nature. All residents had a job function and/or attended vocational or educational classes and were required to participate in peer confrontation groups at various times during the week.

The three phases were orientation, primary treatment and re-entry.

1.  Orientation phase occurred during the first few weeks, when residents would learn about the program and their role within the therapeutic community. The phase included assessment and sentence planning. Participants would begin to examine their behaviour and individual programs would be developed. Contact with family and friends was restricted to letters and telephone calls. Having completed this phase, residents would automatically move on to the treatment phase.

2.  The next phase was primary treatment, which lasted three to four months. The resident lived and worked as a full member of the community, progressing through the work hierarchy and treatment program. Treatment methods would include a variety of groups, such as peer confrontation, didactic sessions (tutorials about issues of personal growth, for example, anger management and conflict resolution), weekly seminars, self-disclosure, phase groups (group work led by staff) and individual sessions with staff and personal officers.

3.  In the final stage, the re-entry phase, residents were prepared for either release into the community or eventual 'graduation' (for those who have completed the program). Residents worked and attended education in the main prison and acted as role models for residents in Phases One and Two. Residents were taught about developing peer support networks, and therapeutic content included 'advanced' staff-led groups. Family members were supposed to be involved in this phase where possible (especially with the young offender group). A relapse prevention plan would

be finalized and throughcare links developed between personal officers and probation officers prior to release.

Movements through the phases were time-related, movement through the work hierarchy related to achievements, behaviour and progress. Peer supporters, prisoners already resident in the therapeutic community, were used; their role was intended to be mainly that of a listener and to befriend and support new residents in the three-week induction period.

## The evaluation

In January 1996 the authors were contracted to evaluate the pilot prison drug treatment programs. The study objectives were to:

o analyse and evaluate drug program processes

o analyse and evaluate the critical success factors of the programs

o evaluate the impact of the program on prisoners, prisons and staff

o compare different types of program

o analyse and offer guidance on service development and contracting

o make recommendations to inform the prison drug strategy.

The evaluation looked at the effectiveness of the projects in delivering a service and meeting their own aims and objectives. The study covered the process of setting up the services, the content and delivery of those services and the impact of the programs. The project involved:

o prison situational assessment. Information was collected on prison characteristics and baseline data on supply and demand indicators.

o contract monitoring. Every three months each service was required to provide standard information on program activity and the progress of participants.

o prisoner study. Questionnaires were given to prisoners on entering treatment and on leaving. The self-completion questionnaires included variables on demographics, drug history, criminal history, dependency, readiness to change and a number of items known to be significant for drug-using offenders.

o site visits. Observations were conducted of elements of the programs, and formal and informal discussions took place with staff and prisoners. A formal interview with the program manager was conducted six months after inception.

o analysis of urine testing data

o cost analysis

○ contract review.

*Prisoners presenting for treatment*

The therapeutic communities' first year performance was assessed by analysing the quarterly contract monitoring forms. 644 applications were recorded and 581 assessments were carried out, the majority from prisoners within the prison where the program was located. The majority of those who were unsuccessful were rejected for security reasons or were not available due to transfer or release. 368 prisoners started the three programs in the year of study and 341 completed orientation and stated the first phase of treatment. The highest dropout rate was prior to completion of Phase 2, representing an average stay of 6 months. Of those who went on to enter Phase 3, the majority (56%) completed. A total of 70% left prior to completion, the majority for drug and discipline offences.

The prisoners entering the therapeutic communities were typically young, male and unemployed (see Table 9.1). The majority had been involved in theft in the month before prison. Burglary was the largest category of main conviction. In-prison drug use was markedly less than drug use prior to imprisonment, particularly daily use.

*Implementation of the therapeutic communities*

Each of the therapeutic communities developed along similar lines but each with its own dominant ethos; all developed their own particular rules and requirements. All the therapeutic communities established hierarchical structures, and staff worked hard to implement the therapeutic community ethos. The therapeutic communities started to change the 'prisoner code' among prisoners through encounter groups and structured self-help, which required prisoners to take and receive instructions from each other in the community and in groups.

The therapeutic communities experienced many similar difficulties and were each started from new. A community takes a long time to establish and a key element is the presence of senior residents who occupy senior positions in the therapeutic community hierarchy and act as role models. As there were no senior residents, the extent to which any of the programs operated as a therapeutic community in the first year was limited.

Due to the constraints of the prison setting, the therapeutic communities were not able to start with a small number of residents and then take on more as the therapeutic community developed. Staff who were unused to working together, and for the most part unused to working in a therapeutic

| Table 9.1: Key characteristics of the therapeutic community sample | | |
|---|---|---|
| Variable | Adults (N=188) | Young Offenders (N=139) |
| Mean age | 26 years old | 19 years old |
| Ethnic origin | 91% white | 86% white |
| Living in own home | 37% | 36% |
| Main source of income: Benefits Crime | 57% 33% | 47% 44% |
| Criminal activity in the month before prison: Theft Property crime Violence Dealing | 53% 40% 36% 33% | 79% 44% 43% 43% |
| In prison before | 84% | 73% |
| Main conviction | 39% burglary | 35% burglary |
| Mean age of first drug use | 15 years old | 13 years old |
| Drug use in the month before prison | 73% heroin 53% cannabis | 69% cannabis 53% heroin 48% crack cocaine |
| Daily drug use in month before prison | 59% heroin 34% cannabis | 54% cannabis 35% heroin 20% crack cocaine |
| Injected in month before prison | 27% | 17% |
| Drug use in last 4 weeks in prison | 47% cannabis 31% heroin | 56% cannabis 13% heroin 12% crack cocaine |
| Daily drug use in last 4 weeks in prison | 13% cannabis 10% heroin | 13% cannabis 4% heroin |

community of any kind, had to quickly set up programs for between 65 and 84 prisoners.

The pressure on bed space meant that the therapeutic communities were not permitted to have empty beds. If program staff were unable to immediately fill the space with a therapeutic community applicant, the prison would 'lodge' another prisoner on the therapeutic community. This would create disruption, as lodgers would not be part of the community, and in some cases were actively using drugs to the detriment of the therapeutic community.

The therapeutic communities undertook various measures to counteract the threat of lodgers. One therapeutic community admitted prisoners who had less than twelve months to serve and would therefore be unable to complete the full program; they were taken through an accelerated program. Staff tended to keep prisoners on the unit rather than risk an unknown lodger. The pressure on beds effectively resulted in the therapeutic communities lowering their requirements for entry to keep the units as full as possible.

There were high levels of institutional resistance to the therapeutic communities from prison staff in the early stages of the review. This was mainly to do with concerns about their cost, the role of the officers on the units, and the integration with external providers. Prison management decisions to utilize therapeutic community program space for prisoners who did not want to be on the unit also had an adverse effect on the development of the communities.

Lack of continuity among prison staff affected all the therapeutic communities. Officers who had received training were often sent to work elsewhere in the prison, while officers who were inexperienced or even antipathetic were detailed to the therapeutic communities. At the prison where the provider was contracted to train prison staff to run the therapeutic community, the training was particularly difficult to deliver as the designated officers were often not detailed to work on the therapeutic community.

The length and intensity of the therapeutic community program placed additional responsibility on the therapeutic community staff to ensure that they selected prisoners who would benefit from the program. Those residents who were ejected to the ordinary location of the prison could potentially not only give other prisoners a negative perspective of the community, but also find themselves at risk from other prisoners.

All residents signed a compact, which included acceptance of voluntary testing of urine. This tended to occur infrequently, due to the large numbers of residents involved, the length of the procedure and the demands on staff time. In addition two programs changed their rules relating to the consequences of positive drug tests. Two units moved to case-by-case assessments which were linked to internal community sanctions, and three positive tests led to expulsion from the therapeutic community.

Although the therapeutic communities were separated from the rest of the prison, full segregation did not occur, which meant residents could be exposed to drugs from outside the therapeutic community. However, a level of isolation did exist and this could potentially increase outside hostility from prisoners not involved in the therapeutic community. Disclosure and group responsibility were integral to the therapeutic community model, and residents could acquire a reputation for 'grassing' which may have dissuaded some prisoners from entering.

### Prisoners' views

Questionnaires given to prisoners as part of the evaluation asked for their views on the therapeutic community. Of the prisoners surveyed, the majority of respondents stated that their major achievement was to stop using drugs: 'This is the longest period, in or out of prison, for years that I have been drug-free and for once, instead of just trying to say the things that want to be heard, I actually now wish to remain drug-free!!'

Over a quarter reported that they had gained more confidence and a more positive view of themselves: 'I've learnt to be open and honest and gained confidence'; 19% stated that they had changed the way they thought about drugs and other people; 16% specifically mentioned that they were now able to 'say no' to drugs, and 12% that they had received information to help deal with future problems. A smaller number reported changes in behaviour, such as being able to control their anger and talk about their problems.

Prisoners were asked if there was anything they felt they had not achieved while they were on the program. Thirty-eight percent of those who responded answered 'no'. The remaining responses were concerned with the failure of the program to address individual issues, for instance, 'problems with family brought out in the open but not dealt with'; 'being able to bring my stress level to an acceptable point'; 'I have not received any pre-release information or support'; and 'anger management'.

The majority of respondents (55%) felt that certain elements of the program were good such as the phase groups: 'Phase groups cos (sic) you can open up more', and the atmosphere; 34% stated that the support of staff ('the staff's commitment') and other prisoners was important, and 11% that being in a drug-free environment was a positive factor. A very small number, five per cent, did not think there was anything good about the program.

Fourteen per cent stated that there were no bad things about the program. Just over half (51%) mentioned elements relating to the structure of the program such as the organization ('disorganized when it comes to groups') that there were not enough groups; 20% stated factors to do with other prisoners, mainly their attitude ('residents who blatantly take the piss and bring drugs on the wing and get away with it'); 19% referred to the staff in negative terms ('staff don't act quickly enough or come down hard enough on the blatant ones') and a small number (4%) mentioned the lack of trust ('lack of trust for some people and lots of trainees are still wearing masks').

Thirty-six per cent of prisoners who responded stated that they did not have any suggestions for improving the program. The majority of respondents (58%) recommended specific program changes such as one-to-one work and things to do ('more things to do instead of cleaning the wing all day when it doesn't need cleaning') and 'change some of the staff, put the age limit up, prisoners who has (sic) been drug-free for at least six months, not so much spare time, structure the evenings'. A small number (9%) suggested better screening of those entering the program. Other areas mentioned were that the prisoners should have closed visits so that it was harder for drugs to get on the wing, and the 'three strikes' policy should be made stricter.

The majority of respondents (78%) suggested specific program changes such as 'more information about drugs because they say you all ready (sic) know about them but don't'; 'more rewards for residents at the top of the hierarchy new residents see that they get the same as every one else which means there is no incentive to move up the structure'; physical exercise, one-to-one work and the provision of incentives were also mentioned; 14% felt that there was a need for more support and 4% that the screening of those entering the program should be improved ('...let's have people properly interviewed to see if there is a hope of them changing before they are allowed onto the therapeutic community'); 15% did not think there was anything missing from the program.

## Aftercare

During the evaluation period 43 prisoners were reported to have graduated from the programs. The majority of these were receiving aftercare in prison, as they had not been released. The aftercare varied considerably, from placement on a voluntary testing unit (VTU) to visits from program staff while in their normal location. In some cases there was no aftercare. Eighteen prisoners were reported to have accessed treatment in the community, and ten were discharged to probation care. In the USA therapeutic communities can offer graduates reduced time in prison, which is then spent in community residential units, but this is not the case in the UK.

## Conclusions

The assessment of performance in the first year of any program must take into consideration the set-up and other development issues that may reduce readiness and effectiveness.

Adaptations of therapeutic communities to special settings does involve changes in techniques, methods and services from the standard regime. When instituting a therapeutic community into the operation of a prison a lot is being asked of the establishment and provider staff. Prison staff are being asked to change their roles and work in situations different from traditional security settings. This may include working with non-prison service staff, some of whom may be ex-offenders, and with program models that may seem unconventional. From the service providers' perspective, they are asked to work in surroundings and in a culture that may not seem conducive to the treatment they have been used to providing in the community.

## Recommendations

The study (Mason and Mason 1999) identified a number of improvements that need to be incorporated into future programs. The strategy should incorporate continuous development as a central approach and method, while involving all programs in creating and sharing improvements to programs. Among the improvements needed are:

*Pre-treatment*

- undertake full needs assessment of prisons and ensure suitable match within each establishment of basic and enhanced services, as required
- review and rationalize existing programs to make goals more explicit
- assign clear roles and responsibilities to prison staff, external provider agencies and participating prisoners
- full review of the time left to serve (less than two years) by prisoners and the number of suitable candidates in the prison system to establish demand for long-term programs.

*During treatment*

- ensure that where officers are employed in the running of programs they are properly trained, supported and supervized

- improve the supervision and monitoring of programs through accreditation and audit
- reduce disruption to programs caused by prisoner transfers, staff allocation to other duties, etc.
- increase treatment intensity
- increase supervision through regular, voluntary, drug urine testing
- review program rules and criteria for discharge or termination from programs.

*Post treatment*

- increase the immediate support for prisoners completing treatment
- standardize outcome-monitoring systems to allow valid comparisons of treatment effectiveness
- improve inter-agency working relationships to improve aftercare
- arrange regular and consistent reviews of performance to ensure planned results are being achieved
- set up support groups (using the task force model) to provide assistance to underperforming programs.

Long-term follow-up inquiry should be built into the routine management of drug services within the prison system and supported by further research.

## References

Chaiken, J. and Chaiken, M. (1990) 'Drugs and predatory crime.' In M. Tonry and J. Q. Wilson (eds) *Drugs and Crime: Crime and Justice*, Vol. 13. Chicago: University of Chicago Press.

Field, G. (1984) 'The Cornerstone Program: a client outcome study.' *Federal Probation 48*, pp. 50–55.

Field, G. (1989) 'A study of the effects of intensive treatment on reducing the criminal recidivism of addicted offenders.' *Federal Probation 53*,10, pp. 51–56.

Gossop, M., Marsden, J., Edwards, C., Wilson, A., Segar, G., Stewart, D. and Lehmann, P. (1995) *The National Treatment Outcome Research Study*. The October report prepared for the Task Force, Department of Health.

Hammersley, R., Forsyth, A., Morrison, V. and Davies, J. B. (1989) 'The relationship between crime and opioid use.' *British Journal of Addiction 84*, pp.1029–1043.

Home Office (1998) *The Prison Population in 1997: Statistical Bulletin 5/98*. London: Home Office.

Home Office (May 2000) *Home Office Research Development Statistics. Prison Population Brief England and Wales*. London: Home Office.

HMSO (1995) *Drug Misuse in Prison*. Prison Service Strategy Document. HMSO: London.

HMSO (1996) *Drug Misusers and the Prison System – An Integrated Approach*. Report by the ACMD.

Lipton, D. S. (1995) 'The effectiveness of treatment for drug abusers under criminal justice supervision.' Presentation at the 1995 Conference on Criminal Justice Research and Evaluation.

Maden, A., Swinton, M. and Gunn, J. (1992) 'A survey of pre-arrest drug use in sentenced prisoners.' *British Journal of Addiction 87*, pp.27–34.

Mason, P. G. and Mason, D. J. (1999) 'Evaluation of prison drug treatment services: review and recommendations.' Unpublished report to Prison Service.

Wexler, H. K., Falkin, G. P. and Lipton, D. S. (1990) 'Outcome evaluation of a prison therapeutic community for substance abuse treatment.' *Criminal Justice and Behaviour 17*, 1, pp.71–92.

Wexler, H., Graham, W., Koronkowski, R. and Lowe, L. (1995) 'Amity therapeutic community substance abuse program: preliminary return to custody data: May 1995.' Report by the Office of Substance Abuse Programs, California Department of Corrections.

# CHAPTER 10

# The modern therapeutic community: dual diagnosis and the process of change

*Rowdy Yates and Jane Wilson*

## Introduction

The therapeutic community movement has had a long and enduring, if somewhat controversial, history. Over the last one hundred years it has evolved from its roots in 'democratic psychiatry' and work with 'maladjusted children' into a major treatment modality with a significant presence in a number of fields. In the addiction field, the therapeutic community movement is more readily associated with the concept-based therapeutic communities which grew out of the work of Dederich in Synanon (Bratter *et al.* 1985; Kooyman, in this volume), although, particularly in Europe, it was undoubtedly the legacy of earlier experiments in self-help community approaches which allowed this new and radical approach to integrate so effectively and be so readily accepted by a field rightly sceptical of new ideas and 'magic bullets' (Jones 1984).

Changes, both in the delivery of treatment services and the profile and potential size of the treatment population, have inevitably resulted in corresponding changes in the structure and content of therapeutic community programs, and the past decade has seen the growth and development of the so-called 'new' therapeutic community (Broekaert *et al.* 1998; Campling and Haigh 1999). Growing recognition that many substance abusers also had serious mental health problems was a significant, though not exclusive, factor in this evolution. An explosion in the numbers of people with drug problems, the shift in drug-using patterns and profiles, the advent of

HIV/AIDS and pressures on the public purse to rationalize resources also contributed to the pressure for change (Toon and Lynch 1994).

Current debates perceive an altered landscape within which a new dependent population, defined as having considerable biopsychosocial problems, is identified as a treatment priority. The multiplicity, severity and chronicity of the problems they experience has created a matrix of disadvantage which has undermined their ability to access or engage in traditional treatment. Whether this group is truly 'new' or the result of an enhanced ability to identify problematic subcultures within the traditional client intake, remains open to question (Yates 1999). This newly identified population has created a growing pool of 'revolving door' clients who shuttle between a range of services, placing an extraordinary burden on public health and social welfare services (Kaplan 1998).

The emergence of this population has brought challenges and opportunities to the traditional therapeutic community (Toon and Lynch, *op. cit.*). The possibilities and pitfalls of adapting concept-based therapeutic communities to meet the needs of those who also have considerable mental health problems is the focus of this chapter.

## Mental health issues in the concept-based therapeutic communities

From the early days of their development, therapeutic communities recognized that dependent drug users suffered psychological, social and behavioural problems: 'Addiction is a symptom of an underlying disturbance. The nature of this disturbance can be psychological, interpersonal and/or social. Psychological problems can vary from a character disorder to neurotic or psychotic disease' (Kooyman 1992).

Initially, evidence of psychological problems in drug users came from studies of therapeutic communities in the USA. In reviewing these studies, De Leon (1989) concluded that they primarily covered three areas: presenting symptomatology, personality features and levels of self-esteem. At that time, however, information on the range and severity of psychiatric problems of drug users was limited. Typically, the dependent drug user entering treatment was seen as having a character disorder. The therapeutic community movement recognized the significance and pervasiveness of the antisocial personality in dependent drug users and this had a primary influence on informing the philosophy, organization and program structure of the early concept-based therapeutic communities.

> The main characteristics constellate around immaturity and and/or antisocial dimensions; ...low tolerance for all forms of discomfort and delay of gratification; problems with authority; inability to manage feelings;

poor impulse control; poor judgment and reality testing; unrealistic self-appraisal in terms of a discrepancy between personal resources and aspirations; prominence of lying, manipulation and deception as coping behaviours; social and personal irresponsibility. (De Leon 1989)

Mainstream psychiatry considered those with a personality disorder as 'untreatable', given the enduring and pervasive nature of these disorders (Linehan 1999). Interestingly, the early democratic therapeutic communities, particularly the Henderson Hospital, were the exception in psychiatric circles in believing that they could work effectively with these issues. Concept-based therapeutic communities also had the wisdom to acknowledge the importance of character disorders in addicts and gave priority to confronting the deviant antisocial behaviours, beliefs and thought processes of addicts in their treatment methods. They also understood the need for a long-term positive social environment in order for change to occur.

However, this conceptualization of the addict as primarily antisocial assumed that all drug users were a homogeneous group who would fit this particular template. Thus, programs were largely standardized in a long-term residential regime which was highly structured, and where stringent behavioural modification techniques were applied. Confrontation and challenge via peer pressure was seen as essential for social rehabilitation: 'The explicit function of the social structure was to break down denial, pathology, and the code of the street, and to replace it with a code of responsibility, honour, trust and helpfulness to each other' (McLaughlin and Pepper 1991).

The approach of the concept-based therapeutic communities may have been appropriate for the traditional heroin addict with an antisocial personality but it might prove to be of limited value for the newly identified group of drug addicts.

### Emergence of 'dual diagnosis'

The term 'dual diagnosis' is ambiguous and has had different meanings at different times. Originally the phrase was used to describe persons with learning difficulties who also had a psychiatric disorder. More recently, the term has been used to describe those with a co-existing mental health disorder and a substance abuse/dependence disorder (Rorstad and Checinski 1996). In addition the word 'dual' can be misleading in that many drug users meet the criteria for multiple psychiatric and/or personality disorders alongside their substance abuse disorder.

The concept has its origins in general medicine in the early 1970s, when it was defined by Feinstein as: 'any distinct additional clinical entity that has existed or that might occur during the clinical course of a patient who has an index disease under study' (Feinstein 1970). It is perhaps understandable that such medical terminology fostered suspicion among many treatment staff. Therapeutic communities, in common with the broad range of non-medical, often non-governmental treatment services, had made strenuous efforts to free themselves from the domains of psychiatry and the stigmatizing label of mental illness. The growing use of such terminology raised concerns about the possibility of a re-medicalization and individual pathologizing of what they recognized as 'the character disordered addict in a social milieu' (Kooyman 1992).

These issues generated considerable debate in the therapeutic community movement. Addiction has traditionally been viewed as a psychosocial problem, not a medical one. Many feared that problems experienced by addicts would be straightjacketed into medicalized psychiatric treatment. Yet others felt it would be a pity if such fears allowed the movement to 'throw out the baby with the bathwater' by only viewing psychological needs within a medical framework (Ravndal and Vaglum, 1995). They took a more optimistic stance and viewed the existence of psychiatric problems in addicts as a challenge which the therapeutic community movement needed to address.

### Prevalence and problems

The study and treatment of 'dual diagnosis' in the USA, Canada and Australia is quite advanced. However, the last decade has seen a rapid growth of European research, much on therapeutic community populations, which also show a high rate of psychiatric and personality disorders in substance abusers (Heindricks 1990; Ravndal and Vaglum 1995; Kokkevi et al. 1998). As studies began to specify the range of psychiatric disorders commonly encountered among substance abusers, it was discovered that the classic symptoms of post-traumatic stress disorder (PTSD), a trauma-based syndrome, were evident at strikingly high rates, ranging from 12% – 34% for men and 30% – 59% for women (Najavits et al. 1997). After antisocial personality disorder, PTSD is now considered the most common diagnosis in substance abusers seeking treatment.

Research in the trauma field has shown that those who have experienced childhood trauma are at high risk of developing both psychological and substance abuse problems. The relationship between adult substance misuse and a history of abuse during childhood has been demonstrated in countless studies. Prevalence figures are shockingly high, ranging from 12% – 42% for men and 33% – 90% for women (Rohsenow et al. 1988; Brown 1995; Gil-Rivas et al. 1996; Porter 1994).

Disturbingly, findings consistently reveal that rates of relapse, readmission and hospitalization are much higher in this group and that they display poor response to traditional treatment (Osher and Kofoed 1989; Brown *et al.* 1995). Furthermore, a number of studies have shown that those 'dually diagnosed' are highly likely to be associated with increased levels of family stress and dysfunction; increased rates of suicide and deliberate self-harm; and increased risk of HIV infection (Anthony and Helter 1991; Zierler *et al.* 1992; Lucks 1997).

By the early 1990s it was clear that traditional treatment provision of all kinds was failing this population. Their interactive symptomatology had a synergistic effect which seemed to create a downward spiral in all areas of functioning (Dansky *et al.* 1995). They had complex and multiple treatment needs which extended beyond what traditional addiction treatment had been able to offer. A new conceptual framework within which more comprehensive models and methods of treatment could be applied needed to be developed, and the therapeutic community movement was very much a part of this process.

Examination of impact and effects of trauma which often include a diagnosis of PTSD offers valuable insights into the tremendous difficulties which this high proportion of drug users are likely to experience in merely surviving the structure of traditional therapeutic communities.

## Trauma, post-traumatic stress disorder and addiction

It had always been acknowledged that the childhood histories of many drug users were characterized by abuse and neglect, and that their life histories continued to reflect high levels of traumatic experiences. With hindsight, it could be said that trauma survivors have probably always constituted a large proportion of those presenting for treatment at therapeutic communities and may also have accounted for a significant proportion of the early dropouts and relapsers. Knowledge of the 'character disordered' addict existed from the early days of concept-based therapeutic communities, but the understanding of trauma 're-emerged' much later and could be said to have its roots in the 'democratic psychiatry' of Maxwell Jones and others at the end of World War II – a development which led to the establishment of the democratic therapeutic community movement:

> Both the Cassel Hospital and the Tavistock Clinic came into being at the end of World War I: the Cassel to meet the increasing needs for psychotherapy for traumatized war veterans and the Tavistock to meet the needs of the civilian population traumatized by the Great War. (Pines 1999)

What had been less well understood until recently was the extent of the trauma produced by these experiences and the severity of problems – across behavioural, interpersonal, physical, psychological and social domains – which could result.

Childhood trauma can have a devastating impact on development. When children are traumatized their physical and psychological boundaries are violated. Their integrity, the very essence of their being, and their separateness is denied (Briere 1988). The exposure to human cruelty, the feelings of dehumanization, and the experience of powerlessness create a diminished, or in the extreme, a fragmented sense of self (Ochberg 1991). These children are deprived of the experience of separateness and an environment that facilitates the development of a sense of self as valuable in its own right.

Victims of physical and sexual abuse are faced with a formidable and complex series of social, emotional, and cognitive tasks in trying to make sense of experiences that threaten bodily integrity and life itself. Confrontations with violence challenge one's most basic assumptions about the self as invulnerable and intrinsically worthy, and about the world as orderly and just. After abuse, the victim's view of self and world can never be the same again (Rieker and Carmen 1986). Disruptions in early relationships caused by trauma may prevent the child from developing solid internal structures of the self.

When trauma occurs in childhood there is an increased likelihood of developing dissociative disorders as well as PTSD (Herman 1992). Without understanding the functional role of dissociation and PTSD, the wide range of symptoms they present may appear bizarre and overwhelming for treatment staff.

The symptoms of post-traumatic stress disorder (American Psychiatric Association 1994) include vivid re-experiencing of the traumatic event(s), avoidance of triggers associated with those event(s), and increased arousal, which often results in debilitating anxiety states. Drug users with PTSD symptoms are generally stuck in time, continually re-exposed to the traumatic event(s) through daytime recollections that persistently interrupt ongoing thoughts, actions, or feelings. Typically, they will be assaulted by terrifying nightmares that awaken them and make them afraid to go back to sleep. During waking hours they may suffer flashbacks or psychotic episodes in which reality dissolves and they are plunged back into the traumatic event(s) that has haunted them for years or decades. During such episodes they may find themselves fighting off rapists, being attacked by enemies or fleeing from explosions – all with the same intense feelings they experienced during the initial trauma.

Most will develop avoidant/numbing symptoms to ward off the intolerable emotions and memories they experience. Many will exhibit dissociative or amnesic symptoms buffering them from painful thoughts and feelings; obsessional defences and other behavioural strategies; drug and alcohol abuse; eating disorders; sexual acting out; and self-harm. Some will display all of these symptoms at one time or another. Autonomic hyperarousal is common in this group and will usually be expressed in such symptoms as insomnia, hyper-vigilance and an enhanced startle reaction. Occasionally, reactions may escalate into acute episodes of aggression and panic (Wilson 1999).

Dissociation is the disconnection from full awareness of self, time and/or external circumstance through fragmentation of the usual connections between behaviour, feelings, sensations and knowledge (Braun 1988). Where dissociation exists, painful memories can be made less intense through dissociative alterations in perceptions (de-personalization and de-realization). They can be 'forgotten' (psychogenic amnesia); diffused through switches in ego states (self-splitting); or disowned as 'someone else's experience (multiple personalities) where parts of the self may assume separate identities. These part-identities, or 'pseudo-identities' are often in conflict with one another (Turkus 1991). Observations that the 'dually diag-nosed' were too fragile in their 'self' structure to sustain the demanding program structure of concept-based therapeutic communities (Toon and Lynch 1994), were astute. Residents experiencing frightening and invasive symptoms of this kind are unlikely to be able to respond in any meaningful and satisfactory way, and it is highly probable that their ability to regulate intense emotional experiences will be seriously compromised. This inability to cope with internal feelings by internal means can result in the tendency to engage in concrete action, externalisation, somatisation and a serious disrup-tion in the ability to care for the self.

The assumption that staff must strongly confront and break down denial through the behavioural modification techniques used in the early therapeu-tic communities – verbal violence, the use of shaming and humiliating tech-niques, etc. – can lead to damaging and counterproductive interventions with this group. Individuals experiencing the symptoms described above may well experience such approaches as invasive and attacking, running a significant risk of reactivating their symptoms. Moreover, confrontative methodology of this type is not only ineffective for this group but, given the difficulties they may be experiencing, could be considered actually abusive.

The proposition that the 'false self' demonstrated in the antisocial addict must be confronted was based on a belief, central to the early philosophy of the therapeutic community movement, in the existence of an intact 'self' hidden within the core. While this belief is entirely appropriate and is critical to the humanity of the self-help approach, the unshakeable faith in the wholeness of this inner self is seriously challenged by these recent findings. What must now be considered is that, for many drug users, treatment must first facilitate the construction of a 'self' from the broken and warring parts before challenging the refraction of a part self which fits the typical addict profile.

Where clients are displaying any or all of the above symptoms, the need for safety and protection will outweigh all other considerations, including intimacy and socialization. The inner world of these drug users is frightening, fragmented and chaotic, though their outward behavioural manifestations may often disguise the terror, isolation and confusion buried inside (Herman 1991; Turkus 1991).

## Overview – treatment for dual diagnosis

The process of program development and implementation for the dually diagnosed has taken shape over the last decade. Given the closely linked nature of addiction and psychiatric problems, it is now widely accepted that both problems need to be addressed simultaneously, and a variety of models have been developed to achieve this: problem-specific services with modifications; linkage programs and integrated programs (Evans and Sullivan 1995; Osher and Kofoed 1989).

Problem-specific services with modifications retain the primary focus of their remit, e.g. addiction, mental health, criminality or homelessness, but extend and adapt their services to include interventions which can address other problem areas as well. Linkage programs connect clients to a network of services providing parallel treatment to cover the range of identified needs, while within integrated programs, clinical resources and systems of care are blended into a single program offering a unified strategy which can deliver individualized and multidimensional assessments, care plans and treatment interventions.

Therapeutic communities have principally adopted the model of problem-specific services with modifications. However, it could be said that the move in European therapeutic communities towards a more open strategy which encourages closer involvement with other services and the community, could also be seen as applying a linkage approach as well.

There is general consensus that the therapeutic process for this group should balance support and confrontation within the context of a strong working alliance, in order to decrease clients' resistance and enhance their motivation for change (Minkoff 1991) as the severity of their problems often results in diminished ability to comply with long-term treatment expectations (Loneck 1997). Osher and Kofoed (1989) developed a process model similar to the stages-of-change model used in substance abuse treatment. This approach has increasingly been adopted for working with those with a dual diagnosis (Hodge 1998). It involves a stepwise progression through four phases:

- engagement, whereby staff strive to develop a therapeutic alliance
- persuasion, during which awareness of their problems and the need for help is enhanced
- active treatment in which clients develop the ability to manage their multiple problems
- relapse prevention, the final phase, in which clients develop skills to maintain gains and avoid relapse.

Within these phases a range of interventions have been identified as pertinent for this population. Multidimensional assessments, intensive case management, motivational interviewing, skills training, relapse prevention, alternative therapies and pharmacotherapy are just some of the interventions which have been either introduced, or given a higher priority in treating dual diagnosis.

This new conceptual framework and the interventions identified presented one of the many challenges the therapeutic community movement needed to face.

### The new – or modified – therapeutic community

The impetus for change and adaptation was fuelled by many internal and external factors. The pressure to address these issues stimulated an increasingly detailed and radical debate about what needs to be changed and what are the fundamental principles which cannot be relinquished.

In their seminal article 'What cannot be changed in a therapeutic community?' (1993) Ottenberg et al. list these principles as:

- self-help and community as cornerstones of the therapeutic process
- the use of staff and peers as role models
- emphasis on social learning to produce behaviour and attitude change
- planned duration of treatment as a necessity for residents to achieve such change.

Two of the essential elements for effective dual diagnosis programs, acknowledgement of the integral role of self-help efforts, and providing a long-term treatment focus with an emphasis on phases of intervention (Evans 1997), dovetail with those recommended by the therapeutic community movement. Many others are reflected in the structural adaptations and new therapeutic methods which are characteristic of the modern therapeutic community.

One of the most significant changes in the European therapeutic community movement has been the shift in emphasis from a behavioural modification approach to the principles of social learning. These principles have had a strategic impact on the transitional process now underway in European therapeutic communities. They are most clearly expressed in the move from excessive use of confrontational methods to a philosophy of engagement and dialogue which would augment motivation for change. While many of the daily regimes in the therapeutic community remain, there is now increased flexibility and tolerance in the application of standard activities and interventions. The use of shaming techniques to produce change has been discarded in favour of more motivational approaches to change (Broekaert *et al.* 1998). Social learning, with its strong emphasis on a collaborative educational process, encouraged the introduction of more psycho-educational approaches, skills development and relapse prevention education into therapeutic community programs.

The process of engagement, persuasion, skills development and relapse prevention suggested for effective dual-diagnosis treatment are consistent with the principles of social learning. Treatment experiences of those dually diagnosed demonstrate that this group will often decompensate in conditions of pressure and confrontation. The fragility of their ego structure, the intensity of their anxiety and the cognitive confusion they experience, require interventions which focus on skills development to manage their multiple symptoms.

The community process, with residents' committed involvement in all aspects of the community, has always been viewed as the primary agent of change. This does not necessarily negate the importance that dual-diagnosis treatment places on individually customized treatment packages. The new therapeutic communities, in recognizing the interactive relationship of the individual to the social whole, view the community process as the development of the individual within the group – the new family.

The community as substitute family and the importance placed on staff as role models who 're-parent' (Kooyman 1992) speak to the concern and connection (Broekaert *et al.* 1998) which the new therapeutic communities aspire to. Importantly, relational healing (Herman 1992) via connectedness is one of the aims in the treatment of trauma resulting from child abuse. The blending of valued fundamental principles and practices with new therapeutic methods introduced by professional staff offers possibilities to develop new and innovative ways to work with this population. However, it will require the creation of a shared philosophy as well as a common language to achieve this.

At present, staff composition in the modern therapeutic community combines a mix of mental health professionals with traditional therapeutic community counsellors, and the importance of integrated training for these blended staff teams has been widely recognized (De Leon 1992; Carroll 1990). In most European therapeutic communities, professionals had always been involved as staff, and this integration was more of an evolutionary process. Therapeutic communities in the USA, however, were staffed almost exclusively by ex-addicts, who were often more resistant, viewing the introduction of professionals as a threat to the basic concept of self-help. Combined training aims to break down barriers and encourage cross-fertilization of ideas and skills, to enable staff teams to offer a range of interventions to augment the basic therapeutic program while maintaining consistency in program delivery.

At a clinical level many new procedures have been adopted to better identify and support these residents. Assessment now receives greater attention than has formerly been the case, and assessment procedures in most therapeutic communities have become much more comprehensive. The process of accurate assessment is essential. Many new screening instruments have been developed which can detect psychiatric problems and are capable of being administered by lay persons without a psychological background.

Without a comprehensive understanding of residents' problems, effective treatment cannot be delivered. The introduction of interventions such as intensive case management, advocacy, crisis intervention skills and the use of pharmacotherapy specifically addresses the needs of residents with a dual diagnosis.

The increased emphasis on research and the relationship between researchers and staff is an important element in the new developments. The therapeutic community movement has accepted the need for a move from the qualitative, soft documenting of their practice to a more scientific approach. De Leon argues this point, claiming it should be a matter of policy to use instruments and methods that are used in the scientific world, since governments and other agencies that provide the funds are asking questions that can only be answered by research findings. More studies which concentrate on individual differences, with particular focus on diagnosis, would help the therapeutic community movement understand what works for which residents, and why certain treatments are successful.

## Conclusion

Internationally, the therapeutic community movement has evolved through both internal and external pressures for change. This change process was different across the globe, and was influenced by the cultural, social, political and historical context within which the therapeutic community was anchored.

The modified therapeutic communities in the USA developed with a primary focus of dual diagnosis and the treatment of these residents, whereas the new therapeutic communities in Europe developed from a broader social agenda with a more political perspective which recognized dual diagnosis as a reflection of the contradictions within the social fabric and one of the many issues which needed to be addressed. At the Second European Conference on Rehabilitation and Drug Policy it was stated that:

> The therapeutic communities are called to maintain an aggressive stance towards the social exclusion that certain categories of the population are facing and the violation of their human rights. Active participation aimed at a change in the present situation is a challenge. The therapeutic communities cannot be systems which strive for internal changes only. (Poulopoulos 1995)

It could be said that the principles and practices of the European therapeutic community movement have always been considered radical. To be radical is to go to the roots. Understanding of the roots of the relationship between addiction and mental health offers an excellent opportunity for therapeutic communities to incorporate a radical psychology which is compatible with and supportive of their aims as a social project.

## References

American Psychiatric Association (1994) *The Diagnostic and Statistical Manual of Mental Disorders: Fourth Edition.* Washington DC: American Psychiatric Press.

Anthony, J. C. and Helzer, J. E. (1991) 'Syndromes of drug abuse and dependence.' In L. Robins, and D. Regier (eds) *Psychiatric disorders in America: The Epidemological Catchment Area Study.* New York: Free Press.

Bohun, E. and Grahn-Bowman, M. (1995) *Treating Sexually Abused Substance Misusing Women: The Connection Centred Model* (Unpublished Ms.).

Bratter, T., Collabolleta, E., Fossbender, A., Pennachia, M. and Rubel, J. (1985) 'The American self-help residential therapeutic community: a pragmatic treatment approach for addicted character-disordered individuals.' In T. Bratter and G. Forrest (eds) *Alcoholism and Substance Abuse.* London: Free Press.

Braun, B. (1988) 'The BASK model of dissociation.' *Dissociation 1*, pp.4–23.

Briere, J. (1988) 'The long-term clinical correlates of long-term sexual victimisation.' *Annals of the New York Academy of Sciences 528.*

Broekaert, E., Bracke, R., Calle, D., Cogo, A., Van Der Straten, G. and Bradt, H. (1996) *De Nieuwe Therapeutische Gemeenschap.* Leuven: Garant.

Broekaert, E., Kooyman, M. and Ottenberg, D. (1998) 'The "new" drug-free therapeutic community: challenging encounter of classic and open therapeutic communities.' *Journal of Substance Abuse Treatment 15*, 6, pp.595–597.

Brown, P., Stout, R. and Mueller, T. (1996) 'Post-traumatic stress disorder and substance abuse relapse among women: a pilot study'. *Psychology of Addictive Behaviours 10*, pp.124–128.

Campling, P. and Haigh, R. (1999) *Therapeutic Communities: Past, Present and Future*. London: Jessica Kingsley Publishers.

Carroll, J. (1990) 'Treating drug addicts with mental health problems in a therapeutic community: managing the dually diagnosed patient.' *Journal of Chemical Dependency Treatment 3*, pp. 237–259.

Dansky, B., Saladin, M., Brady, K., Kilpatrick, D. and Resnick, H. (1995) 'Posttraumatic stress disorders among substance users from the general population.' *International Journal of the Addictions 30*, pp.1079–1099.

De Leon, G. (1989) 'Psychopathology and substance abuse: what is being learned from research in therapeutic communities.' *Journal of Psychoactive Drugs 21*, pp.177–187.

De Leon, G. (1993) 'Modified therapeutic communities for dual disorders.' In J. Solomon, S. Zimberg and E. Shollar (eds) *Dual Diagnosis: Evaluation, Treatment, Training, and Program Development*. New York: Plenum Medical Press.

Edens, J., Peters, R. and Hills, H. (1997) 'Treating prison inmates with co-occuring disorders: an integrative review of existing programs.' *Behavioural Sciences and the Law, 15*, pp.439–457.

Evans, K. and Sullivan, J. (1995) *Treating Addicted Survivors of Trauma*. New York: Guilford Press.

Feinstein, A. R. (1997) 'The pre-therapeutic classification of co-morbidity in chronic disease.' *Journal of Chronic Disease 23*, pp.455–468.

Finkehlor, D., Hotaling, G., Levis, I. and Smith, C. (1990) 'Sexual abuse in a national survey of adult men and women: prevalence, characteristics, and risk factors.' *Child Abuse and Neglect 14*, pp.19–28.

Gil-Rivas, V., Fiorentine, R. and Anglin, M. D. (1996) 'Sexual abuse, physical abuse and post-traumatic stress disorder among women participating in outpatient drug abuse treatment.' *Journal of Psychoactive Drugs 28*, pp.95–102.

Heindricks, V. M. (1990) 'Psychiatric disorders in a Dutch addict population: rates and correlates of SAM-III diagnoses.' *Journal of Consulting and Clinical Psychology 58*, pp.158–165.

Herman, J. L. (1992) *Trauma and Recovery*. New York: Basic Books.

Jones, M. (1984) 'Why two therapeutic communities?' *Journal of Psychoactive Drugs 16*, pp.23–26.

Kaplan, C. (1998) 'Methodological aspects and theoretical background of improving psychiatric treatment in residential programmes for emerrging dependency groups: the EWODOR roots of Biomed 2 project.' In J. Marques Teixeira, J. Negreiros De Carvalho and L. Machado Rodrigues (eds) *Proceedings of the Workshops EWODOR Portugal*. Porto: Gabinete de Planeamento e de Coordenacao do Combate a Droga.

Kohut, H. (1971) *The Analysis of the Self: A Systematic Approach to the Psychoanalytic Treatment of Narcissistic Personality Disorders*. New York: International University Press.

Kokkevi, A., Stefanis, N., Anastasopoulou, E. and Kostogianni, C. (1998) 'Personality disorders in drug abusers: prevalence and their association with Axis I disorders as predictors of treatment retention.' *Addictive Behaviours 23*, pp.841–853.

Kooyman, M. (1992) *The Therapeutic Community for Addicts: Intimacy, Parent Involvement and Treatment Outcome*. Rotterdam: Universiteitsdrukkerij Erasmusuniversiteit.

Linehan, M. (1999) *Cognitive-Behavioural Treatment of Borderline Personality Disorder*. New York: Guilford Press.

Lucks, N. (1997) *HMP Cornton Vale: Research into Drugs and Alcohol Violence, Bullying, Suicides, Self-injury and Backgrounds of Abuse – Scottish Prison Service Occasional Papers: Report No. 1/98.* Edinburgh: Scottish Office/HMSO.

Mclaughlin, P. and Pepper, B. (1991) 'Modifying the therapeutic community for the mentally ill substance abuser.' *New Directions for Mental Health Services 50,* pp.85–93.

Najavits, L. M., Weiss R. D. and Shaw, S. R. (1997) 'The link between substance abuse and post-traumatic stress disorder in women: a research review.' *American Journal on Addictions 6,* pp.273–283.

Ochberg, F. M. (1991) 'Post-traumatic therapy.' *Psychotherapy 28,* pp.107–124.

Osher, F. C. and Kofoed, L. L. (1989) 'Treatment of patients with psychiatric and psychoactive substance abuse disorders.' *Hospital and Community Psychiatry 40,* pp.1025–1030.

Ottenberg, D., Broekaert, E. and Kooyman, M. (1993) 'What cannot be changed in a therapeutic community?' In E. Broekaert and G. Van Hove (eds) *Special Education Ghent 2: Therapeutic Communities.* Ghent: vzw OOBC.

Pines, M. (1999) *Forgotten Pioneers: The Unwritten History of the Therapeutic Community Movement.* http://www.pettarchiv.org.uk/atc-journal-pines.htm: Association of Therapeutic Communities.

Porter, S. (1993) 'Assault experiences among drug users.' *Substance Abuse Bulletin 8,* 1, pp.1–2.

Poulopoulos, C. (1995) 'The new challenges for therapeutic communities.' *Proceedings of the 2nd European Conference on Rehabilitation and Drug Policy: Europe in Transition – TC In Transition.* Thessaloniki: Europe Against Drug Abuse.

Ravndal, E. and Vaglum, P. (1995) 'The influence of personality disorders on treatment completion in a hierarchical therapeutic community for drug abusers: a prospective study.' *European Addiction Research 1,* pp.178–186.

Rohsenow, D. J., Corbett, R. and Devine, D. (1988) 'Molested as children: a hidden contribution to substance abuse?' *Journal of Substance Abuse 5,* pp.13 –18.

Rorstad, P. and Checinski, K. (1996) 'The care of people with a dual diagnosis of mental illness and substance misuse.' In O. McGeachy and M. Ward (eds) *Dual Diagnosis: Facing the Challenge.* London: Wynne Howard Publishing.

Toon, P. and Lynch, R. (1994) 'Changes in therapeutic communities in the UK.' In J. Strang and M. Gossop (eds) *Heroin Addiction and Drug Policy: The British System.* Oxford: Oxford University Press.

Turkus, J. (1991) 'Psychotherapy and case management for multiple personality disorder: synthesis for continuity of care.' *Psychiatric Clinics of North America 14,* 3, pp.649–660.

Wilson, J. (1998) 'Abuse and misuse: the ultimate hidden population.' *Druglink 13,* 4.

Wilson, J. (1999) 'Trauma, Mental Health and Addiction.' In E. Broekaert, W. Vanderplasschen and V. Soyez (eds) *Proceedings of the International Symposium on Substance Treatment and Special Target Groups.* Ghent: Universiteit Gent.

Yates, R. (1999) 'Multi-drug use: a new problem or the recognition of how it always was?' In E. Broekaert, W. Vanderplasschen and V. Soyez (eds) *Proceedings of the International Symposium on Substance Treatment and Special Target Groups.* Ghent: Universiteit Gent.

Zeirler, S., Feingold, L., Laufer, D., Velentgas, P., Kantrowitz, G. and Mayer, K. (1991) 'Adult survivors of childhood sexual abuse and subsequent risk of HIV infection.' *American Journal of Public Health 81,* 5, pp.572–575.

# CHAPTER 11

# The significance of resettlement support on completion of a drug rehabilitation therapeutic community program

*Paul Goodman and Karen Nolan*

## Introduction

The provision of resettlement support on completion of a therapeutic community program has never been an integral part of the therapeutic community movement. Originally the therapeutic community movement in the USA during the 1960s evolved a quasi-cult culture whereby 'members' retained over years a close association with the community that encouraged separateness from mainstream society, and inflated the importance of key personalities. Members saw their recovery in the context of the therapeutic community. They remained within the community and upheld the rules and expectations over lengthy periods of time (Kennard 1998, pp.96–98).

In recent years, therapeutic communities have been concerned with preparing residents for the return into the wider community. The therapeutic community movement recognizes that the processes within the treatment program have the inevitable effect of 'removing' residents for a time from the normal pressures of living, and provide an alternative society within which new behaviours, attitudes, beliefs and values can be developed. The therapeutic community structure provides the framework through which residents have the opportunity to work through issues at the core of their addiction, and learn new ways of coping without resorting to destructive behaviours. The process takes place within the safety of rigid rules that are primarily managed and enforced by other residents in treatment. While the culture provides the containment to allow the process of healing to take place, it bears little resemblance to the 'real world' to which residents return on completing their program.

Unlike the twelve-step residential programs which provide structured and available resettlement support to ex-residents through the network of Alcoholics Anonymous and Narcotics Anonymous meetings held daily throughout the country, little support has historically been available to ex-therapeutic community residents following completion of their program. The internalized message is that the resident who has successfully completed the long and challenging program is equipped to face the real world and the challenges ahead. So long as relapse does not occur, therapeutic communities have been happy for ex-residents to drop in, both to provide ex-residents with a little support, and to be seen as successful role models for current residents – examples of what can be achieved if you strive hard enough to keep with the program even when the demands of the community feel impossibly difficult.

Ex-residents who relapse have traditionally been seen as a threat to the therapeutic community, and banned from the site through the desire to protect current residents from either the sight of 'failure', or, more realistically, the risk of drugs being brought onto the premises. A similar position is taken with residents who 'split' against advice. Such people are warned that the consequences of leaving their program early against advice are likely to be dire. At some time, nearly all residents hit a point in their program when the desire to run away becomes almost overwhelming, and both staff and other residents take time out, both to confront the resident about the likely outcome of leaving, and to provide support and reassurance. One of the risks of underlining the possible negative consequences of leaving is to set up a self-fulfilling prophecy. Residents are reminded about the state they were in when admitted, and the situation they will be returning to if they leave. They are told about the likelihood that they will quickly relapse, and subsequently many do so. As far as the therapeutic community is concerned, the decision to leave is the end of the line in respect of the therapeutic community's responsibility for ex-residents who leave against advice: they are on their own and take the full consequences for their decision.

Ultimately, of course, any drug rehabilitation program should be judged not on the numbers who successfully complete their program, but on long-term rehabilitation. Research undertaken at the Ley Community (Wilson and Mandelbrote 1978, 1985; Small (in preparation) has demonstrated that there is a correlation between the length of time residents remain in treatment and subsequent offending behaviour. Certainly, ex-residents who remain in treatment for six months or more have a hugely reduced chance of re-offending even if they do not complete the full program successfully. It clearly makes sense, then, to maximise treatment gains by ensuring that resettlement support is available to build on learning achieved during the program.

## The Ley Community program: building in 'resettlement'

The Ley Community, a therapeutic community founded in 1971 near Oxford, provides treatment to a maximum of 60 men and women over eighteen years old. In 1999/2000, 81 residents were admitted on to the program, 30 residents successfully completed their program, and 39 left the program early. The Ley Community program underwent a major review in 1998 and, in the process, the issue of resettlement was tackled. To understand how resettlement support has been structured into the program, it will be necessary to briefly outline the structure of the program itself.

The Ley Community program is structured into six stages, summarized in Table11.1. It should in particular be noted that Stage 6, 'Resettlement', is marketed to potential residents as an integral part of the program.

The Ley Community employs two full-time resettlement officers, who work closely with the two house care teams located within the therapeutic community. They become directly involved with the residents when residents reach Stage 4 of the program and are beginning to start the process of re-integration with the 'outside world'. At this stage, residents undertake voluntary work off site, take on speaking engagements with community groups and with the local prison drug rehabilitation program, and begin to socialize away from the Ley. The resettlement officers are involved in running a weekly Stage 4 group in which residents are provided with an opportunity to share as a peer group their current experience and frustrations. For much of the time, Stage 4 residents are required to be 'good role models' as senior residents within the community, so it is important for them to have an opportunity to let off steam without having a negative effect on more junior residents. The involvement of the resettlement officers with the Stage 4 group allows for relationships to build with them prior to residents receiving permission to look for work.

The resettlement officers take over responsibility for individual residents from their key worker at the point that a resident moves into Stage 5 of the program, and into full-time employment. No resident leaves the Ley Community on successful completion without being in three months' full-time employment. Many residents, prior to joining the Ley Community program, had not worked, and while they are given support with compiling *curricula vitae*, and with interview technique, all gain employment on the open job market. The link between employment and offending has been

| Table 11.1 The six-stage program | | |
|---|---|---|
| **Stage 1:**<br>Safety Net | 2 weeks | Enabling residents to settle into the community. Sleep patterns are stabilized and relationships with staff and residents established. |
| **Stage 2:**<br>Induction | 8 weeks | Enabling residents to integrate themselves into the therapeutic program. Residents attend seminar programs, participate in individual key work sessions, participate in groups and the work structure, and complete daily diary entries. |
| **Stage 3:**<br>The work | Approx. 22 weeks | Taking on increased responsibility. Residents participate in the full range of therapeutic activities. They are encouraged to explore the past with the purpose of coming to terms with their own feelings, beliefs, attitudes and behaviour, and thus developing personal qualities, self-awareness, self-worth, self-confidence and self-discipline. |
| **Stage 4:**<br>Preparing for the future | Approx. 8 weeks | Enabling residents to plan and prepare for their future, start socializing outside the community and go to voluntary work. During this stage, residents are expected to act as role models and undergo auxiliary staff training. They attend specific workshops aimed at preparing them for moving out of the Ley, which includes finance and budgeting, alcohol use and cross-addiction, education, leisure, voluntary work and employment. |
| **Stage 5:**<br>Re-entry | Approx. 12 weeks | At this stage, residents are expected to be in full-time employment and living financially independent from the Ley. Stage 5 residents attend a group once a week and act as auxiliary staff. |
| **Stage 6:**<br>Resettlement | | This is an open-ended period, offering support to residents who have completed the program. There is a weekly group run by a member of the Ley staff at a venue in Oxford City. |

clearly established (Lipsey 1995; Bridges 1998), and there can be no doubt that the geographical location of the Ley Community in an area of buoyant employment has proved of real benefit.

Residents in Stage 5 of the Ley program live in three self-contained houses and take full responsibility for budgeting and managing themselves.

In addition to full time employment, Stage 5 residents are expected to support staff on a rota at weekends and in the evenings in the capacity of auxiliary staff. They also have to attend a weekly group facilitated on Monday evenings by the resettlement officers. The three months in Stage 5 play a crucial role as a bridge between living within the tight framework of the community and moving out and on. Many will move out with their peers, though others will choose to move into their own separate accommodation on completing their program at the Ley. The vast majority decide to settle locally after their program, though referrals to the Ley Community come from throughout the country. A recent snapshot between November 1999 and February 2000 indicated that of the 20 residents successfully completing the program during that period, 19 settled locally. The advantage of making a fresh start on completing a long rehabilitation program is self-evident. The advantage of moving on in employment, surrounded by supportive peers, adds to the potential for consolidating treatment gains achieved during the program.

During 1999, 44% of residents leaving the Ley Community did so on successfully completing the program in an average period of fourteen months. In the same year, the average length of time for all residents leaving the program was just under nine months, a figure that includes the 25% of residents who left within four weeks of arrival – without giving themselves the opportunity to settle into the community structure. It follows that a significant number left during the latter part of Stage 3, and during Stages 4 and 5. The reasons for leaving vary hugely, from an inability to cope with a particular issue, to concern about a partner, child or relative, to an impulsive wish to escape the confines of the demanding regime. The research, however, indicates that treatment gains can be sustained even if the program is not completed, and so subsequent support offered by the resettlement officers to those leaving early is aimed at providing advice and assistance, as well as referral on to other appropriate agencies.

## The resettlement project

The resettlement project was originally set up in late 1998. The following year, a partnership agreement was negotiated with another local voluntary sector agency to broaden the project to include people returning to Oxford after completing other drug rehabilitation programs in other parts of the country – whether in the community or in prison. We anticipate that the project will grow substantially during the next few years as a consequence of a major Government initiative to set up 21 new prison-based drug rehabilitation programs in late 1999. The importance of resettlement work following on from prison-based drug treatment programs was highlighted in the largest study of prison-based treatment for drug users (Inciardi *et al.* 1997), which found that when followed up by a substantial aftercare program in the community, the prison-based program was very effective. When no aftercare was provided, the in-prison treatment program had no discernible impact on levels of drug use on release.

What does the Ley Community resettlement project look like? While it is still early days, a number of issues have already emerged. Initially, the Ley re-settlement officers set up a weekly 'Stage 6' group in Oxford – well away from the Ley Community premises. Attendance at the group from January 1999 to March 2000 is illustrated in Table 11.2.

| Table 11.2: Attendance at Stage 6 group, January 1999 – March 2000 | |
|---|---|
| Total number of ex-residents who attended groups | 37 |
| Average number of ex-residents attending in each group | 5 |
| Highest attendance at any one group | 9 |
| Lowest attendance at any one group | 1 |

The hope was that recent ex-residents would use the facility of the group to share their experiences, challenge each other and provide support when individuals were struggling. Attendance at the group was voluntary, based on the assumption that people who had recently been through an intensive therapeutic program would wish to make use of the opportunity to talk and gain support from others who had also had a treatment program in common with them. In the event, ex-residents tended not to go to the group if the rest of their lives seemed to be generally satisfactory. The view emerged that to attend the group was an acknowledgement of failure, of feeling needy.

It soon became apparent that it was not possible to run a 'therapeutic community' encounter group in the community without the structure, framework and sanctions that are explicitly part of the structured residential program. The Stage 6 group resembled a traditional approach to community work more than a therapeutic community group. The level of honesty and openness, which had been second nature within the therapeutic community program, was compromised by 'life' – relationships, jealousies, half-truths and fears of admitting to fears. People chose not to attend if this was simply to provide support to others who might be struggling. The long program was over, and football was a greater attraction after work than a two-and-a-half-hour group.

But, of course, at other times all ex-residents have periods of being inten-sively needy. In reviewing the first six months of the resettlement project, we decided to change the structure to move more overtly to a community work model. The resettlement officers moved away from providing the weekly resource of a group that would take place (however few ex-residents chose to attend), to a program of activities that ex-residents would have an opportu-nity of opting into on a needs basis. In addition, the revised program provides 'private time' on an individual basis with one of the resettlement officers, if booked in advance, while the other resettlement officer partici-pates in an open group.

Other evenings have been allocated for social events. A busload of fourteen ex-residents, all in work and living full and independent lives, went bowling together. The activity provided an opportunity for re-establishing a sense of 'community' – of having had a significant shared experience – while allowing for a number of important conversations to take place between ex-residents and between ex-residents and the resettlement officers. A further development planned is a women-only group to take place for women ex-residents on a six-weekly basis. This will also focus around a shared activity, and allow for serious contacts to be made in the context of 'having fun'.

The penultimate section of this chapter describes briefly a typical week for one of the Ley Community resettlement officers. This provides an illus-tration of how the work is managed in practice. While the project still remains in its early days, Tables 11.3 and 11.4 provide a guide as to how it has developed. The first resettlement officer post was set up in November 1998, the second post from September 1999.

## Resettlement and relapse

It is not surprising that a significant number of ex-residents relapse even after completing the intense rehabilitation program. For some, the experience of relapse can prove the final hiccup on the way to recovery. Indeed, such people can often gain a great deal from the experience. For others, it can mean a quick spiral back into addiction. The experience at the Ley Community is that ex-residents who get into difficulty are more likely to do so through alcohol misuse, rather than returning to drugs. The resettlement officers with the program director at the weekly resettlement team meeting will discuss any ex-resident who has relapsed. Decisions will be made about the extent of intervention to be followed. An ex-resident who has used illegal substances or relapsed on alcohol will not be allowed to visit the community. However, the resettlement officers can continue to work with

### Table 11.3: Workload carried by resettlement officers (1 January 1999 – 31 March 2000)

| Resident category | Total | Residents accessing resettlement services |
|---|---|---|
| Residents completed program | 33 | 31 |
| 'Split' at Stage 5 | 1 | 0 |
| Asked to leave at Stage 5 | 6 | 3 |
| Ex-residents who completed prior to 1 Jan. 1999 accessing resettlement services | | 14 |
| Ex-residents who 'split' prior to 1 Jan. 1999 accessing resettlement services | | 1 |

### Table 11.4: Resettlement officers' caseload on 31 March 2000:

| | |
|---|---|
| Stage 6 (ex) residents accessing resettlement services | 26 |
| Stage 5 residents (key-worked by resettlement officers) | 8 |
| Stage 4 residents looking for work | 4 |
| 'Splittees' accessing resettlement services | 1 |

### Table 11.5: Involvement with ex-residents who have successfully completed the program and then relapsed, January 1999 – March 2000

| | |
|---|---|
| Percentage of ex-residents who have completed the program and experienced relapse | 34% (11 out of 32) |
| Number of ex-residents re-admitted to the program | 1 |
| Number of ex-residents who have recovered from relapse | 2 |
| Number of ex-residents who have experienced relapse, but who are still in employment, and accessing support | 6 |

them until such time as a period of stability has been established, and they are considered 'safe' to return to visit. If it becomes clear that the ex-resident is not responding to support, the resettlement officers will refer on to other front-line support services. Table 11.5 summarizes the involvement of the resettlement officers with ex-residents who have successfully completed the program and then relapsed between 1 January 1999 and 31 March 2000.

## The significance of public milestones and demonstrating effectiveness

On their final day in the community, a resident stands 'on the table' in front of all the staff and residents and receives a standing ovation for their achievement. In addition to family members attending, numerous ex-residents also return to share in the celebration. It is a powerful and moving experience. The resident 'on the table' experiences a range of emotions as they receive acknowledgement for their achievement in working through the demands of the program. However, it is the public graduation ceremony which takes place between twelve and eighteen months after completing the program which underlines that the program does not end when the resident moves out. The graduation ceremony takes place twice a year at the Ley Community in front of a large number of invited guests. Each graduate receives a silver ring engraved with the Ley emblem. The graduation marks the achievement not only of completing the program, but of building on the program subsequently. In a very overt way, the fact that the graduation takes place over a year after a resident leaves the Ley Community illustrates the understanding that it is how a resident puts into place the learning achieved on the program that is ultimately the gauge of success.

One further comment on demonstrating effectiveness, and the potential for an integrated resettlement project to feed into the process. The Ley Community commenced in April 1999 a major research project into the impact of the program on the values, beliefs and attitudes of residents. Shortly after arrival, all residents complete a battery of psychological tests, and then repeat the battery at six-monthly intervals. This builds on the National Treatment Outcome Research Study (NTORS) which is comparing the effectiveness of a number of different treatment modalities over time. The NTORS project, which the Ley Community is part of, was set up by the British Government in 1995 to study treatment outcomes over a period of time, from a range of treatment facilities, with the intention of informing guidance to treatment purchasers based on effectiveness research (Gossop *et al.* 1999). The NTORS project has inevitably had difficulty in keeping in touch with people after completion of treatment, and it is reasonable to posit that the large number of ex-Ley Community residents in contact with the resettlement project will greatly assist the process of follow-up and retesting. It is interesting to note, in passing, how much residents have appreciated their involvement with the research project. They have found their improved scores on re-testing hugely validating in providing them with 'objective evidence' for the improvements that they know themselves they have made.

## The shape of a resettlement officer's week

The posts of resettlement officers have been designed to ensure that the post-holders are fully integrated into the Ley Community staff team, and are involved in the day-to-day life of the community as well as undertaking outreach work with Stage 6 ex-residents. Wherever possible, the resettlement officers attend the staff handover meetings that take place every weekday at 9.00am and 4.45pm (4.30pm on Mondays and Thursdays) when the 'day staff' hand over to the staff on overnight duty.

For the post-holder, there is a great deal of variety in any week's work. One way to bring the resettlement project alive is to describe the work of the people involved. The following is based on the recorded activities of a resettlement officer over one working week.

## *MONDAY*

9.00am    Handover meeting – Ley Community.

9.30am    Catch up on contact sheets, redirect post to ex-residents, take phone calls, check Stage 5 box for receipts and memos to be made up.

10.45am    Attend fortnightly staff seminar facilitated by consultant psychiatrist reviewing individual residents' care plans.

12 noon    Lunch.

12.30pm    Make phone calls to agencies and Stage 6 ex-residents.

1.00pm    Visit Stage 6 ex-resident who has lapsed, used heroin twice, and has been smoking large quantities of cannabis. Has not used in past 9 days. Discuss relapse prevention. Joined by Stage 6 housemate for practical discussion about housing options – considering relinquishing tenancy.

2.15pm    Receive phone call on mobile from another Stage 6 ex-resident asking to meet.

2.20pm    Off duty.

5.00pm    Visit Stage 6 ex-resident at one of the Stage 5 houses rented by the Ley Community. This ex-resident currently returned for 'respite' after developing a co-dependent relationship with another ex-resident who relapsed and is now back in the program. Discuss issues and feelings.

6.00pm    Individual session with another Stage 6 ex-resident. This ex-resident is trying to support others in Stage 6, but feeling overwhelmed. Needs to make space for own needs.

6.30pm    Weekly Stage 5 group facilitated jointly with resettlement officer colleague. The main issues from the group: two people 'grounded' for breaking rules and going to a nightclub with Stage 6 ex-residents;

three people discussing move-on plans; one person discussing a home visit to see her children, and the tensions with her ex-partner; one person discussing concerns over family members with health problems. In addition, there was general discussion about room changes in the three Stage 5 houses, rent payments and savings payments.

8.30pm    Brief individual slots with Stage 5 residents over issues not suitable for group discussion because of need for confidentiality.

9.00pm    Finish.

## TUESDAY

9.00am    Handover.

9.15am    Pay in rents, write up weekly movements.

10.00am   Visit 'splittee' at home. Having met regularly for individual sessions over the last ten days, 'splittee' is now returning to the program. Bring 'splittee' back to the Ley Community – focus on the task ahead.

11.00am   Hand over 'splittee' to her key worker and prepare her for a general meeting of the House to raise issues about her return.

11.30am   General Meeting.

12 noon   Lunch.

12.30pm   Meet up with Stage 5 resident who has had an extension owing to difficulty in finding suitable move-on accommodation. Take him to various places looking for accommodation, gathering information from notice boards, housing rights, etc. Talk about fears around moving-on. Drop resident at bus stop.

2.30pm    Attend Oxford Resettlement Forum – an inter-agency information-sharing meeting for frontline workers employed by a wide range of local voluntary and statutory services.

4.30pm    Finish.

## WEDNESDAY

9.00am    Handover.

9.30am    Meet up with Stage 4 resident to discuss job which has been offered, wages, hours, and long-term plans.

10.00am   Meet another Stage 4 resident who has been offered two jobs. Discuss merits. Resident makes phone calls. Discuss response.

10.30am   Phone calls to a Stage 6 ex-resident and to his landlord.

11.30am   Stage 5 resident drops in to withdraw savings and pay balance of rent. Arrange to meet the next day for an exit interview.

11.45am   Drive to Oxford to meet Stage 5 resident whose move-on plans have collapsed. Discuss possibilities over lunch.

| 12.45pm | Pick up Stage 6 ex-resident in town and bring back to office at the Ley. Ex-resident has experienced relapse on alcohol and heroin, and has been receiving support from other ex-residents. Discuss progress made and support received through Alcoholics Anonymous. Discuss practical changes (i.e. accommodation). Arrange acupuncture appointment. Says he did not drink the previous night because of meeting up today. Asked to attend Stage 6 group tonight. |
| 2.00pm | Catch up with colleague resettlement officer. |
| 2.30pm | Off duty. |
| 6.00pm | Individual session with Stage 6 ex-resident. |
| 6.30pm | Stage 6 group. Focus of group on sharing experiences of relapse and feeling around identity. Share positive interventions. |
| 8.30pm | Finish. |

## THURSDAY

| 9.00am | Handover. |
| 9.30am | Three way handover with Stage 4 resident and their key worker as resident prepares to move into Stage 5. |
| 10.45am | Stage 4 group. Discuss tensions between residents, fears about moving on and into work, and feelings about visits. |
| 12 noon | Lunch. |
| 12.30pm | Write up discharge summaries. Draft reference. Write up memos to Stage 5. Phone calls. |
| 2.00pm | Meet up with Stage 6 ex-resident. No further relapse. Discuss feelings around relationship with long-standing partner, and whether the relationship has a future. Looking for full-time work – currently working part-time. |
| 3.00pm | Weekly resettlement team meeting. Discuss residents in Stages 4, 5 and 6. Discuss interventions, room changes, rent arrears. Discuss issues from the two rented Stage 5 properties. Allocate workers to meetings. Agree time back. |
| 4.30pm | Handover. |
| 5.00pm | Finish. |

## FRIDAY

| 9.00am | Handover. |
| 9.15am | Phone calls. |
| 9.30am | Formal interview with Stage 4 resident prior to permission being given to look for work. Rules for Stage 5 spelt out. Discuss curriculum vitae and what kind of work, and how to approach job hunting. |

10.30am    'House run' (house check) in allocated Stage 5 rented house. Fill sheets identifying where standards of maintenance and cleanliness need to be improved.

12 noon    Lunch.

12.30pm    Phone calls. Complete contact sheets.

1.00pm    Staff training seminar.

3.00pm    Stage 5 exit interview. Discuss what has been learned on the program. Relapse prevention. Arrange follow-up interview for two weeks after the resident has left the program.

4.00pm    Catch up with colleague resettlement officer, data input, residents' files, etc.

4.45pm    Handover.

5.00pm    Finish.

7.00pm    Return to the Ley Community to support Stage 5 resident 'getting on the table'. Present certificate of completion to Stage 5 resident in front of all residents, ex-residents and colleagues.

## Conclusion

Each stage of the program confronts residents with new challenges and anxieties. Recovery is not a straightforward progression, but more akin to a rollercoaster. It is normal for residents to 'regress' as Stage 4 is reached, and the prospect of leaving the secure and familiar structure of the community beckons. It is a time for encouragement and reassurance. The knowledge that Ley Community staff will remain in contact during the process of resettlement provides significant support during this critical phase. All treatment programs must be judged ultimately on their effectiveness in preparing participants to successfully cope in the months and years after completing their program. Adequate and targeted resettlement support will be seen to have played an important role in achieving the long-term effectiveness of treatment programs, and consequently must be integrated into the therapeutic community structure.

## References

Bridges, A. M. (1998) *Increasing the Employability of Offenders: An Inquiry into Probation Service Effectiveness.* Probation Studies Unit Report No. 5. London: Probation Studies Unit.

Gossop, M., Marsden, J., Stewart, D. and Rolfe, A. (1999) *NTORS: Two-Year Outcomes. The National Treatment Outcome Research Study: Changes in Substance Use, Health and Crime.* Fourth Bulletin. London: Department of Health.

Inciardi, J., Martin, S., Butzin, C., Hooper, R. and Harrison, I. (1997) 'An effective model of prison-based treatment for drug involved offenders.' *Journal of Drug Issues 27,* 2, pp.261–278.

Kennard, D. (1998) *An Introduction to Therapeutic Communities.* London: Jessica Kingsley Publishers.

Lipsey, M. (1995) 'What do we learn from 400 research studies on the effectiveness of treatment with juvenile delinquents?' In J. McGuire (ed) *What Works in Reducing Offending: Guidelines from Research and Practice.* Chichester: John Wiley and Sons.

Small, M. A. 'Two year follow-up study of criminal re-convictions in a residential therapeutic drug/alcohol rehabilitation centre: a retrospective study of 1996–1997 admissions.' (In preparation.)

Wilson, S. and Mandelbrote, B. (1978) 'The relationship between duration in a therapeutic community for drug abusers and subsequent criminality.' *British Journal of Psychiatry 132,* pp.487–491.

Wilson, S. and Mandelbrote, B. (1985)'Reconviction rates of drug dependent patients treated in a residential therapeutic community: a ten-year follow-up.' *British Medical Journal* 1985, 291, p.105.

Part 5

# Research and Evaluation

# CHAPTER 12

# Evaluative research in therapeutic communities

## Barbara Rawlings

## Introduction

In this chapter I will introduce and describe evaluative research on the therapeutic community. I will not set out to comprehensively review this research,
but to highlight the various research approaches which have been used. It is
clear from studies of the literature that most research has come from North
America, and the studies chosen in this chapter to illustrate the research approaches will reflect this. However, work has also been done outside the
USA, and to acknowledge this I have chosen some examples from other
countries. It should be borne in mind, though, that North American therapeutic community research is far more professionalized, organized and
well-funded than anywhere else in the world, and by choosing to cite studies
from elsewhere, I am not trying to give the most up-to-date view of research
findings. However, several reviews, far more comprehensive than this, have
been published elsewhere (Anglin *et al.* 1996; Anglin and Hser 1992;
Gerstein 1992, 1994; Lees *et al.* 1999; Rawlings 1999).

### What is evaluative research?

At its most basic level, evaluative research aims to discover whether a
program or intervention does what it sets out to achieve. For any kind of
treatment program, the major aims of evaluation are to discover first of all
whether or not clients have improved, and secondly whether this improvement is truly a result of the treatment. Much of the methodological debate
which goes on between researchers concerns how these two questions can
best be answered.

Client improvement is a qualitative phenomenon, and concerns things like how much better the client feels, or gets on with people, or copes with crises. Staff or peers who know the client can 'know' how much he or she has improved, but an evaluation generally needs to put this qualitative knowledge into figures, so that the extent of improvement can be measured and used for comparisons. Thus researchers look for markers of improvement. These can be external markers, such as drug relapse or reconviction, or markers devised by the researchers, such as changes on psychological test scores. The issue of whether any change can be attributed entirely to the treatment in question is complicated, since individuals can be affected by so many different influences.

## What is the purpose of evaluative research?

There are two main reasons for carrying out evaluations. The first is to see whether a program or intervention works effectively enough for people to continue to put their efforts and resources into it. The history of public services suggests that even those who can unequivocally demonstrate their success are not guaranteed funding, but nevertheless evaluation findings can provide the means of judging where funds and policy priorities should go. The second reason is to demonstrate to program staff where the strengths and weaknesses of the program seem to be, and what kinds of changes they could make to improve it. Thus, for example, research which finds that certain types of client are likely to leave early because they in particular cannot tolerate the pressures of confrontation, could lead to staff making changes in their approach, in order to maximize the chances that such clients will stay longer.

## What is 'successful outcome'?

In the eyes of the therapeutic community staff, the successful therapeutic community graduate may be someone who takes no drugs, has no further convictions, and leads a busy and orderly life, and many evaluative studies reflect this expectation. Studies of reconviction rates are usually done by checking information about ex-residents using their criminal records. This is particularly the case with evaluation studies done for in-prison therapeutic communities, as one of the main reasons for setting up any kind of treatment in a prison is to lower the likelihood that a person will be reconvicted, so reconviction rates are of particular interest to prison authorities. However, using re-arrests or reconvictions as a measuring tool has to be done sensitively, because often an ex-prisoner is re-arrested and imprisoned for breaching the terms of parole, or for a crime committed before treatment took place, and not for a new crime. There are other problems in using reconviction rates (Gunn *et al.* 1978), which include the finding that ex-prisoners may lead a life of crime and never get re-arrested, while others, struggling to stay crime-free, are re-arrested for their first minor infringement. Nevertheless, reconviction rates are considered a reasonable measure of treatment effectiveness.

Thus, in a retrospective study of one program, Swartz *et al.* (1996) compared outcomes for long-stay and short-stay clients of IMPACT (Integrated Multiphase Program of Assessment and Comprehensive Treatment) in Cook County Jail, Chicago. By examining the treatment records and criminal records of 1991–92 clients, they found that the shortest-stay group was most likely to be re-arrested, and that the rate of re-arrest decreased with increasing lengths of stay in IMPACT. In a comparative study, Wexler *et al.* (1992) looked at re-arrests, and time until re-arrest, for inmates released from the Stay'n Out therapeutic community, which operates programs for male and female inmates in New York State. The researchers compared outcomes for therapeutic community inmates with three other prison treatment groups: milieu therapy, counselling and no treatment. (The authors define milieu therapy as less structured, less regimented and less hierarchical than the therapeutic community.) Using parole records and treatment records, they found that the hierarchical therapeutic community was the most effective means of reducing recidivism for both men and women, and that the longer an inmate spent in the program, the greater the success rate.

Drug abstinence and relapse is usually judged by self-report or by examination of records. However, some American studies (Inciardi *et al.* 1997; Knight *et al.* 1997) use urinalysis or hair sampling in order to establish abstinence, and often the subjects are paid a fee for assisting with the research.

### Research studies of treatment outcome

The literature on evaluation of therapeutic communities mainly comprises statistical studies of post-treatment outcome, and psychological studies of in-treatment changes. Indeed, it is largely concerned with post-treatment outcome, possibly because reduction in drug use and reconviction reflects the real concern of funding agencies and public interest. The rest of this chapter will look at some of these studies, from prison and community settings, and at the major findings which have been derived from them.

#### Pre-test/post-test design

This means taking a 'snapshot' of a client's psychological functioning and social skills profile at the beginning and end of treatment. This is done by using standard psychological tests and staff reports, comparing the two and measuring the difference. For example, following a study at the Ley Community in England (Wilson 1977) which found that introverts who left early did particularly badly, and which suggested that perhaps the program style was too highly pressured for introverted personalities, Kennard (1978) carried out a pre-test/post-test study. This compared the scores of residents at different stages in their treatment, and found that those introverts who stayed tended to become more extroverted over time. In a study of program graduates and program dropouts at Phoenix House, New York (De Leon 1984) it was found that while signs of personality disorder and poor self-esteem improved significantly at the two-year follow-up, these did not reach normative or healthy levels. Improvements were greatest for those who stayed longest. In a later study De Leon (1989) studied 53 graduates of Phoenix House, New York, and 371 dropouts. He compared psychological profiles obtained early in treatment with test results obtained at two-year follow-up, and found that while graduates improved most, dropouts had also improved, and that their improvements correlated positively with the length of time they had spent in treatment.

*Post-treatment outcome study*

Here the researcher tracks ex-residents for a set time to see how they behave. Many such studies use a 'single case study' method. The research is confined to one therapeutic community, and no attempt is made to compare it to another or to a different form of treatment. Nevertheless, the comparative method is strongly embedded in research practice, and many of the single case studies devise a means of presenting comparative results, by classifying residents into different groups, and comparing their outcomes. A typical study might group residents according to how long they stayed in treatment, or according to their individual profiles, and then subject the data to statistical tests to see which groupings seem to be related to outcome. For example, Wilson and Mandelbrote (1978) carried out a study of reconviction after treatment in a concept-based therapeutic community, the Ley Community in Oxford, England. This looked at people admitted to the Community between 1971 and 1973 (n = 62) using information from the Criminal Records Office. Reconviction data was correlated with social characteristics, history of criminality and history of drug use. The sample was divided into three groups according to duration of residence: a short-stay group of those who had stayed less than one month (n = 22), a medium-stay group of those who had stayed between one and six months (n = 20), and a long-stay group of those who had stayed over six months (n = 20). The maximum duration of residence was two years. Rates of conviction before admission and following departure were obtained and compared. Conviction rates following departure were also compared with length of stay. The long-stay group had a pre-admission conviction rate of 60% which was significantly reduced to 10% during the follow-up period; the conviction rate of the medium-stay group was reduced from 70% to 45%, and the conviction rate of the short-stay group remained constant at 57%. The authors concluded that concept-based therapeutic community treatment is effective in reducing criminal activity in drug abusers who remain in residence for longer than six months. The reconviction findings from this study have been echoed by many others in America, including Holland (1978) who studied the Gateway Houses in Illinois, and found that after discharge early dropouts showed no change in arrest rates, late dropouts showed an 81% reduction in arrest rates and program graduates showed a 97% reduction. A later study at ten-year follow-up confirmed that the longer a person had stayed in the program, the better the outcome (Holland 1983). In the Phoenix House study cited above, De Leon (1984) examined outcomes for 525 graduates and dropouts using interviews and records at two and five years after residents had left the program. Again, improvements were greatest for those who had stayed longest.

*Comparative studies*
These two basic kinds of evaluation study are often refined in various ways. For example, the researcher may attempt to show that the difference in behaviour or test scores really is a consequence of treatment by comparing the treated group with a 'non-treatment group' or by comparing one treatment method (say therapeutic community) with another (perhaps methadone maintenance). However, it is often very difficult to find groups which can properly be compared, since the critical factor in treatment outcome may be related to exactly the personality characteristics which lead someone to come to a therapeutic community for treatment (such as motivation and preparedness to change). In particular, it is difficult to properly compare treatment and non-treatment groups, since non-treatment groups may not be motivated to change anyway. (Moreover, the literature often notes that the non-treatment group is not a pure type, since its members often get treatment at some point during the study, even if this is only going into prison.) One example of comparative research is a study by Kooyman (1993) who compared the outcomes of two therapeutic communities in the Netherlands, Emiliehoeve (n = 172) and (Essenlaan (n = 47) and two no-treatment groups (n = 44). Follow-up information at six months found

much better outcomes for the therapeutic community clients, and some differences between the therapeutic communities which related to differences in the programs and the types of client.

Where statistics from other organizations are already available, the researcher can use these as comparative material. For example, in the Ley Community study above (Wilson and Mandelbrote 1978), the authors went on to compare their results with results from other treatment programs, and showed that their post-treatment conviction rates were substantially lower than those reported from other types of treatment.

*Relationship between outcome and individual characteristics of clients*

Evaluation research has also focused on examining outcome scores in relation to personal information about the individuals they relate to, such as their social, educational, mental health and employment background, in a bid to discover whether the program works better for one kind of person rather than another. Thus, for example, Kooyman, in a later addition to his comparative study, went on to interview ex-residents at three- and five-year follow-up, and found that it was not only the length of time people spent in the program which seemed to predict a positive outcome, but also the parental involvement and a higher level of education. A large-scale American study (Simpson and Sells 1982) described later in this paper, found that clients with lesser criminal histories did better.

Research on the relationship between client characteristics and outcome has also thrown light on the nature of the client group, and in particular has identified that for many clients, the presenting problem of drug abuse co-exists with a mental illness or personality disorder. In 1989, De Leon reviewed the research evidence on the prevalence of psychological disorder in admissions to therapeutic communities, and distinguished three groups of the dually diagnosed. These were mentally ill chemical abusers (MICA), whose primary problem is a mental disorder; chemical abusers with a mental illness (CAMI), whose primary problem is chemical abuse, although they also have a severe psychological or psychopathic disorder; and chemical abusers (CA) whose primary problem is chemical abuse, although they exhibit mild pathological signs or personality disorders. De Leon noted that generally therapeutic communities tended to exclude MICAs and chose to treat CAMIs and CAs. The best outcomes seemed to be for CAs (De Leon 1989).

*Relationship between outcome and treatment characteristics of program*

Some research has focused on particular aspects of the program in a bid to see not just whether it works, but how and why it works. There has, however, been less work on characteristics of the treatment than there has been on characteristics of the patients. George De Leon (1994) argued that 'the primary therapist and teacher in the therapeutic community is the community itself', thus specifying what is meant by the dictum 'community as method'. In a bid to specify the particular components of this treatment method, he went on to outline a number of features, such as the use of role models, open communication, feedback and active participation, which distinguish therapeutic communities from other forms of treatment. He noted that for change to occur, certain things need to happen to individuals, in particular essential experiences (healing, nurturing, physical safety) and critical experiences in therapy. Using a form of social learning theory, he looked at the mechanisms and processes of change for individuals, and considered the stages in the program in terms of how this relates to an individual's internalization of new learning. More recently he has provided an account of how therapeutic communities have developed and changed their approaches, and how treatment models are currently organized in the USA (De Leon 2000; see also De Leon, this volume).

Nielson and Scarpitti (1997) criticized this social learning model, on the grounds that it describes the separate components of a program, and what these components are intended to do, rather than looking at the components in use. They argued that these components interact with each other, with the community and with the individuals, and that a more dynamic research method was needed to capture and understand this. They describe a process analysis which they carried out at the CREST Outreach Centre in Delaware, USA, in which they spent fifteen months in intensive fieldwork which involved participant observation, informal discussions with clients and staff members, formal interviews and analysis of formal documents relating to the program. From this they were able to identify the core elements of the program and show how they interacted with one another, and how this operated within the context of a sense of community and a set of rules and expectations. This very detailed description is one of the few attempts to apply qualitative research methods (i.e. research methods which describe processes rather than produce statistics) to the problems of evaluating a therapeutic community.

## Cost–benefit analysis

A different research approach is to use some form of cost–benefit analysis. This might entail comparing the cost of treating a client in one type of treatment compared to another (for example, is it cheaper to keep a drug user in prison or in a therapeutic community?). Cost–benefit analysis can be extended to evaluate treatment outcome, by providing a comparison of the costs of treating an individual and those of tolerating his or her civic behaviour before and after treatment.

In therapeutic community research, cost–benefit methods have mainly been used to ascertain the financial savings to the general community made through keeping drug users off the streets. Griffin (1983) looked at figures from Gaudenzia House, West Chester, USA. She estimated the costs relating to the clients' criminal lifestyle (costs of crime, imprisonment, etc.) and added these to the costs of their unemployment, and costs of street crime avoided during the residents' stay in the therapeutic community. Set against the costs of therapeutic community treatment, she estimated that over the five-year inclusive period 1982 to 1986, Gaudenzia House had saved the state a total of 9 million dollars. Gerstien (1992) reviewed several cost-benefit studies, and found that therapeutic communities were cost-beneficial compared to prisons, less cost-beneficial than methadone maintenance, cost-effective insofar as they reduced crime costs and unemployment costs, and paid for themselves by simply keeping street crime off the streets.

A cost–benefit methodology has also been applied to therapeutic communities in prisons. A study of the Comprehensive Alcohol and Substance Abuse Treatment Program (CASAT) by the State of New York Department of Correctional Services (1996) includes a preliminary model for ascertaining cost savings that may be attributed to the operation of the CASAT program. The CASAT initiative comprises seven therapeutic community-style facilities which each have 200 beds. The basic assumption of the model was that no CASAT inmate would have been approved for temporary release program participation without participation in the CASAT program. Thus the major savings calculated are the difference between the cost of temporary release, and the greater cost of full-time incarceration. While the in-prison therapeutic community treatment is more costly than general confinement, the earlier date of temporary release makes the CASAT program cheaper to run overall. Overall the authors estimated that approximately $153 million in cost savings to the Correctional Department has resulted from the operation of the CASAT program from its initiation in 1990 to the end of year 1996. The model is based solely on 'hotel' costs, and does not estimate other possible savings, such as lower costs of re-incarceration or lower costs of crime and unemployment.

A different cost–benefit methodology, known as cost-offset, has been used at Henderson Hospital in England, a democratic therapeutic community for personality-disordered clients. This method involves calculating the cost of services received by patients in the year before admission, calculating the cost of services received in the year after leaving, and comparing the difference with the cost of the residential therapeutic community treatment received at Henderson. Personality-disordered patients tend to have a particularly high level of unplanned service usage, such as prison and emergency medical and mental health services. In a study of 24 patients Dolan *et al.* (1996) found that the actual cost of psychiatric and penal services had dropped from £13,966 per person during the year before admission to £1,308 in the year after discharge. This represented a cost-offset of £12,658 per patient per year. Since the average cost of treatment at Henderson was £25,641 per year, treatment costs could be recouped within two years, and savings made thereafter.

### Research reviews and meta-analysis

Research reviews set out to collect up all the research on a particular subject, and describe the methods employed and the findings. They can be useful for finding out how much is known about a field, and what kind of research has generally been carried out. They cannot cover everything in the field, though, and usually the search criteria for studies is fairly narrow, so that the researcher is not overwhelmed by a wide variety of information. A study which examined the published research on methadone maintenance and therapeutic communities in America found that the most overwhelming evidence produced for therapeutic communities was that they could significantly affect the behaviour of clients, provided they retained them for several months. The actual number of months varied from program to program (Gerstein 1994). The study did not compare the two treatment modalities in terms of outcomes, but found that no single treatment 'works' for a majority of people who seek treatment. Provided a client found a treatment which worked for them, and stayed with it long enough, positive change would occur. Rawlings (1999) reviewed the research on democratic and concept-based therapeutic communities in prisons in Britain, Europe, North America and Canada, and concluded that therapeutic communities can reduce offending, but that outside of the USA they tend to be sparingly employed and in prisons especially are often short-lived.

A systematic literature review is a review of research carried out according to certain stringent criteria about what should be included and excluded, and is based on a model developed for medical research. Lees *et al.*

(1999) used this approach in an international study of therapeutic communities for personality disorder and mentally ill offenders. This study concluded with a meta-analysis of the collected research studies, which used further statistical tests on the original findings in order to summarize them. When subjected to this methodology, the studies showed strong evidence for the effectiveness of therapeutic communities. Meta-analysis is methodologically a complicated procedure, since different studies will use different research techniques and these may not be easy to compare with one another. However, studies of research findings can help to reduce the risks of relying on a single piece of research, and can help to increase confidence in findings which support one another.

*Large-scale studies*

In the USA, a large-scale comparative study, known as the Drug Abuse Reporting Program (DARP) was undertaken between 1969 and 1973, and looked at the progress of almost 44,000 admissions to 52 treatment programs. The programs were divided into types: therapeutic communities, methadone maintenance, outpatient drug-free and outpatients detoxification. In 1974, follow-up evaluation of clients began, and was carried out in stages so that different cohorts of the DARP clients could be compared. On average, clients were interviewed four years after termination of treatment. The study found that effective treatments were methadone maintenance, therapeutic communities and outpatients drug-free programs. Outpatients detoxification and a comparison no-treatment group had the poorest outcomes. The research found that the main predictor of success was the extent of previous criminal history – the lower the better. In addition, there was a positive correlation between the length of time in any program and outcome (Simpson and Sells 1982).

There is little to match this research output outside the USA. Recently however, two major projects have been initiated in Europet. NTORS (National Treatment Outcome Research Study) is a prospective longitudinal cohort study which is monitoring the progress of 1,075 clients who entered treatment in the UK in 1995. Four treatment modalities were selected to be representative of the main types of treatment in the UK: specialist inpatient, residential rehabilitation, methadone maintenance and methadone reduction. At one-year outcome, the research found that treatment in residential programs (these included inpatient and rehabilitation programs) had substantially decreased clients' use of opiates, psychostimulants and benzodiazepines. There were also improvements in related problem behaviours of injecting, sharing injecting equipment, heavy drinking and criminal behaviour at follow-up. The researchers noted that time in treatment is predictive of improved outcome and found that for longer-stay rehabilitation programs, the critical time was 90 days. They recommended that attempts to maximize the cost-effectiveness of residential services should not seek to reduce treatment duration, but to increase rates of client retention in treatment (Gossop *et al.* 1999). Outcomes at two-year follow-up are very similar to those found at one year. (NTORS: Bulletin 4, 2000).

The IPTRP (Improving Psychiatric Treatment in Residential Programs) is a project funded through the BIOMED II program of the European Commission and has partners in 9 universities and 33 residential treatment centres across Europe. The UK partner is the Scottish Drugs Training Project at the University of Stirling. The study aims to standardize psychiatric protocols for relapse prevention, and to provide information on the extent of co-morbidity or dual diagnosis among substance abusers. The final phase of this project will be an outcome study. Neither NTORS or IPTRP focus explicitly on therapeutic communities, but like some of the large American studies, therapeutic communities is one of the major treatments included.

## Major findings of evaluative research

### Time in treatment

In reviewing the literature, three findings stand out. The first is that the longer the amount of time spent in the program (shortened to TIP in some papers) the better the outcome. This finding has been repeatedly confirmed in successive studies (De Leon *et al.* 1979 and 1982: Simpson 1979 and 1980, Gossop *et al.* 1999), and has become widely accepted by practitioners. Occasionally, though, a new study may question this wisdom. For example, some recent work from Australia has suggested that it may not be simply the amount of time spent in treatment that predicts good outcome. Toumbourou *et al.* (1998) interviewed 255 ex-residents who had left Odyssey House in Melbourne between 1984 and 1988. These interviews were held an average of 5.6 years after their first entry to Odyssey House. They argue it is not so much the length of time spent in the program that is critical, as how much progress the resident had made in that time. Those who progressed faster tended to do better than those who had stayed just as long, but progressed slower. They conclude from this that level attainment on exit is a better predictor of outcome than time in treatment.

The finding that time in treatment is so critical to good outcome has sparked a number of issues. A methodological concern is that perhaps what is really going on is a self-selection of people who are better disposed to benefit from treatment, and that those who are less willing or able to change are the ones who leave early. This would equally well explain why longer treatment times lead to better outcomes. This concern has fed back into research and practice, with the development of admission policies designed to more accurately assess the 'circumstances, motivation, readiness and suitability' of clients (De Leon 1994), and with the design of modified therapeutic communities aimed at providing a regime which potential early leavers may be able to tolerate for longer. The thinking here is that if it is time in the program rather than predisposition which predicts good outcome, then the more time in treatment the better.

### The extent of co-morbidity

A second major finding is the extent of co-morbidity among drug users and the discovery through research that therapeutic communities may have been systematically losing particular groups of very damaged people through early leaving or strict admission criteria (De Leon 1989). This has led to substantial changes in aspects of therapeutic community programs, and in some cases the creation of modified programs for different client groups. (See Yates and Wilson, this volume.) Harbour House, for example, in the Bronx, New York, is a therapeutic community for homeless drug abusers with a mental health problem which employs a mix of mental health professionals and therapeutic community staff, and provides a regime gentler than that ordinarily found in a North American therapeutic community, and which is designed to cope with the psychotic episodes of the residents (McLaughlan and Pepper 1991).

### The added-value of aftercare programs

A third finding is that while prison inmates who complete treatment in a therapeutic community in prison do better than those who do not, those who go on from there to a therapeutic community on the outside, do very much better (Inciardi et al. 1997: Nielsen et al. 1996; Swartz et al. 1996; Wexler et al. 1995). This is closely related to the finding that time in treatment affects outcome, and has led to the creation of post-release therapeutic communities for prisoners. One of these, CREST (see Inciardi, this volume) was set up jointly between the University of Delaware and the prison services as a research experiment. The researchers have had opportunities to randomly allocate prisoners to CREST or to a conventional work-release centre, and as a result have been able to build up some robust evidence that therapeutic community treatment achieves far more positive results than conventional treatment.

## Conclusion

Over the past thirty years, a number of widely-used research methodologies have developed for concept-based therapeutic communities. Markers of successful outcome include reconviction, relapse and employment, and studies pay particular attention to client characteristics and the length of time clients spend in treatment. The extent of evaluative research is greatest in the USA, where research has been closely tied to treatment development and where large-scale studies have tended to confirm the findings of smaller studies.

## References

Anglin, D., Cardozo, A., Di Mienza, S., De Leon, G., Gawin, G., Havassey, B., Heaps, M., Hoffman, N., Hubbard, R., Inciardi, J., McBride, D., McClellan, T., McCloud, A., Miller, N. and Simpson, D. (1996) 'Treatment protocol effectiveness study.' *Journal of Substance Abuse Treatment 13*, 4, pp.297–319.

Anglin, M. D. and Hser, Y-I. (1992) 'Drug abuse treatment.' In R. R. Watson (ed) *Drug Abuse Treatment*. Totowa, NJ: Human Press.

De Leon, G. (1984) *The Therapeutic Community: Study of Effectiveness*. National Institute on Drug Abuse Research Monograph. DHHS Publication No. (ADM) 84–1286. Washington, DC: Supt. of Docs., U.S. Government Print Office.

De Leon, G. (1989) 'Psychopathology and substance abuse: what is being learned from research in therapeutic communities.' *Journal of Psychoactive Drugs 21*, 2, pp.177–187.

De Leon, G. (1994) 'The therapeutic community: toward a general model.' In F. M. Tims, G. De Leon and N. Jainchill (eds) *Therapeutic Community: Advances in Research and Application*. Government Printing Office, NIDA Research Monograph 144, pp. 16–53.

De Leon, G. (2000) *The Therapeutic Community: Theory, Model and Method*. New York: Springer Publishing Inc.

De Leon, G., Andrews, M., Wexler, H. K., Jaffe, J. and Rosenthal, M. S. (1979) 'Therapeutic community drop-outs: criminal behaviour 5 years after treatment'. *American Journal of Drug and Alcohol Abuse 6*, 3, pp.253–271.

De Leon, G., Wexler, H. and Jainhill, N. (1982) 'Success and improvement rates five years after treatment in a therapeutic community.' *International Journal of Addictions 17*, 4, pp.703–747.

Dolan, B., Warren, F.M., Menzies, D. and Norton, K. (1996) 'Cost-offset following specialist treatment of severe personality disorders.' *Psychiatric Bulletin 20*, pp.413–417.

Gerstein, D. R. (1992) 'The effectiveness of drug treatment.' In C. P. O'Brien and J. H. Jaffe (eds) *Addictive States*. Research Publications: Association for Research in Nervous Mental Disease, Vol. 70. New York: Raven Press.

Gerstein, D. R. (1994) 'Outcome research: drug abuse.' In M. Gallanter and H. D. Kleber (eds) *The American Psychiatric Press Textbook of Substance Abuse Treatment*. Washington, DC: American Psychiatric Press Inc.

Gossop, M., Marsden, J., Stewart, D. and Rolfe A. (1999) 'Treatment retention and one-year outcomes for residential programs in England.' *Drug and Alcohol Dependence 57*, pp.89–98.

Griffing, K. S. (1983) 'The therapeutic community: an exploratory cost benefit analysis'. *International Journal of Therapeutic Communities 4*, 4, pp.276–284.

Gunn, J., Robertson, G., Dell, S. and Way, C. (1978) *Psychiatric Aspects of Imprisonment*. London: Academic Press.

Holland, S. (1978) 'Gateway Houses: effectiveness of treatment on criminal behaviour.' *International Journal of the Addictions 13*, 3, pp.369–381.

Holland, S. (1983) 'Evaluating community-based treatment programs: a model for strengthening inferences about effectiveness.' *International Journal of Therapeutic Communities 4*, 4, pp.285–306.

Inciardi, J. A., Martin, S. S., Butzin, C. A., Hooper, R. M. and Harrison, L. D. (1997) 'An effective model of prison-based treatment for drug-involved offenders.' *Journal of Drug Issues 27*, 2, pp.261–278.

Kennard, D. (1998) *An Introduction to Therapeutic Communities.* London: Jessica Kingsley Publishers.

Knight, K., Simpson, D. D., Chatham, L. R. and Camacho, L. M. (1997) 'An assessment of prison-based drug treatment: Texas in-prison therapeutic community program.' *Journal of Offender Rehabilitation 24*, 3/4, pp.75–100.

Kooyman. M. (1993) *The Therapeutic Community for Addicts: Intimacy, Parent Involvement and Treatment Success.* Amsterdam: Swets and Zeitlinger.

Lees, J., Manning, N. and Rawlings, B. (1999) *Therapeutic Community Effectiveness: A Systematic International Review of Therapeutic Communities for People with Personality Disorders and Mentally Disordered Offenders.* CRD Report 17, NHS Centre for Reviews and Dissemination, University of York, England.

McLaughlin, P. and Pepper, B. (1991) 'Modifying the therapeutic community for the mentally ill substance abuser.' *New Directions for Mental Health Services 50*, pp.85–93.

Nielsen, A. L. and Scarpitti, F. R. (1997) 'Changing the behaviour of substance abusers: factors influencing the effectiveness of therapeutic communities.' *Journal of Drug Issues 27*, 2, pp.279–298.

Nielsen, A. L., Scarpitti, F. R. and Inciardi, J. A. (1996) 'Integrating the therapeutic community and work release for drug involved offenders: the CREST program.' *Journal of Substance Abuse Treatment 13*, 4, pp.349–358.

NTORS Bulletin 4 (2000) Internet site: http: //www.ntors.org.uk/ publications.htm

Rawlings, B. (1999) 'Therapeutic communities in prisons.' *Policy and Politics 27*, 1, pp.97–111.

Swartz, J. A., Lurigio, A. J. and Slomka, S. A. (1996) 'The impact of IMPACT: an assessment of the effectiveness of a jail-based treatment program.' *Crime and Delinquency 42*, 4, pp.553–573.

Simpson, D. D. (1979) 'The relation of the time in drug abuse treatment to post-treatment outcomes.' *American Journal of Psychiatry 136*, pp.1449–1453.

Simpson, D. D. (1980) *Follow-up Outcomes and Length of Time Spent in Treatment for Drug Abuse.* Fort Worth, Texas: Institute of Behavioural Research, Texas Christian University. (Cited in Wexler, H. K. and Love, C. T. (1994) 'Therapeutic Communities in Prison.' *NIDA Research Monograph 144*, pp.181–208.

Simpson, D. D. and Sells, S.B. (1982) 'Effectiveness of treatment for drug abuse: an overview of the DARP Research Program.' *Advances in Alcohol and Substance Abuse 2*, 1, pp.7–29.

State of New York Department of Correctional Services (1996) *The Comprehensive Alcohol and Substance Abuse Treatment Program, as of June 30, 1996.* New York, State of New York: Department of Correctional Services.

Toumbourou, J. W., Hamilton, M. and Fallon, B. (1998) 'Treatment level, progress and time spent in treatment in the prediction of outcomes following drug-free therapeutic community treatment.' *Addiction 93*, 7, pp.1051–1064.

Wexler, H. K., Falkin, G. P., Lipton, D. S. and Rosenblum, A. B. (1992) 'Outcome evaluation of a prison therapeutic community for substance abuse treatment.' *NIDA Research Monograph 118*, pp.156–175.

Wexler, H., Graham, W., Koronkowski, R., and Lowe, L. (1995) *Amity Therapeutic Community Substance Abuse Program: Preliminary Return to Custody Data: May 1995*. Report by the Office of Substance Abuse Programs. California: California Department of Corrections.

Wilson, S. (1977) 'An investigation of factors related to the outcome of treatment in a therapeutic community for drug dependence.' MSc. thesis, Oxford University. (Cited in Wilson, S. and Mandelbrote, B. (1978) 'Drug rehabilitation and criminality.' *British Journal of Criminology 18,* 4, pp. 381–386.

Wilson, S. and Mandelbrote, B. (1978) 'The relationship between duration of treatment in a therapeutic community for drug abusers and subsequent criminality.' *British Journal of Psychiatry 132,* pp.487–91.

# CHAPTER 13

# An outcome study of a therapeutic community based in the community: a five-year prospective study of drug abusers in Norway

*Edle Ravndal*

## Introduction

The hierarchical therapeutic community as a treatment model for drug abusers was introduced in Norway in the late 1970s. In 1982 the first Norwegian treatment program based on the Phoenix House model started with nine residents. Since then there have been established at most seven treatment programs in Norway based on the model. Phoenix House, Oslo, or Veksthuset, which was the first program, is based upon the Phoenix House model as it is formulated in England and in the United States (De Leon and Ziegenfuss 1986). The program is intended to provide treatment for substance abusers with a long history of addiction. The essential dynamic in the program is mutual self-help, work as therapy, peers as role models and staff as rational authorities.

In 1985, when an external program evaluation of Phoenix House, Oslo started, the program had a capacity of 38 beds. During the observation period the total treatment program lasted on average one-and-a-half years. The inpatient period, Phase 1, took one year, and the outpatient period lasted for half a year. The treatment in Phase 1 was an intensive, highly confrontational and group-oriented program, while in the outpatient period the program was less confrontational, and the clients attended only one group meeting once a week.

The subjects in the first study were 200 drug abusers who consecutively applied for treatment at Phoenix House, Oslo, during the years 1986–88 (Ravndal 1994a). None of the applicants were refused entry to treatment as long as they were able to attend a waiting group once a week and cut down on their drug abuse. The intake evaluation consisted of a structured research interview for background information, and completion of three self-report schedules measuring psychological health.

The main conclusions from the client part of the first study were that females completed the program significantly more often than males, that clients with a frequent use of amphetamines completed the program more often than clients with a frequent opiate use/polydrug use, and that clients with high scores on a dramatic personality style completed the first year of the program more often (Ravndal 1994a). Clients with a high frequency of schizotypal traits,[1] and clients with a high consumption of alcohol had a higher dropout rate than other clients. Also, clients with major depression, and clients with a typical antisocial personality style, more often dropped out during the last six months of the program (Ravndal 1994a).

Since there are few strong follow-up studies of this model, we decided in 1993 to follow up all the 200 clients who had been interviewed at application for treatment, on average, five years later. The instruments were mainly the same as we used in the first study. The follow-up study is a quasi-experimental study, where we are comparing non-beginners and dropouts with treatment completers. Since it is not an experimental study with a matched control group, we cannot come to final conclusions about the independent effect of therapeutic community (TC) treatment compared to other treatment or no treatment.

The present study aimed to examine five outcomes for those people who had applied to the program. These outcomes were:

o level of substance abuse

o level of social functioning

o overdoses

o suicide attempts

o death.

In order to understand the effect of background characteristics on these individual outcomes, background information on subjects was correlated with the five outcome criteria. Then in order to investigate the effect of the TC treatment on outcomes, further calculations were done which allowed the effect of 'treatment completion' to be isolated from the background characteristics, and assessed against the five outcome criteria. Thus the study identifies whether particular background characteristics and treatment completion can be used to predict outcomes for drug users.

## Material and methods
### Previously collected data
The original sample consisted of 200 subjects who consecutively applied for treatment in the period 1986–1988 at Phoenix House, Oslo. At application to the program all subjects (n = 200) had been personally interviewed according to a structured research interview covering socio-demographic data, family background, education, employment, substance abuse, legal problems, social adjustment, treatment received, prostitution and sexual assaults. All substance use had been recorded as frequency of use during the six months prior to application. Alcohol use had been calculated as litres of pure alcohol consumed during the six months before application. In addition the subjects had completed two self-report instruments measuring personality disorders and psychopathology: the Millon Clinical Multiaxial Inventory (MCMI-I) (Millon 1982) and the Symptom Checklist–90 (SCL–90) (Derogatis et al. 1973).[2] Clients who scored as 'cases' on the depression subscale on both SCL–90 and the MCMI Dysthymia scale were then defined as 'depressed clients' (Ravndal and Vaglum 1994b).

### Characteristics of this original sample
The mean age of the original 200 subjects was 27.5 years (range: 18–46); 31 % were women. Drugs had been used for an average of 10.4 years (range: 1–22). During the last six months before application, 78% had used opiates and 70% had used amphetamines. Sixty-seven per cent had been in prison. Seventy-one per cent of the clients were classified as depressive. With regard to personality disorders, the highest scores on the MCMI were found on the passive–aggressive[3] (BR score 86) and the borderline[4] (BR score 80) scales (Ravndal and Vaglum 1991).

### Entering and completing treatment
After the intake evaluation, one hundred and forty-four of the 200 subjects actually entered the program. Of these, forty-three clients (30%) completed the one year inpatient phase, and twenty-nine clients (20%) completed the 1½ year program.

## The follow-up sample

The follow-up study consisted of all 200 drug abusers, on average five years (mean = 5.9; range: 4.3–7.2 years) after application to treatment. Twenty-two persons died before the follow-up study started, and two before we were able to interview them in 1993, in all 12.4%. One person had emigrated to an unknown country. We tried to contact the remaining 175 persons by mail through addresses obtained from Statistics Norway, through the social security system and through the prison administration. One hundred and thirty-nine of 175 possible live subjects were personally interviewed (79%), and twenty-seven persons did not want to take part in the study for various reasons.

## Data collection

At follow-up 139 persons were personally interviewed using a structured schedule. The interview covered, among other things, accommodation, employment/education, economy, marital status, social network, substance abuse and criminality. As for psychopathology, the clients completed the MCMI-I and SCL–25 for a second time.

Substance use was registered by the same kind of questions as were asked at application to treatment, but now the questions covered frequency of use of all substances for the whole year prior to the follow-up interview. Based on this information we constructed a weighted index which divided the use of substances into light, moderate and heavy use. *Light* use is defined as no use, or the use of some of the substances at most two to three times yearly, *moderate* use as a few times a month or less, and *heavy* use as several times a week, daily or almost daily. Use of cannabis and alcohol several times a week qualifies for the moderate group, while corresponding use of psychoactive drugs, amphetamines and/or opiates qualifies for the heavy group.

We also used a rating scale for social functioning, constructed by Petersen (1974) and used in previous Scandinavian studies of drug abusers (Holsten 1984; Ravndal, Hammer and Vaglum 1984; Vaglum 1979). The scale of 1–5 covered housing, work and education, treatment, employment, and social life during the year prior to the follow-up interview.

The interviews lasted between two and four hours, depending on the subjects' psychological and social condition. Most of the people in the sample were interviewed in their own home. Some were interviewed in prison, in treatment institutions or in cafés. Each person received two hundred Norwegian kroner for being interviewed. Ten trained interviewers took part, most of them students majoring in social science and/or with experience of working with substance abusers.

## Results

### Gender, age, place of residence

Of the 139 interviewed subjects 37 (27%) were women. The average age was 33 years (range: 24–52 years). At follow-up approximately 45% were living in Oslo, the rest all over the country.

### Status in the treatment program

Of the 29 persons who had completed the total 1½ year Phoenix House program, 26 were interviewed. Two of the completers had died prior to the follow-up, both women. Of the 115 clients who started in the program, but dropped out, eighty (70%) were followed up. Of the 56 who never started treatment, 33 (59%) were followed up.

Because non-beginners and dropouts from the program had almost similar scores on the substance use index the year prior to follow-up, we combined them into a non-completion group (NC-group = 113), to be compared with the group of completers of the program (C-group = 26).

### Outcome criterion 1: substance abuse

#### Substance abuse by all subjects during the year prior to follow-up

Since we knew that almost all the subjects who had died (n = 24) had died in connection with heavy substance use, and 15 of the persons we tried to interview, but who broke all appointments or said no, had a heavy substance use the year prior to follow-up, we decided to add these two groups to the group with heavy substance use. Using this procedure, 20% had no use or light use of substances at follow-up, 25% moderate use, and 56% had heavy use or were deceased (n = 178). There were no significant gender differences.

Using this information on substance abuse, we divided the subjects into two groups: a 'good outcome group' (no or light use) and a 'poor outcome group' (moderate or heavy use). We then compared these groups to the C-Group and the NC-Group. Thirty-six per cent in the C-group had a good outcome, as opposed to 17% of the NC-group (p<0.5). There were no significant gender differences.

We have previously reported that being a woman, having low scores on MCMI schizotypal, having frequent use of amphetamines and an infrequent use of alcohol before start of treatment, were significantly correlated with completion of the program (Ravndal and Vaglum 1991). We now found that frequent use of amphetamines before start of treatment was also correlated to a good five-year outcome (no use or light use) (p<0.5). The correlation was strongest among the women (p<0.1). There was also a positive correlation for men between frequent use of alcohol before start of treatment and a poor outcome (heavy use) at five-year follow-up (p<0.5).

*Effects of background characteristics and treatment completion on substance abuse*

The next stage was to isolate and assess the effect of these particular background variables (gender; alcohol and amphetamine use; MCMI scores) and treatment completion on substance abuse. In theory, if any significant relationship could be established between some of these variables and substance abuse, when corrected for the others, then these could be used to make predictions about which kinds of people might become heavy substance abusers, and which might not. The method used for this assessment was logistic regression analysis.[5] This involved devising a model in which gender, frequency of amphetamine and alcohol use, MCMI score and treatment completion were entered and compared. Of these, the only significant predictor was amphetamine use. When treatment completion and gender were corrected for, clients who had made frequent use of amphetamines before start of treatment had 3.4 more chances of having no or light use of substances at follow-up than clients without frequent use of amphetamines.

## Outcome criterion 2: social functioning

### Social functioning the year prior to follow-up

The social functioning scale used goes from 1 (low) to 5 (high). The five areas covered are: own dwelling or living at home; in work/school or part-time work; earns his/her own living or receives sickness benefit; not receiving treatment; no contact with a drug-abusing milieu. A positive response to all five areas indicates an optimal social condition and scores the full five points.

The average score on social functioning, the year prior to follow-up, was 1.9 in the sample that was interviewed (n = 139). Only 31% of the sample had a score of 3 to 5, and 69% a score of 0 to 2. There were no gender differences. There was no significant difference in the score for social functioning between the clients in the 'good outcome group' (no use or light use) (mean 2.1) compared with the 'poor outcome group' (heavy use) (mean 1.8).

There was no difference in the score for social functioning the year prior to follow-up between the subjects who did not start treatment and the dropouts from treatment. They were therefore combined into the same group (NC-group). The C-group scored significantly higher on social functioning (mean 2.4) the year prior to follow-up than the NC-group (mean 1.8) (p<0.5). When men and women in the C-group and NC-group were compared separately, we found that the women in the C-group scored significantly higher on social functioning (mean 2.3) than the women in the NC-group (mean 1.4) (p<0.1). Among the men in the corresponding groups, there were no significant differences.

*Effect of background characteristics and treatment completion on social functioning*

Again, logistic regression analysis was used in order to investigate whether background characteristics or treatment completion could predict relatively 'good' social functioning (score: 3–5) the year prior to follow-up. The previously identified background characteristics (gender, MCMI score, use of amphetamines and alcohol before start of treatment) and treatment completion were entered and compared. Only treatment completion had a significant independent impact as predictor. The best model consisted of two predictors: treatment completion and gender. When corrected for the influence of gender on social functioning, clients in the C-group had 2.7 more chances than clients in the NC-group for having a score between 3 and 5 on social functioning.

Then we repeated the analysis with a bigger sample (n = 178), including the deceased (n = 24) and a group of un-interviewed clients (n = 15), who we knew all had heavy substance abuse problems when they died during the follow-up year. They were therefore included in the poor social functioning group (0–2). Now the chances for having 'good' social functioning among completers of the program was even higher (3.7 against 2.7). Gender was, then, also significant as predictor. When corrected for the influence of treatment completion, males had 2.5 more chances than females for having 'good' social functioning at follow-up.

*Outcome criterion 3: overdoses*

*Overdoses before application and during the observation period*

During the five years observation period 40 persons out of 139 (29%) reported they had been hospitalized for accidental overdoses. Of these 40 persons, 21 (53%) had also taken overdoses before application to treatment.

*Relationship between background characteristics and overdoses*

There were no significant differences in background data before application to treatment between these clients and the rest of the sample. The number of years with a daily use of hard drugs before application was not related to overdoses, but number of years with a daily use of hard drugs in the observation period was related to overdoses ($p < 0.5$). However, frequency of use of opiates in the observation period was not related to overdoses.

*Relationship between treatment completion and overdoses*

Only six of the program completers (11%) had overdosed during the observation time, compared with 20 of the non-completers (24%). There was no difference between the number of times those in the C-group and those in the NC-group took overdoses in the observation period.

To investigate if treatment completion could have an independent impact on overdoses in the observation period, logistic regression analysis was used. In the model we corrected for the possible simultaneous influence of gender, age, and number of years with daily use of hard drugs in the observation period. When correcting for the other variables, treatment completion could not predict overdoses. The only variable which was found to have a significant impact on overdoses after treatment was number of years with daily use of hard drugs during the observation period.

## Outcome criterion 4: suicide attempts

*Suicide attempts before application and during the observation period*

38 persons out of 139 (27%) reported having attempted suicide during the observation period (the 'suicide-group'). All of these clients, except for nine, also reported having attempted suicide once or more before application for treatment.

*Relationship between background characteristics and suicide attempts*

As for background data before application to treatment, only the total length of time in prison significantly differentiated between clients who made later suicide attempts, and those who did not. To establish this, the mean time for those who had spent less time in prison (6 months) was compared with the mean time of those who had spent more time in prison (19 months). We found that clients who had spent less time altogether in prison before applying for treatment committed significantly more suicide attempts during the observation time (6 months *vs* 19 months, $p < 0.5$).

*Relationship between psychopathology and suicide attempts*

We began this part of the analysis by looking at the effects of depression and MCMI scores on suicide attempts separately. In the 'suicide-group', 79% (n = 74) of the clients were depressed at application, compared to 60% (n = 64) in the 'non-suicide group'. However, there was no correlation between MCMI borderline, or other MCMI scores at application, and suicide attempts.

Because stability of suicidal behaviour has been found in subgroups of borderline patients (Mehlum *et al.* 1994), we wanted to investigate the relationship between depression, borderline and suicide attempts further. We therefore looked at the effects of different combinations of depression and MCMI borderline on suicide attempts. We divided the material into a depressive group (n = 90) and a non-depressive group (n = 49). Among the depressive clients, who were not cases on borderline, 67% (n = 8) had attempted suicide, while among the depressive clients who were also cases on borderline, only 28% (n = 22) had attempted suicide (see Table 13.1). Among the clients who were neither depressed nor cases on borderline, 14% (n = 6) had attempted suicide, while among clients who were only a case on borderline, 40% (n = 2) had attempted suicide.

Table 13.1: Percentages of those attempting suicide during the observation period in each group.

|  | Borderline | Not borderline |
|---|---|---|
| Depressive | 28% | 67% |
| Not depressive | 40% | 14% |

*Relationship between treatment completion and suicide attempts*

Only 8% of the 'suicide group' completed the treatment program compared to 23% (n = 24) in the 'non-suicide group'. As for number of suicide attempts in the observation period, non-completers of the treatment program had attempted suicide more often (0.6 attempts) than completers (0.1 attempts).

To investigate if treatment completion could have an independent impact on suicide in the observation period, logistic regression analysis was used. To do this, we constructed a psychopathology variable with the following four categories: 0 – not depressed and not borderline; 1 – depressed but not borderline; 2 – depressed and borderline; 3 – not depressed but borderline.

We then constructed a model into which we entered gender, age, treatment completion, the psychopathology variable (depression/border-line) and number of years in prison before application to treatment. Lifetime suicide attempts at application to treatment was left out of the model because there was such a strong correlation between previous suicide attempts and suicide attempts in the observation period that the more subtle correlations with the other variables would have been obscured. We found that both the psychopathology variable and treatment completion were significant inde-pendent predictors.

When the other variables in the model were corrected for, clients who were depressed but not borderline had 19.4 more chances of attempting suicide in the observation period compared with clients who were neither depressed nor borderline. When all the other predictors in the model were corrected for, clients who had completed the treatment program had only 0.20 chances for committing suicide attempts in the observation period, compared with non-completers. This last finding suggests that this lower likelihood of attempting suicide is a treatment effect regardless of pathology.

*Outcome criterion 5: death*

### The deceased clients

Altogether 24 persons (12.4%) had died by the end of 1993; 16% (n = 10) of the women were dead, and 10% (n = 14) of the men. The average age was 30 years (range: 21–37 years). The women were on average three years younger than the men when they died (28 against 31 years) (p<0.5). Almost half of the subjects lived in Oslo.

For half of the group the primary cause of death was directly related to substance abuse, while for the other half death was caused more indirectly from substance abuse problems. Only two persons died from AIDS, while two others were HIV-infected, but died from other causes. For four persons the cause of death is unknown.

Two of the 29 completers (7%) of the program and 22 (13%) of the 171 non-beginners/completers were dead. The average time between the intake interview and the time of death was 33 months (range: 0–76 months) (48 months among completers compared to 32 months among non-completers). Before application to treatment the deceased clients had spent significantly more time in inpatient treatment than the rest of the sample (mean: 14 months as against 7 months) (p<0.5). Significantly more of them had overdoses (64% as against 39%) (p<0.5). When compared to the rest of the sample, the greater amount of time the deceased people had spent in prison before application was almost significant (mean: 24 months as against 14 months). There was no significant difference in the number of suicide attempts before application to treatment between the deceased group and the rest of the sample.

As for psychopathology measured at application, the deceased clients had significantly higher scores on MCMI passive-aggressive ($p<0.5$), antisocial ($p<0.5$), and almost on histrionic ($p = 0.05$) and narcissistic ($p = 0.06$), which group together into a dramatic/impulsive cluster. They also scored significantly lower than the rest of the sample on MCMI compulsive ($p<0.5$).

To investigate which variables had an independent relationship with death, logistic regression analysis was used. We found that none of the variables that were related to a good outcome at follow-up (no or light substance abuse), including completion of treatment, were related to death, either positively or negatively.

We then investigated the predictive power of the MCMI personality variables together with gender, overdoses, time in prison, treatment before application, and treatment completion. We found that a high narcissistic score, a greater length of time spent in prison, and gender (female) had a significant impact as predictors. Specifically these were as follows. When time in prison, gender and treatment completion were corrected for, persons with high scores on narcissistic (above 75) had 4.8 more chances of dying compared with persons with lower scores on the scale. The likelihood of dying for persons who had spent 25 months or more in prison, before the intake interview, was 3.7 compared with those who had spent less time in prison, when correcting for the other variables in the model. As for gender, females had 2.9 more chances of dying compared with males, when corrected for the narcissistic score, time in prison and treatment completion.

## Discussion

The present follow-up study builds on a prospective treatment study of 200 drug abusers applying for treatment at Phoenix House, Oslo. The follow-up rate was 79%. The study aimed to identify predictors of five outcomes: level of substance abuse; level of social functioning; overdoses; suicide attempts; and death.

In the year prior to follow-up, 20% of the sample had no or light use of substances and 56% had heavy use. (This heavy use group included the deceased group, which made up 12.4% of the sample.) In a similar five-year follow-up study of 141 drug abusers in Oslo in 1983 (Ravndal *et al.* 1984), 27% of the sample was drug-free the year prior to follow-up and 26% had heavy substance use or had died (9%). This group of drug abusers was very similar in background characteristics to our sample, but with a lower mean age. The poorer outcome in our sample may partly be connected to a different social and cultural situation for Norwegian drug abusers in the 1990s compared to the 1980s. Today more drugs are available at lower prices, and there is more unemployment, more violence and more crime. On the other hand our results are much in line with international follow-up studies of drugs abusers who have been in treatment, indicating that only a small percentage (20–22%) report abstinence from all substances for at least a year (Hser, Anglin, Powers 1993; Oppenheimer, Sheehan and Taylor 1990). Altogether there are few tendencies in our study which indicate that the percentage of drug-free persons, or those with light substance use, increases as the years go by, or that drug abusers 'mature out' of substance abuse problems. This is in accordance with other treatment studies of drug abusers (Haastrup and Jepsen 1988; Hser *et al.* 1993; Maddux and Desmond 1980).

Frequent use of amphetamines was the only significant baseline predictor of a 'good outcome' (no or light substance use) at follow-up. It was also the best predictor for completion of the inpatient year of the program (Ravndal and Vaglum 1991). At application to treatment, there were no gender differences or differences in background characteristics or personality disorders which could indicate that the frequent amphetamine users were less socially deprived than the non-frequent users. Swedish follow-up studies show that the prognosis is far better for amphetamine users than for opiate users, when background characteristics have been corrected for (Frykholm 1980; Berglund *et al.* 1991; Ågren *et al.* 1993). One explanation of our finding may be, as indicated in the literature, that the use of opiates is far more intense than use of amphetamines (Ravndal 1994a), and therefore has more negative biological and social consequences. This suggests that it is not that a different kind of person chooses amphetamines in preference to opiates, but that it is something about the use or effects of amphetamines which predisposes their users to better outcomes. Significantly more of the subjects who had completed treatment had 'good' outcomes (no or light substance use, and high scores on social functioning) the year prior to follow-up than non-completers of the program, and only a few had died.

Treatment completion could not, however, predict which persons might become light users of substances at follow-up, because the effect of frequent use of amphetamines on a 'good' outcome (no or light substance use) was much stronger.

On the other hand, treatment completion was the only variable that could predict 'good' social functioning the year prior to follow-up. The finding indicates that this type of treatment program exerts its main influence on social functioning and only indirectly on substance use. This may also indicate that systematic training in how to abstain from different drugs and alcohol is not emphasized adequately in the Phoenix House model. This was, in fact, observed in our qualitative study of the program (Ravndal and Vaglum 1994c).

During the five years' observation period 29% reported having been hospitalized for overdoses. Fewer of the completers of the treatment program had overdosed during the observation period than non-completers, but the difference was not significant. However, our material is small and firm conclusions should be avoided. Twenty-seven per cent reported having attempted suicide during the observation period. Almost significantly fewer of the completers of the program had committed suicide attempts, and they had also committed fewer suicide attempts than the non-completers in the observation period. Most persons who had attempted suicide during the observation period were found among depressive, non-borderline cases at application (67%), and not in the group that were both depressive and borderline (28%). This may indicate that the depression reported by the borderline cases seems to be more fluctuating and less serious than the depression reported by non-borderline persons. This is in line with the assumptions of Gunderson and Phillips (1991) that there is a surprisingly weak and non-specific relationship between depression and borderline disorder.

Completion of treatment also reduced the risk of suicide attempts in the observation period. Although this is not an experimental study, it indicates that adequate treatment interventions for this subgroup might be of great importance to hinder further risk of suicide attempts. In depressive, non-borderline clients, it seems that depression should be treated in order to prevent further suicide attempts, while in borderline clients it seems to be impulsivity, rather than depression, that should be the main focus (Linehan et al. 1991).

Twenty-four persons (12.4%) had died during the observation period, which represents a yearly death rate of 2.4%. When compared to a yearly death rate of 1.8% in our former treatment study in the late 1970s and the beginning of the 1980s (Ravndal et al. 1984), the increase has been relatively small. A death rate of two per cent per year has been usual in this population for years, both in Scandinavia and internationally (Oppenheimer et al. 1994; Rossow 1994; Tunving 1988; Vaillant 1988). This finding is important. We would have expected a higher death rate, since our sample consists of an older age group, where most sudden deaths are supposed to occur. Also taking into consideration the low abstinence rate, the poor social functioning and the fact that there was almost no methadone treatment in Norway at the time, the death rate is lower than we would have predicted.[6]

Contrary to what we expected, the women had a higher chance of dying than the men, and at a significantly younger age. Considering that being female was one of the best predictors for completing the treatment program (Ravndal and Vaglum 1991), this finding is worrying, but is in line with another Norwegian study of death among drug abusers (Rossow and Kielland 1995), which showed that the excess mortality was greater among women below thirty years of age than among men. This may indicate that stigmatization and marginalization are greater for female drug abusers than for male abusers. Almost twice as many of the non-completers of the program were dead at follow-up compared with the completers. However, treatment completion was not significant as a predictor of death, but having a narcissistic or antisocial personality style was. Analysis of the original test scores of those who had died showed that all scales in the dramatic cluster were highly correlated. It seems, then, that a self-reported impulsive/dramatic personality style is important information in relation to risk of death.

## Summary and recommendations

Altogether these findings indicate that clients who completed the Phoenix House program had fewer substance abuse problems and better social functioning at five-year follow-up than those who had not entered the program or had dropped out. Fewer completers had overdosed or attempted suicide during the observation period and fewer of them were dead. However, the findings indicate that there should be more emphasis on systematic training in how to control the use of substances. We would also recommend a long-term outpatient program of social skills training, aiming at following these clients for years. Our findings also underscore the importance of diagnosing psychopathology because of its influence on both suicide attempts and death.

The study has certain methodological limitations. It has a small sample, and it is not an experimental study with a matched control group. However, by comparing treatment completers with a group who had either not started treatment, or who dropped out of treatment, and by isolating the effect of treatment completion from the effects of other variables, we were able to show the effect of treatment completion on substance abuse, social functioning, overdoses, suicide attempts and mortality. Despite some methodological weaknesses, the study provides further evidence for treatment effectiveness.

## Notes

1. Socially detached, eccentric behaviour; emotional flatness.

2. The MCMI comprises a 175 true–false item inventory based on Millon's theory of personality. It consists of 20 clinical scales, which are designed to reflect the integration of longstanding personality characteristics and symptoms of briefer duration. Scores on the MCMI are reported as base rate (BR) scores. A BR score of 75–84 indicates that a particular trait is present, and a BR score of 60 represents the median score for all patients in the original normative group.

The SCL–90 is a 90-item self-report inventory with nine subscales, for assessing different types of current mental symptoms.

3. Unstable and rapidly changeable emotional state, behavioural contrariness, discontented self-image.

4. Very unstable and rapidly changeable mood; impulsivity. Is either depressed or excited or has recurring periods of dejection and apathy interspersed with spells of anger, anxiety or euphoria. Reveals recurring self-mutilating and suicidal thoughts.

5. With logistic regression, the statistician looks at the relationship of one variable and the dependent variable, while simultaneously correcting for the relationship of the others to the dependent variable. This produces an expression (odds ratio) for how strong the relationship is between this variable and the dependent variable. Thus the effect of each separate variable can be isolated, and its strength assessed.

6. The lack of methadone treatment is included here as a factor because it is known that methadone, in combination with psychosocial treatment, may have given these older drug abusers a better life and a lower risk of death. In Norway the overdose rate among older drug abusers is very high, compared to countries like Denmark and the Netherlands, where methodone has been used for many years.

## References

Ågren, G., Anderzon, K., Berglund, E. and Dundar, A. (1993) *Narkotika i Stockholm (Narcotics in Stockholm)*. Stockholm: FoU-byrån, Socialtjänsten, Report 17.

Berglund, G. W., Bergmark, A., Björling, B., Grönbladh, L., Lindberg, S., Oscarsson, L., Olsson, B., Segraeus, V. and Stensmo, C. (1991) 'The SWEDATE-project: interaction between treatment, client background, and outcome in a one-year follow-up.' *Journal of Substance Abuse Treatment 8*, pp.161–169.

De Leon, G. and Jainchill, N. (1981–82) 'Male and female drug abusers: social and psychological status two years after treatment in a therapeutic community.' *American Journal of Drug and Alcohol Abuse 8*, pp.465–479.

De Leon, G. and Ziegenfuss, J. T. (eds) (1986) *Therapeutic Communities for Addictions*. Springfield, IL: Charles C. Thomas.

Derogatis, L. R., Lipman, R. S. and Covi, L. (1973) 'SCL-90: an outpatient psychiatric rating scale – preliminary report.' *Psychopharmacology Bulletin 9*, pp.13–28.

Frykholm, B. (1980) 'Changes in short-term prognosis – a comparison between Swedish amphetamine and opiate abusers.' *Drug and Alcohol Dependence 5*, pp.123–128.

Gunderson, J. G. and Phillips, K. A. (1991) 'A current view of the interface between borderline personality disorder and depression.' *American Journal of Psychiatry 148*, pp.967–975.

Haastrup, S. and Jepsen, P. W. (1988) 'Eleven years follow-up of 300 young opioid addicts.' *Acta Psychiatrica Scandinavica 77*, pp.22–26.

Holsten, F. (1984) *Forløpet ved stoffmisbruk hos ungdom. En etterundersøkelse (The progress of drug abuse in adolescents)*. Oslo: National Institute for Alcohol and Drug Research. Thesis.

Hser, Y. I., Anglin, M. D. and Powers, K. (1993) 'A 24-year follow-up of California narcotics addicts.' *Archives of General Psychiatry 50*, pp.577–584.

Linehan, M. M., Armstrong, H. E., Suarez, A., Allmon, D. and Heard, H. L. (1991) 'Cognitive-behavioural treatment of chronically parasuicidal borderline patients.' *Archives of General Psychiatry 48*, pp.1060–1064.

Maddux, J. F. and Desmond, D. P. (1980) 'Few light on the maturing out hypothesis in opioid dependence.' *Bulletin on Narcotics 32*, pp.15–25.

Mehlum, L., Friis, S., Vaglum, P. and Karterud, S. (1994) 'The longitudinal pattern of suicidal behaviour in borderline personality disorder: a prospective follow-up study.' *Acta Psychiatrica Scandinavica 90*, pp.124–130.

Millon, T. (1982) *The Millon Clinical Multiaxial Inventory Manual*. Minneapolis: National Computer Systems.

Oppenheimer, E., Sheehan, M. and Taylor, C. (1990) 'What happens to drug misusers? A medium-term follow-up of subjects new to treatment.' *British Journal of Addiction 85*, 1, pp.255–1260.

Oppenheimer, E., Tobutt, C., Taylor, C. and Andrew, T. (1994) 'Death and survival in a cohort of heroin addicts from London clinics: a 22-year follow-up study.' *Addiction 89*, pp.1299–1308.

Petersen, E. (1974) *Stofmisbrugere – frivillig behandling (Drug abusers – voluntary treatment)*. København: Mentalhygienisk Forlag.

Ravndal, E. (1994a) *Drug Abuse, Psychopathology and Treatment in a Hierarchical Therapeutic Community. A Prospective Study*. University of Oslo: Department of Behavioural Sciences in Medicine.

Ravndal, E., Hammer, T. and Vaglum, P. (1984) *Arbeid isteden for rus? Om arbeidstrening, arbeid og rusmiddelbruk (Work instead of drugs? About vocational training, work and drug abuse)*. Oslo: University Press.

Ravndal. E. and Vaglum, P. (1991) 'Psychopathology and substance abuse as predictors of program completion in a hierarchical therapeutic community.' *Acta Psychiatrica Scandinavica 83*, pp.217–222.

Ravndal, E. and Vaglum, P. (1994b) 'Self-reported depression as a predictor of dropout from a hierarchical therapeutic community.' *Journal of Substance Abuse Treatment 11*, pp.471–479.

Ravndal, E. and Vaglum, P. (1994c) 'Why do drug abusers leave the therapeutic community? Problems with attachment and identification in a hierarchical therapeutic community.' *Nordic Journal of Psychiatry*, Supplement 33, 48, pp.4–55.

Rossow, I. (1994) 'Suicide among drug addicts in Norway.' *Addiction 89*, pp.1667–1774.

Rossow, I. and Kielland, K. B. (1995) 'Dødlighet blant stoffmisbrukere i Norge (Mortality among drug abusers in Norway).' *Tidsskrift for Den Norske Lægeforening 115*, pp.1050–1054.

Tunving, K. (1988) 'Fatal outcome in drug addiction.' *Acta Psychiatrica Scandinavica 77*, pp.551–556.

Vaglum, P. (1979) *Unge stoffmisbrukere i et terapeutisk samfunn (Young drug abusers in a therapeutic community)*. Oslo: University Press.

Vaillant, G. E. (1988) 'What can long-term follow-up teach us about relapse and prevention of relapse in addiction?' *British Journal of Addiction 83*, pp.1147–1157.

# CHAPTER 14

# Therapeutic communities in prisons and work release: effective modalities for drug-involved offenders

*James A. Inciardi, Steven S. Martin and Hilary L. Surratt*

## Introduction

The problems of implementing drug treatment programs in correctional settings is often difficult because, despite any arguments to the contrary, the primary task of prisons is custody. The internal order of the prison is maintained by strictly controlling the inmates and regimenting every aspect of their lives. In addition to their loss of freedom and basic liberties, goods and services, heterosexual relationships and autonomy, they are deprived of their personal identities. Upon entering prison, inmates are stripped of their clothing and most of their personal possessions; and they are examined, inspected, weighed, documented, classified, and given a number. Thus, prison becomes painful, both physically and psychologically (Clemmer 1958; Sykes 1965).

The rigours and frustrations of confinement leave but a few paths open to inmates. They can bind themselves to their fellow captives in ties of mutual aid and loyalty, in opposition to prison officials. They can wage a war against all, seeking their own advantage without reference to the needs and claims of others. Or they can simply withdraw into themselves. Ideally, these alternatives exist only in an abstract sense, and most inmates combine characteristics of the first two extremes. Within this balance of extremes an inmate social system emerges and functions, and one of the fundamental elements of this social system is the prison subculture.

Every correctional facility has its subculture, and every prison subculture has its system of norms that influence prisoners' behaviour, typically to a far greater extent than the institution's formally prescribed rules. These subcultural norms are informal and unwritten rules, but their violation can evoke sanctions from fellow inmates ranging from simple ostracism to physical violence and death. Many of the rules revolve around relations among inmates and interactions with prison staff, while others reflect preoc-cupations with being 'smart,' 'tough,' and streetwise. As such, this prison code often tends to militate against reform in general, and drug rehabilitation in particular (Inciardi, Lockwood and Martin 1991).

In addition, there are many other phenomena in the prison environment that make rehabilitation difficult. Not surprisingly, the availability of drugs in prisons is a pervasive problem. Moreover, in addition to the one-to-one assaults that seems to be a concomitant of prison life, there is the violence as-sociated with inmate gangs, often formed along racial lines for the purposes of establishing and maintaining status, 'turf,' and unofficial control over certain sectors of the penitentiary. Within this setting, it would appear that if any drug rehabilitation approach had a chance of succeeding, it would be the therapeutic community.

## Therapeutic communities in prisons

The therapeutic community is a total treatment environment that can be isolated from the rest of the prison population – separated from the drugs, the violence, and the norms and values that rebuff attempts at rehabilitation. Like therapeutic communities in free society, the primary clinical staff of the therapeutic community are typically former substance abusers – 'recovering addicts' – who themselves were rehabilitated in therapeutic communities. The treatment perspective of the prison therapeutic community is also the same, that drug abuse is a disorder of the whole person – that the problem is the person and not the drug, that addiction is a symptom and not the essence of the disorder. In the prison therapeutic community's view of recovery, the primary goal is to change the negative patterns of behaviour, thinking and feeling that predispose towards drug use. As such, the overall goal is a re-sponsible, drug-free lifestyle (De Leon and Ziegenfuss 1986; Yablonsky 1989).

## The staging of prison-based therapeutic community treatment

Based on experiences with correctional systems and populations, with prison-based drug treatment, and with the evaluation of a whole variety of correctional programs, it would appear that the most appropriate strategy for effective therapeutic community intervention with inmates would involve a three-stage process (Inciardi, Lockwood and Martin 1991). Each stage in this regimen of treatment would correspond to the inmate's changing correctional status – incarceration, work release, and parole (or whatever other form of community-based correction operates in a given jurisdiction).

## The primary stage

The primary stage should consist of a prison-based therapeutic community designed to facilitate personal growth through the modification of deviant lifestyles and behaviour patterns. Segregated from the rest of the penitentiary, recovery from drug abuse and the development of pro-social values in the prison therapeutic community would involve essentially the same mechanisms seen in community-based therapeutic communities. Therapy in this primary stage should be an ongoing and evolving process. Ideally, it should endure for nine to twelve months, with the potential for the resident to remain longer, if necessary. As such, recruits for the therapeutic community should be within 18 months of their work release date at the time of treatment entry.

It is important that therapeutic community treatment for inmates should begin while they are still in the institution, for a number of reasons. In a prison situation, time is one of the few resources that most inmates have an abundance of. The competing demands of family, work, and the neighbourhood peer group are absent. Thus, there is the time and opportunity for comprehensive treatment – perhaps for the first time in a drug offender's career. In addition, there are other new opportunities presented – to interact with 'recovering addict' role models; to acquire pro-social values and a positive work ethic; and to initiate a process of education, training, and understanding of the addiction cycle.

Since the 1970s, work release has become a widespread correctional practice for felony offenders. It is a form of partial incarceration whereby inmates are permitted to work for pay in the free community but must spend their non-working hours either in the institution, or, more commonly, in a community-based work release facility or 'halfway house'. Inmates qualified for work release are those approaching their parole eligibility or conditional release dates. Although graduated release of this sort carries the potential for easing an inmate's process of community reintegration, there is a negative side, especially for those whose drug involvement served as the key to the penitentiary gate in the first place.

This initial freedom exposes many inmates to groups and behaviours that can easily lead them back to substance abuse, criminal activities, and reincarceration. Even those receiving intensive therapeutic community treatment while in the institution face the prospect of their recovery breaking down. Work release environments in most jurisdictions do little to stem the process of relapse. Since work release populations mirror the institutional populations from which they came, there are still the negative values of the prison culture. In addition, street drugs and street norms tend to abound.

### The secondary stage

Graduates of prison-based therapeutic communities are at a special disadvantage in a traditional work release centre, since they must live and interact in what is typically an antisocial, non-productive setting. Without clinical management and proper supervision, their recovery can be severely threatened. Thus, secondary therapeutic community treatment is warranted. This secondary stage is a 'transitional therapeutic community' – the therapeutic community work release centre.

The program composition of the work release therapeutic community should be similar to that of the traditional therapeutic community. There should be the 'family setting' removed from as many of the external negative influences of the street and inmate cultures as is possible; and there should be the hierarchical system of ranks and job functions, the rules and regulations of the environment, and the complex of therapeutic techniques designed to continue the process of resocialization. However, the clinical regimen in the work release therapeutic community must be modified to address the correctional mandate of 'work release'.

### The tertiary stage

In the tertiary stage, clients will have completed work release and will be living in the free community under the supervision of parole or some other surveillance program. Treatment intervention in this stage should involve outpatient counselling and group therapy. Clients should be encouraged to return to the work release therapeutic community for refresher/reinforcement sessions, to attend weekly groups, to call on their counsellors on a regular basis, and to participate in monthly one-to-one and/or family sessions. They should also be required to spend one or more days each month at the program, and a weekend retreat every three months.

## The therapeutic community continuum in the Delaware correctional system

This three-stage model has been made operational within the Delaware correctional system, and is built around three therapeutic communities – the KEY Arena, the KEY Village, and CREST Outreach Center.

### The KEY Arena

The KEY Arena is a prison-based therapeutic community for male inmates located at the Multi-Purpose Criminal Justice Facility in Wilmington, Delaware. Also known as 'KEY North', it represents the primary stage of therapeutic community treatment, and was established in 1988 through a Bureau of Justice Assistance grant. In 1990, the State of Delaware assumed the funding of the program, expanding it from its original 40 beds to 70, with further expansions in subsequent years. By 2000 the KEY Arena (or KEY North) had a capacity of 240 beds and a staff of 15. During 1999, furthermore, two additional prison-based therapeutic community programs for men were established: KEY West, a 90-bed facility in central Delaware; and KEY South, a 300-bed facility in the southern part of the state.

In general terms, the treatment regimen at the KEY Arena follows an holistic approach. Different types of therapy – behavioural, cognitive, and emotional – are used to address individual treatment needs (Hooper, Lockwood and Inciardi 1993). Briefly:

1. *Behavioural therapy* fosters positive demeanour and conduct by not accepting antisocial actions. To implement this, behavioural expectations are clearly defined as soon as a new resident is admitted to the program. At that time, the staff's primary focus is on how the resident is to behave. The client works with an orientation manual which he is expected to learn thoroughly. Once again, the focus is on his behaviour as opposed to thoughts and feelings. As the client learns and adjusts to the routines of the therapeutic community, more salient issues are dealt with in the treatment process.

2. *Cognitive therapy* helps individuals recognize errors and fallacies in their thinking. The object is to help the client understand how and why certain cognitive patterns have been developed across time. With this knowledge the client can develop alternative thinking patterns, resulting in more realistic decisions about life. Cognitive therapy is accomplished in both group and individual sessions.

3. *Emotional therapy* deals with unresolved conflicts associated with interactions with others and the resulting feelings and behaviours. To facilitate this treatment strategy, a non-threatening but nurturing manner is required so that clients can gain a better understanding of how they think and feel about themselves as well as others.

A number of techniques are employed to implement these three alternative therapeutic approaches and to motivate individuals to change, including transactional analysis, psychodrama, and branch groups. Transactional analysis involves a detailed assessment of the roles that one plays in interactions with others. The ego states affecting behaviour are defined in terms of 'parent', 'adult', and 'child'. Through group and individual sessions, clients are taught how to recognize which ego state they typically select for certain interactions and the effects of allowing their behaviour to be controlled by that ego state.

In psychodrama, individuals re-live and explore unresolved personal feelings and thoughts. Through this process, clients are helped to bring to closure unresolved issues which have prevented them from developing more adequate life-coping skills. Group and individual sessions are used as the vehicle for this treatment.

In branch groups, clients meet on a routine basis to share both feelings and thoughts about the past and present. In-depth thoughts and feelings are dealt with so that there can be a better understanding of how a person is perceiving his world. With this understanding, he is in a better position to develop more adequate coping skills.

### The KEY Village

The KEY Village is a prison-based therapeutic community for women inmates located at the Baylor Women's Correctional Institution in New Castle, Delaware. Like The KEY Arena, the KEY Village represents the primary stage of therapeutic community treatment, and was established during the closing months of 1993 through a Center for Substance Abuse Treatment grant. The Village follows a treatment regimen similar to that at the KEY Arena, but with adaptations designed specifically for women. The capacity of the KEY Village is currently 42 beds.

### CREST Outreach Center

During the closing months of 1990, the Center for Drug and Alcohol Studies at the University of Delaware was awarded a five-year treatment demonstration grant from the National Institute on Drug Abuse to establish a work release therapeutic community. Known as 'CREST Outreach Center', it represented the first dedicated work release therapeutic community in the nation, and it was designed to incorporate Stages 2 and 3 of the treatment process outlined above (Inciardi and Lockwood 1994).

The treatment regimen at CREST Outreach Center follows a five-phase model over a six-month period.

*Phase One* is composed of entry, assessment and evaluation, and orientation, and lasts approximately two weeks. New residents are introduced to the house rules and schedules by older residents. Each new resident is also assigned a primary counsellor, who initiates an individual needs assessment. Participation in group therapy is limited during this initial phase, so that new residents can become familiarized with the norms and procedures at CREST.

*Phase Two* emphasises involvement in the therapeutic community, including such activities as morning meetings, group therapy, one-to-one interaction, confrontation of other residents who are not motivated toward recovery, and the nurturing of the newer people in the environment. During this phase, residents begin to address their own issues related to drug abuse and criminal activity, in both group sessions and during one-to-one interactions. In addition they begin to take responsibility for their own behaviours by being held accountable for their attitudes and actions in group settings and in informal interactions with residents and staff. Residents are assigned job functions aimed at assuming responsibility and learning acceptable work habits, and they continue to meet with their primary counsellors for individual sessions. However, the primary emphasis in Phase Two is on becoming an active community member through participating in group therapy and fulfilling job responsibilities necessary to facilitate operations. This phase lasts approximately eight weeks.

*Phase Three* continues the elements of Phase Two, and stresses role modelling and overseeing the working of the community on a daily basis (with the support and supervision of the clinical staff). During this phase, residents are expected to assume responsibility for themselves and to hold themselves accountable for their attitudes and behaviours. Frequently, residents in this phase will confront themselves in group settings. They assume additional job responsibilities by moving into supervisory positions, thus enabling them to serve as positive role models for newer residents. They continue to have individual counselling sessions, and in group sessions they are expected to help facilitate the group process. Phase Three lasts for approximately five weeks.

*Phase Four* initiates preparation for gainful employment, including mock interviews, seminars on job-seeking, making the best appearance when seeing a potential employer, developing relationships with community agencies, and looking for ways to further educational or vocational abilities. This phase focuses on preparing for re-entry to the community and lasts approximately two weeks. Residents continue to participate in group and individual therapy, to be responsible for their jobs in the CREST facility. However, additional seminars and group sessions are introduced to address the issues related to finding and maintaining employment and housing as well as returning to the community environment.

*Phase Five* involves 're-entry', i.e. becoming gainfully employed in the outside community while continuing to live in the work release facility and serving as a role model for those at earlier stages of treatment. This phase focuses on balancing work and treatment. As such, both becoming employed and maintaining a job are integral aspects of the therapeutic community work release program. During this phase, residents continue to participate in house activities, such as seminars and social events. They also take part in group sessions addressing issues of employment and continuing treatment after leaving CREST. In addition, residents begin to prepare to leave CREST. They open a bank account and begin to budget for housing, food, and utilities. At the end of approximately seven weeks, which represents a total of 26 weeks at CREST Outreach Center, residents have completed their work release commitment and are free to live and work in the community as program graduates.

The CREST Outreach Center community is comprised of women and men at a variety of stages of treatment. Through this interaction, newer residents are given hope and encouragement for changing their lifestyles, and the older residents can assess their own changes and become positive role models. Moreover, beginning in Phase Two, residents are encouraged to engage family and significant others in the treatment process through family and couples groups led by CREST counsellors.

At the beginning of 2000, CREST Outreach Center had three co-educational facilities: CREST North, housing 112 work release clients; CREST Central, housing 125 clients; and CREST South, housing 148 clients.

### Aftercare North and South

Because the majority of CREST graduates have probation and/or parole stipulations to follow after their period of work release, an aftercare component was developed to ensure that graduates fulfilled probation/parole requirements. This represents the tertiary phase of treatment, providing continued treatment services so as to decrease the risk of relapse and recidivism. This aftercare program endures for six months, and requires total abstinence from illegal drug use, one two-hour group session per week, individual counselling as scheduled, and urine monitoring.

Graduates must return once a month to serve as role models for current CREST clients. Participation in a 12-step AA (Alcoholics Anonymous) and/or NA (Narcotics Anonymous) program is also encouraged.

## Early research

The Center for Drug and Alcohol Studies at the University of Delaware has been funded for more than a decade by the National Institute on Drug Abuse (NIDA) to evaluate the relative effectiveness of the prison and work release treatment programs described above. In recent years, evaluation funding has also come from the National Institute of Justice and Center for Substance Abuse Treatment. All of these US Government agencies have a continuing interest in treatment alternatives for drug-involved offenders.

Client selection for study has involved both random assignment and purposive sampling, and previous studies have included four client groups:

1. those participating only in the KEY Arena or KEY Village

2. those receiving treatment in either the Key Arena and KEY Village, followed by transitional treatment at CREST Outreach Center

3. those assigned directly to CREST, without the benefit of in-prison treatment

4. a 'no treatment' comparison group.

Groups 1 and 2 are purposive samples. The initial KEY-only clients all had volunteered for treatment, and all were included in the sample design. When CREST was established, all KEY Arena and KEY Village graduates were compelled to enter the work release therapeutic community. By contrast, samples 3 and 4 – CREST-only and the comparison group – were randomly assigned from the institutional population eligible for work release.

Previous evaluation analyses have demonstrated that participation in the Delaware therapeutic community programs is associated with reductions in the likelihood of both relapse and recidivism for drug-involved offenders. Specifically, analyses of the 18-month follow-up data suggested that clients receiving treatment in either the two-stage (CREST and aftercare) or the three-stage (in prison, CREST and aftercare) model had significantly lower rates of drug relapse and criminal recidivism than the comparison sample, even when adjusting for other risk factors (such as criminal history and severity of prior drug use). In addition, when examining the frequency of drug use at the 18-month follow-up, the average was significantly higher for the comparison group than for the two-stage and three-stage treatment participants (Inciardi et al. 1997). Other benefits of exposure to the therapeutic community programs indicated by analyses of follow-up data include significant reductions in the use of injection drugs, fewer returns to prison for new convictions, fewer hospital stays for drug and alcohol problems, and greater likelihood of having employer-provided health insurance.

## Current research and methods

Although previous examinations of the outcome data clearly indicated that participation in the therapeutic community programs had a positive impact on the likelihood of relapse and recidivism, the initial group distinctions on which these analyses were conducted (comparison, KEY, CREST, and KEY–CREST) were felt to be somewhat conservative in that CREST group membership was based on *assignment* to CREST, regardless of whether the client dropped out after only a short time or completed the entire program. Consequently, the initial grouping categories do not account for the potential cumulative effect of length of time in treatment. In addition, the aftercare component of the treatment continuum was not instituted until 1996, and therefore long-term follow-up analyses which include these data have become possible only recently. As such, the treatment groupings have been analytically restructured to include the comparison group, treatment dropouts, treatment graduates, and treatment graduates with aftercare.

Participation in the project is voluntary, and clients are protected by a certificate of confidentiality issued by NIDA. About 95% of all eligible clients have agreed to participate in the study at baseline, and over 80% of those interviewed also provided a urine specimen. Follow-up rates for all study participants have been about 80%. The data presented here pertain only to those clients who have completed the 42-month follow-up interview, resulting in sample sizes of 210 for the comparison group, 109 for the treatment dropout group, 101 for the treatment graduate group, and 69 for the treatment graduate group also participating in aftercare.

The baseline interview was administered in prison, just prior to the client's transfer to CREST Outreach Center or regular work release. The baseline assessment collected self-report data on basic demographics, prior living situation, criminal history, drug use history, treatment history, sexual behaviour history, sexual attitudes, HIV risks, and physical and mental health. Previous use of a series of illegal drugs was measured on an ordinal scale ranging from 0 (no use) to 6 (use more than once a day) in the six months prior to incarceration.

The first follow-up assessment occurred six months after release from prison, corresponding with graduation from CREST (for the treatment groups) or completion of regular work release (for the comparison group). Subsequent interviews were conducted 18 months and 42 months after release. Treatment dropouts were also followed up at these time points. Follow-up surveys elicited detailed information about drug use and criminal activity during the intervening time periods. In addition, the follow-up interviews collected information on the amount of time spent in any drug treatment program since release from prison. This is important because the comparison group was not truly a no treatment group. Many of these offenders sought treatment on their own during work release, and this treatment status should be controlled for in outcome analyses.

The dependent variables for the analyses presented here are dichotomous measures of relapse to illegal drug use and re-arrest at the 42-month follow-up. Each outcome measure was constructed from repeated self-report data and objective criteria. To be considered 'drug-free', the respondent must have reported *no* illegal drug use *and* have tested negative for drugs on the urine screen at each follow-up point. As such, this is an extremely conservative criterion, since drug use on even one occasion during the follow-up period would negate the 'drug-free' status. Similarly, the criteria for 'arrest-free' included no self-reports of arrest and no official arrest records for new offences since release from prison.

The data were analysed using a multivariate logistic regression technique, with treatment status (treatment graduates with aftercare, treatment graduates with no aftercare, treatment dropouts, and no treatment), and a number of other putative predictors of relapse and recidivism included as possible explanatory variables in the model. These additional predictors include age, gender, race/ethnicity, age at first arrest, number of previous arrests, number of times in prison, frequency of prior drug use, and history of drug treatment. These control variables are not only potential predictors of treatment outcome but, more importantly, they are factors that may differ across groups since group membership was not randomly assigned.

## Results

Table 14.1 presents the baseline sample characteristics by treatment status for those study participants with 42-month follow-up data. Sample attrition has generally been low (less than 10% between the 18- and 42-month follow-ups) and, importantly, does not differ significantly between the treatment and comparison groups.

There do appear to be some differences in group characteristics, primarily in terms of their gender and racial composition, but also with regard to prior drug treatment history. In order to control for these differences, the logistic regression models predicting drug use relapse and recidivism incorporated each factor displayed in Table 1, as well as treatment group status. Looking first at the control variable effects in the multivariate logistic regression analyses, age and previous arrest history predicted new arrest, and there was also a small effect of previous drug history on the likelihood of recidivism. That is, older participants were less likely to be arrested for new crimes, while those with more previous arrests were more likely to have been re-arrested by 42 months after release. For the logistic regression model predicting drug relapse, the only significant control variable was prior drug history.

Figures 14.1 and 14.2 present the results of the logistic regressions predicting re-arrest and relapse to drug use by treatment status, holding the control variables constant.

An examination of the arrest-free panel reveals that treatment dropouts are just as likely as the comparison group to be arrested on a new charge.

**Table 14.1: Baseline characteristics of comparison and treatment samples**

|  | Comparison | Treatment dropouts | Treatment graduates | Treatment graduates with aftercare |
|---|---|---|---|---|
| N | 210 | 109 | 101 | 69 |
| Age (mean) | 29 | 29 | 31 | 31 |
| Age at 1st arrest | 22 | 20 | 21 | 23 |
| Mean # of times in prison | 4 | 4 | 4 | 4 |
| Mean # of arrests | 10 | 13 | 13 | 11 |
| Males (%) | 82 | 83 | 76 | 67 |
| Whites (%) | 28 | 21 | 15 | 20 |
| Hispanic (%) | 3 | 4 | 2 | 2 |
| African-Americans (%) | 68 | 74 | 83 | 74 |
| Other races (%) |  |  |  | 4 |
| Scale of drug use 6 mos. prior to prison, ranging from 0 (none) to 6 (several times/day) | 4 | 4 | 5 | 4 |
| Prior drug treatment (%) | 74 | 79 | 79 | 88 |

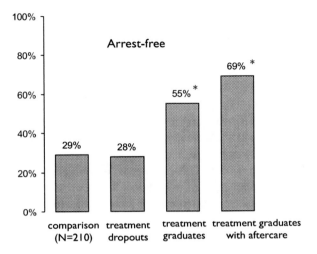

Figure 1. Per cent arrest-free 42 months after release from prison (adjusted for control variables)

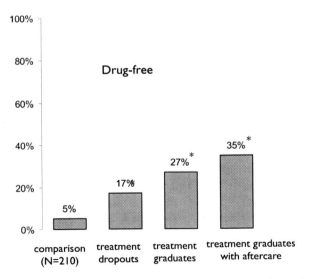

Figure 2. Per cent drug-free 42 months after release from prison (adjusted for control variables)

*Significantly different from comparison group p<0.5

However, those that complete treatment fare significantly better (p =.004), and those who complete treatment *and* get aftercare are the most likely to be arrest-free (p =.000). Less than one-third of the clients completing treatment with aftercare have been re-arrested, while more than two-thirds of the comparison group have been re-arrested by the 42-month follow-up.

The beneficial effects of the both treatment and aftercare are equally apparent when drug-free status is examined in Figure 14.2. When contrasted with the comparison group in which only 5% have remained drug-free since release from prison, treatment dropouts are more than three times as likely to be drug-free (p =.017), treatment graduates more than five times as likely (p =.001), and treatment graduates with aftercare are seven times more likely to be drug-free (p =.000). These data provide compelling evidence that participation and completion of transitional and aftercare treatment programs provides a significant and incremental protective factor against both relapse and recidivism.

## Discussion

The typically long-standing drug and criminal careers of offenders coming to the attention of the criminal justice system in Delaware necessitates that the successful substance abuse treatment approach be both intensive and extensive, comprising a continuum of *primary* (in prison), *secondary* (work release), and *tertiary* (aftercare) therapeutic community treatment corresponding to sentence mandates. The outcome data presented here indicated that clients who completed secondary treatment (some of whom also completed primary treatment) were significantly more likely than those with no treatment, or those who dropped out of treatment, to remain drug-free and arrest-free three years after release from prison. In addition, preliminary analyses of data now available on Delaware clients who received tertiary treatment (a therapeutic community aftercare program implemented in 1996) suggest that treatment graduates who participate in aftercare programming surpass treatment graduates who do not receive continuing care in terms of remaining drug- and arrest-free at 42 months. These results provide continuing support for the beneficial effects of participation in institutional, transitional and community therapeutic community treatment for drug-involved offenders.

It should be noted, however, that the 42-month outcome data presented here are preliminary, as follow-ups are still underway. As we collect long-term follow-up data on more clients, several more comprehensive analyses will be conducted. In particular, the effects of length of time in each phase of treatment, as well as completion of each phase, will be examined more fully. For example, the analyses presented here do not delineate the effects of participating in the in-prison therapeutic community program, although there is some indication that graduates of the institutional therapeutic community are more likely to remain in treatment through work release and aftercare. As more follow-up data are collected and the sample sizes increase, it will be possible to model the effects of all stages of the treatment continuum simultaneously.

There are other limitations to the present analysis that will be addressed in future work. In particular, it is clear that the models estimated, although significant, are not accounting for all of the variance in predicting relapse and recidivism. It is likely that important control variables and possible confounding variables for group effects have not been modelled. One such area that will be considered in future analyses is the compulsory or voluntary nature of the treatment entry (Leukefeld and Tims 1988; De Leon, Inciardi and Martin 1995). The Delaware therapeutic community programs contain both treatment volunteers and mandates, and this status needs to be incorporated into future models of treatment effects predicting relapse and recidivism. Yet, despite these limitations, the present data support the value of treatment in work release and parole settings and the importance of retention in treatment in increasing long-term abstinence from drug use and criminal activity. More generally, the data also support some long-held beliefs about the beneficial effects of aftercare (De Leon 1990–1991; Inciardi and Scarpitti 1992; Wexler et al. 1999).

## Notes

This research was supported by HHS Grants DA06124 and DA06948 from the US National Institute on Drug Abuse and by Cooperative Agreement 97-RT-VX-K004 from the National Institute of Justice.

## References

Clemmer, D. (1958) *The Prison Community.* New York: Rinehart and Co.

De Leon, G. (1990–1991) 'Aftercare in therapeutic communities.' *International Journal of the Addictions 25*, pp.1225–1237.

De Leon, G., Inciardi, J. A. and Martin, S. S. (1995) 'Residential drug treatment research: are conventional control designs appropriate for assessing treatment effectiveness?' *Journal of Psychoactive Drugs 27*, 1, pp.85–91.

De Leon, G. and Ziegenfuss, J. T. (1986) *Therapeutic Communities for Addictions: Readings in Theory, Research and Practice.* Springfield, IL: Charles C. Thomas.

Hooper, R.M., Lockwood. D. and Inciardi, J. A. (1993) 'Treatment techniques in corrections-based therapeutic communities.' *The Prison Journal 73*, pp.290–306.

Inciardi, J. A., Lockwood, D. and Martin, S. S. (1991) 'Therapeutic communities in corrections and work release: some clinical and policy considerations.' National Institute on Drug Abuse technical review meeting on therapeutic community treatment research, Bethesda, Maryland, May 16–17.

Inciardi, J. A. and Lockwood, D. (1994) 'When worlds collide: establishing CREST outreach center.' In B. Fletcher, J. Inciardi and A. Horton (eds) *Drug Abuse Treatment: The Implementation of Innovative Approaches.* Westport, CT: Greenwood Press.

Inciardi, J. A., Martin, S. S., Butzin, C. A., Hooper, R. M. and Harrison, L. D. (1997) 'An effective model of prison-based treatment for drug-involved offenders.' *Journal of Drug Issues 27, 2,* pp.261–278.

Inciardi, J. A. and Scarpitti, F. R. (1992) 'Therapeutic communities in corrections: an overview.' Paper presented at the annual meeting of the Academy of Criminal Justice Sciences, Pittsburgh, Pennsylvania.

Leukefeld, C. G. and Tims, F. M. (1988) 'Compulsory treatment: a review of the findings.' In C. G. Leukefeld and F. M. Tims (eds) *Compulsory Treatment of Drug Abuse: Research and Clinical Practice.* NIDA Research Monograph 86, pp.236–254. Rockville, MD: US Department of Health and Human Services.

Sykes, G. M. (1965) *The Society of Captives: A Study of a Maximum Security Prison.* New York: Atheneum.

Wexler, H. K., Melnick, G., Lowe, L. and Peters, J. (1999) 'Three-year reincarceration outcomes for Amity in-prison therapeutic community and aftercare in California.' *The Prison Journal 79,* 3, pp.321–336.

Yablonsky, L. (1989) *The Therapeutic Community: A Successful Approach for Treating Substance Abusers.* New York: Gardner Press.

# About the contributors

**Eric Broekaert** is a professor in the faculty of Psychology and Educational Sciences of Ghent University where he teaches orthopedagogics (special education). He is co-founder of the therapeutic community 'Die Kiem', a therapeutic community in Belgium, and was the first president of the European Federation of Therapeutic Communities. He is interested in qualitative and quantitative aspects of therapeutic community research, and has published several books and articles.

**Nadia Brookes**, BA MSc, was researcher on the evaluation of the pilot prison drug treatment services project. She has worked in the drugs field as a practitioner, in a development role and as a researcher. Nadia is currently Best Practice Senior Researcher at University Hospital, Lewisham, London, and is due to take up a research post with the Home Office Research Division.

**Keith Burnett,** an Arrest Referral Team Leader at CAN, Northampton, credits his introduction to 'people-work' to Swansea Student Community Action, who stretched his horizons as a volunteer. After initially graduating in history and politics he juggled a number of jobs, most importantly as an outreach youth-worker, which led on to full-time work in housing, working with probation service clients. Therapeutic community enlightenment came while training as a social worker at Durham, where tutor Jeannine Hughes suggested that Phoenix House might be interesting, and it was. Since completing his MA, Keith has been a drugs worker, again working with people at varying stages within the criminal justice system, and trying to introduce some of the lessons of concept-based therapeutic community experience to non-residential settings.

**George De Leon** is director of the Center for Therapeutic Community Research (CTCR) at National Development and Research Institutes Inc. in New York City, and clinical professor at New York University. He has authored over 165 papers and chapters, one book and several edited volumes and monographs, and is one of the originators of systematic research into therapeutic community process and outcome. He is the recipient of several awards, the most recent of which is the New York State Governor's Lifetime Service Award, presented to him in 2000.

**Paul Goodman** has been chief executive of the Ley Community in Oxford, England, since 1998. He originally graduated in law from Cambridge University in 1974, and worked as a drug and alcohol counsellor for the Health Commission of New South Wales, Australia. He then returned to England where he qualified as a social worker from Barnett House, Oxford University. He went on to join the Probation Service, where he became Assistant Chief Probation Officer for Berkshire.

**James Inciardi** is director of the Center for Drug and Alcohol Studies at the University of Delaware. He has a background in sociology, law enforcement, corrections, drug abuse treatment, HIV/AIDS prevention, and research. He is currently involved in the development and evaluation of prison-based treatment programs for drug–involved offenders, and field studies of HIV seroepidemiology and prevention in South Florida and Brazil. He is the author of 50 books and 250 articles and chapters in the areas of substance abuse, criminology, criminal justice, history, folklore, public policy, AIDS, medicine, and law.

**Martien Kooyman** has a private psychotherapy practice, is a Teaching Fellow of the International Society for the New Identity Process (bonding psychotherapy) and works as a consultant for addiction treatment programs. He began his career working as a psychiatrist in Uganda and then returned to the Netherlands, where he set up many treatment centres for addicts, including the Emiliehoeve Therapeutic Community, a day centre in The Hague and a crisis-detoxification centre and a family system therapy project in Rotterdam. He has been medical director of several programs, including the Jellinek Centre for drug and alcohol treatment, a clinic for World War II victims and a centre for refugees with psychiatric problems. He has taught in the Department of Preventative and Social Psychiatry at the Erasmus University in Rotterdam and published a thesis on a follow-up study of the Emiliehoeve Therapeutic Community.

**The Ley Community** is one of the longest-running concept-based therapeutic communities in England. The Community is located in a spacious rural setting ten minutes from the centre of Oxford. It accommodates up to 64 men and women who on average take 14 months to complete. The self-help programme integrates group therapy, a structured timetable, a resident hierarchy, work around the houses and grounds, and activities. All residents are required to be in full time employment for the final three months of their programme, and have access to resettlement support provided by the Ley Community following completion.

**Clive Lloyd** is a researcher and practising psychologist specializing in the treatment of addicted individuals and their families. He has held senior clinical positions in a number of therapeutic communities, and has published articles on therapeutic community treatment effectiveness. Currently he is researching attrition rates in Australian therapeutic communities, and implementing controlled trials of a motivational enhancement program designed to increase therapeutic community retention. Clive is the co-ordinator of the Drug Court Program with the Gold Coast Drug Council.

**Steven Martin** is a scientist with the Center for Drug and Alcohol Studies, University of Delaware. He is working on several research projects including an evaluation of the Therapeutic Community Continuum for Offenders in Delaware, a new HIV prevention intervention among probationers, and an assessment of the validity of self-report of drug use in a national sample. He is also the evaluator for several youth initiatives in Delaware and supervises some of the school surveys for the state. He is the author/co-author of over 50 articles on substance abuse, treatment effectiveness, delinquency, and methodology.

**Diana Mason** BA, RGN is a director of PDM Consulting in London. She carried out much of the evaluation of the therapeutic communities pilot project for drug users in prisons. She has extensive experience of research and project management in health and social care and specialist knowledge of primary, community and secondary health care, the prevention and treatment of problem drug use, and the prison system.

**Peter Mason** BSc, RGN, RMN holds the Diploma in Adult Behavioural Psychotherapy and is the director of PDM Consulting in London. In 1992 he studied international drug policy and prison health care as Harkness Fellow at the Centre on Addiction and Substance Abuse at Columbia University in New York. His company, PDM Consulting, specializes in improving drug treatment and prison health care through development, training and research projects.

**Karen Nolan** is a resettlement officer for the Ley Community. After graduating from Oxford Brookes University she worked in Oxfordshire as a home support worker with young people with multiple disabilities in a community setting. She went on to become the activities and life skills co-ordinator at Simon House, a hostel for the homeless, providing opportunities to improve independent living skills and enable participation in decision-making processes.

**Frances O'Callaghan** is a lecturer in the School of Applied Psychology at Griffith University on the Gold Coast of Australia. She worked for two years as a teacher and consultant with the Alcohol and Drug Programs Unit in Queensland, and has published primarily in the area of adolescent and young adult substance abuse. She is currently undertaking an evaluation of the Gold Coast Drug Court Program. Frances is a member of the management committee and clinical advisory committee of the Gold Coast Drug Council, which operates Mirikai, a therapeutic community for young people.

**Salvatore Raimo** is the General Director of CEIS (Centro Italiana di Solidarietà) in Verona. He began working with CEIS in Modena as a staff member in 1986, and moved on to become head of the day care unit and then head of residential treatment. He went on from there to the Ruedli e. V. therapeutic community in Switzerland, where he reorganised their treatment program and management. He is vice-president of the European Federation of Therapeutic Communities, and has published papers on therapeutic communities, social networks and migrant populations in several languages.

**Edle Ravndal** is senior researcher at the National Institute for Alcohol and Drug Research in Norway. She has a Ph.D in clinical sociology, and long experience of drug and alcohol research, particularly treatment evaluation, process evaluation and outcome evaluation, and has published a number of papers in these fields. Between 1982 and 1997 she was a researcher in the Department of Behavioural Sciences in Medicine at the University of Oslo.

**Barbara Rawlings** is an independent qualitative researcher and Honorary Fellow in the Department of Sociology at the University of Manchester, England. She has worked as a social-work assistant at Alpha House in Portsmouth, Hampshire, an information officer at the Institute for the Study of Drug Dependence in London, a therapist/researcher at a democratic therapeutic community for adolescents, and is currently engaged on two research projects relating to the organizational and clinical processes of therapeutic communities. She is a member of the Advisory Group for the therapeutic community at HMP Gartree, a prison for life-sentenced offenders, and a member of the editorial board of the journal *Therapeutic Communities*.

**Hilary Surratt** is an associate scientist with the Center for Drug and Alcohol Studies at the University of Delaware. Prior to joining the centre, she was a senior research associate in the Department of Epidemiology and Public Health at the University of Miami School of Medicine, where she directed research projects on HIV/AIDS prevalence and prevention in Rio de Janeiro, and a female condom multi-site study. She is director of a major study into risk reduction of HIV/AIDS for drug-involved probationers. She has published widely in both English and foreign-language journals and other media in the areas of AIDS, substance abuse, and drug policy.

**Jane Wilson** is Research Fellow at the Scottish Drugs Training Project at the University of Stirling in Scotland. She has previously worked as a senior counsellor at Marin ACT (Addiction Counselling Treatment) in California, and as a community psychologist at the Muirhouse/Pilton Drug Project in Edinburgh. She has published a number of papers on women and HIV/AIDS, dual diagnosis and substance abuse and therapeutic communities.

**Alan Woodhams** is a team senior at the New Directions Therapeutic Community at HMP Channings Wood, a Category C prison in Devon, England. A professional counsellor, he has worked as an alcohol counsellor in Southampton and as a team member counsellor at Alpha House, which is a long-standing community-based therapeutic community in Hampshire. He has always had an interest in change, and finds that in his present job the processes of bringing about change for inmates, staff and prison officers are demanding, challenging and rewarding. He advocates the development of training and supervision for therapeutic community staff, to ensure good practice, and believes that accreditation and auditing will ensure the continuing development of therapeutic communities.

**Rowdy Yates** is the director of the Scottish Drugs Training Project based at the University of Stirling. He has worked in the drugs field for more than twenty-five years and, prior to this appointment, he was the director and co-founder of the Lifeline Project, one of the longest established drug specialist services in the UK. He has published widely on addiction issues, including a chronicle of drugs, music and popular culture since the 1960s. He has travelled and lectured in Africa, the USA, South America and Western Europe, and in 1994 was awarded the Order of Member of the British Empire (MBE) for services to the prevention of drug misuse. He is Executive President of EWODOR (the European Working Group on Drugs Oriented Research).

# Subject Index

# Author Index

Printed in the United Kingdom
by Lightning Source UK Ltd.
121800UK00001B/154-171/A